Excellence in Wareh ouse

Excellence in Warehouse Management

How to Minimise Costs and Maximise Value

By Stuart Emmett

John Wiley & Sons, Ltd

Other Wiley Editorial Offices

John Wiley & Sons Inc., 111 River Street, Hoboken, NJ 07030, USA

Jossey-Bass, 989 Market Street, San Francisco, CA 94103-1741, USA

Wiley-VCH Verlag GmbH, Boschstr. 12, D-69469 Weinheim, Germany

John Wiley & Sons Australia Ltd, 33 Park Road, Milton, Queensland 4064, Australia

John Wiley & Sons (Asia) Pte Ltd, 2 Clementi Loop #02-01, Jin Xing Distripark, Singapore
129809

John Wiley & Sons Canada Ltd, 22 Worcester Road, Etobicoke, Ontario, Canada M9W 1L1

Wiley also publishes its books in a variety of electronic formats. Some content that appears in
print may not be available in electronic books.

Library of Congress Cataloging-in-Publication Data

Emmett, Stuart.
 Excellence in warehouse management : how to minimise costs and maximise value / by Stuart
Emmett.
     p. cm.
 Includes bibliographical references and index.
 ISBN 13 978-0-470-01531-5 (pbk. : alk. paper)
 ISBN 10 0-470-01531-4 (pbk. : alk. paper)
 1. Warehouses — Management.   2. Business logistics.   3. Materials management.   I. Title.
 HF5485.E46 2005
 658. 7'85 — dc22

                                                                                    2005005164

British Library Cataloguing in Publication Data

A catalogue record for this book is available from the British Library
 ISBN 13 978-0-470-01531-5 (PB)
 ISBN 10 0-470-01531-4 (PB)

Typeset in 11/15 Goudy by SNP Best-set Typesetter Ltd., Hong Kong
Printed and bound in Great Britain by TJ International Ltd, Padstow, Cornwall, UK

This book is printed on acid-free paper responsibly manufactured from sustainable forestry in
which at least two trees are planted for each one used for paper production.

Contents

Introduction

My interest in handling freight goes back to childhood and was fostered and matured during employment. Starting out in shipping and forwarding in the days of conventional cargo shipping in the early 1960s, an early responsibility was in arranging transport to the docks. We were quickly forced to change to roll-on roll-off and lift-on lift-off methods as containers and trailer methods of transport largely took over and also moved activities inland, involving the setting up of inland warehouses for cargo consolidation.

With the UK making the decision to join the EU in 1972, this also changed my work and I moved into consultancy, giving distribution advice to those people who previously had only traded in the UK and now had the view that the whole continent was soon to become a domestic market. This consultancy work was also widened out to include worldwide export/import movements.

After completing studies with the Open University in 1978, I then moved out to Nigeria where I was employed by the country's largest Forwarding and Shipping Agency, with over 1000 staff in Lagos alone. I was involved with different responsibilities: clearing, containers deconsolidation/warehousing, and lighterage/road transport of strategic imports. It was never a dull place in which to work, and fascinating also to be able to work where skills in distribution were highly appreciated and well rewarded.

The time in Nigeria ran its course and on my return to the UK I took one year out to complete an MSc at Cranfield, before joining a third party company in a commercial development role on UK Distribution, working for such companies as Heinz, Pedigree Petfood and Boots the Chemist.

This role continued until 1990 when I moved into training, with work associated largely with the, then, Institute of Logistics and Distribution Management (now the Chartered Institute of Logistics and Transport).

Since 1998 I have been a freelance independent mentor/coach, trainer and consultant trading under the name of Learn and Change Limited (www.learnandchange.com). I now enjoy working all over the UK and on four other continents, principally in Africa and the Middle East, but also in the Far East and South America. Additional to undertaking training, I am also involved with one to one coaching/mentoring, consulting, writing, assessing and examining for professional institutes' qualifications and as an external MSc examiner for Purchasing and Logistics.

The journey, while an individual one, could not have happened without the involvement of other people, and I am grateful when I recall the assistance they offered. Additionally, during the lifetime of learning and meeting people, the original source of an idea or information can be overlooked. If I have, in this book, omitted to give some people the credit they deserve, I apologise and hope they will contact me to enable me to correct that omission in, hopefully, a future edition.

Therefore, anyone who has ever had contact with me can be assured that they will have contributed to my own learning, growing and developing. While thanking you all, my hope is that in this book I have given you back something positive.

I am pleased to say, and acknowledge, that my learning still continues, both with formal pieces of paper as evidence to the CV viewers, but more importantly, in trying to find something new in every day.

I have made great endeavours to ensure that nothing in this book, if used, would be in any way injurious or cause financial loss to the users. The users are, however, strongly recommended to check and verify their own company policy/requirements before applying or using any of the items mentioned. No liability will be accepted by the author for the use of any of the contents.

Throughout this book, there are some Action Times, Challenges/ Thinking Points and Case Studies. These are designed to enable the students to think and reflect. Without this, there is unlikely to be any learning. Additionally, I have including typical training topics/content plans to highlight the appropriate knowledge that is needed for the given topics. Again, my hope is that this will encourage study and eventual learning with specific application.

Abbreviations

The following is a list of the abbreviations used in this book. The list does not include Acts or Regulations.

3PLSP	third party logistics service provider company
4PL	fourth party logistics provider
ABC	ABC analysis or 80/20 rule or Pareto analysis
ACOP	approved codes of practice
AFT	articulated fork-lift truck
AGV	automated guided vehicle
APR	adjustable pallet racking
AS/RS	automatic storage and retrieval system
BOM	bills of materials
CBT	counter-balance truck
CCTV	closed circuit television
CPD	continuing professional development
CR	continuous review
CRM	customer management
DIR	drive in racking
DV	demand variability
EDI	electronic data interchange
EOQ	economic order quantity
ERP	enterprise resource planning
FCL	full container load
FLT	fork-lift truck

FMCG   fast-moving consumer goods
FMS   fast, medium, slow
FOQ   fixed order quantity
FOT   fixed order time
G-O   goods to operator
HD   hoist down
HPT   hand pallet truck
HU   hoist up
ICT   information and communications technology
IMS   inventory management system
KPD   key productivity driver
KPI   key productivity indicator
LT   lead time
LTV   lead time variability
MBWA   management by walking about
MESC   materials and equipment standards and codes
EPOS   equipment at point of sale
MHE   material handling equipment
MPS   master production schedule
MRO   maintenance, repair and overhaul
MRP   materials requirement planning
MRPII   manufacturing resource planning
MRPT   man riser picking truck
NART   narrow aisle reach truck
NRA   no-returns agreement
O–G   operator to goods
OTIF   on time, in full
PMPR   powered mobile pallet racking
PPE   personal protective equipment
PPT   powered pallet truck
PR   periodic review
PU   put down
QC   quality control
R&D   research and development
R&R   rent and rates
RA   returns agreement
RDC   regional distribution centre

RFID	radio frequency identification
RL	reverse logistics
ROL	re-order level
ROP	re-order point
RT	reach truck
SD	standard deviation
SKU	stock keeping unit
SLT	supply lead time
SLTV	supply lead time variability
SM	standard minute
TAC	total acquisition cost
TRAMS	transport management system
ULD	unit load device
VDU	visual display unit
VOQ	variable order quantity
VOT	variable order time
WMS	warehouse management system
XML	extensible mark-up language

Acknowledgements

I am grateful for help and assistance from friends and colleagues in checking contents and giving suggestions for this book. In particular to Jeremy Mant on the inventory topics and I shall be forever grateful to Barry Crocker of Salford University for his support and expert editorial eye on the text.

1

The Role of Warehousing and Stores

WAREHOUSING AND THE SUPPLY CHAIN

Warehousing is actively involved in the supply chain. In demand-driven supply chains this may be mainly by storing goods, or involve more sorting activities; both being required to largely feed external customers. In the supply-driven supply chains, then warehouses get renamed as stores, and hold stocks required to feed internal activities like production.

Warehouses are therefore an integral part of the supply/demand chain/pipeline infrastructure.

The term 'supply chain' is the process that integrates, coordinates and controls the movement of goods and materials from a supplier to a customer to the final consumer (Figure 1.1). The essential point with a supply chain is that it links all the activities between suppliers and customers to the consumer in a timely manner. Supply chains therefore involve the activities of buying/sourcing, making, moving and selling. Therefore, the supply chain 'takes care of business' following from the initial customer/consumer demand. Nothing happens with supply until there is an order; it is the order that drives the whole process. Indeed some people logically argue that the term 'supply chain' could be called the demand chain.

Additionally, as supply chain management is all about the flow of goods and information, then perhaps a better analogy than chain is a pipeline, as this better emphasises flow. Also to emphasise the flow aspects,

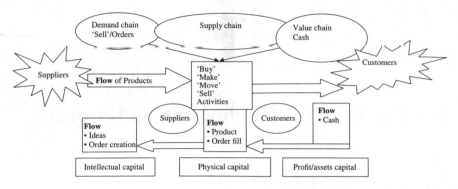

Figure 1.1   *The supply chain*

warehouses should perhaps be better thought of as undertaking sorting and not storing products.

It is also important to realise that each company has not one supply chain but many, as it deals with different suppliers and has different customers. For each finished product, while some of the buying, making, moving and selling processes will be identical or very similar, the total supply chain for each product will be different. Multiple supply chain management is therefore a better description but it is a cumbersome one. In supply chain management, therefore, there are many different supply chains to manage, with the varied goods being 'combined' in the warehouse.

CHALLENGE

How many supply chains exist in your company?

TRAINING TOPICS

Topic: Supply chains – Awareness of the key impacts and developments
Duration: 1 day

Course content

- *Understanding what the supply chain is about*
  - Definitions: The interrelations and connections of buying, making, moving, and selling activities
  - History of the supply chain and its development
  - A view of the future.

- *The key aspects*
  - The cost/service balance
  - Customer service principles
  - Lead times throughout the supply chain
  - Adding value
  - Production options/changes
  - Trade-off opportunities.

- **The benefits of adopting a supply chain approach**
  - The sub-functional conflicts
  - Benefits within functions
  - A supply chain view of total acquisition costs.

- **Why traditional ways are changed**
  - Demand amplifications and the 'Forester' effect
  - Uncertainty and unresponsiveness.

- **Impacts to the supplier/customer relationships**
  - Practical effects on lot sizes/order quantities
  - Reducing costs
  - Sharing developments
  - Eliminating internal and external barriers
  - Interfacing versus integrating relationships.

- **Supplier relationship case studies**
  - Manufacturing and retailer case studies
  - Lessons and key aspects from experience.

- **Implementing a supply chain management approach**
  - The changes needed
  - Potential action needed.

- **What happens if we do nothing?**
  - The 'do nothing' future of adversary relationships
  - Higher stock levels
  - Competition gains
  - Silo closed management approaches.

- **A 5-step approach to supply chain development**
  - The model ('should we?; benefits and drawbacks; internal issues; key issues; and finally')

DEFINITIONS

Definitions can be important to clarify thought and are especially so when one person understands a term to mean one thing but another person understands the same term to mean something different. This has been happening, for example, in the UK from the early 2000s with the word 'Logistics'. This term, which originally encompassed the whole supply chain, is now being referred to by many companies as a new name for transport, or for warehousing/stores or for distribution. Third-party transport companies are also beginning to call themselves supply chain management companies. Confusing, isn't it?

In the UK, one can observe the new name on a freight transport vehicle that was previously called 'Fred Smith Transport' and is now called 'Fred Smith Logistics'. Logistics can therefore be a confusing word and, additionally, some people use the term 'logistics' to describe their own internal company process, and use the supply chain term, when they are dealing with external suppliers/customers. At the risk of further confusion, others also call their internal logistics processes an internal supply chain!

Distribution is meant to be about delivering the right goods to the right place at the right time and at the right cost. This definition is the 'rights of distribution' and represents, in a simple way, the objectives for distribution. Distribution therefore involves the combining of transport with warehousing, and is a term that is often applied to finished goods. However, it may also be used by suppliers who are delivering product to their customers, perhaps of raw materials and semi-finished work-in-progress goods. Suppliers are also concerned with getting the 'rights' correct and, as far as that supplier is concerned, the raw materials can, for them, be the finished goods.

Meanwhile, when readers hear the three terms 'logistics', 'supply chain' and 'distribution', they are strongly recommended to ensure that they have the full understanding of what the originator means when each term is being used. This can be very important and prevent confusions; for example, 'Fred Smith Logistics' is unlikely to have a clue about whether to outsource the manufacture of sub-assemblies or whether these can be manufactured internally. This would often be a strategic supply chain decision (but then again, some would say it is strategic logistics decision).

THINKING POINT

How are the terms 'logistics', 'supply chain' and 'distribution' used in your company and with the suppliers/customers with whom you deal?

With warehousing and stores, we can usefully define a warehouse as 'a planned space for the storage and handling of goods and materials'. It should not be 'a place where buyers keep their mistakes' – an observation from a major retail company in the early 1990s. Throughput and sorting are often of more importance than storing (especially in demand driven operations). The effective and efficient use of both time and the warehouse/site space are also important. The emphasis should therefore be on the planning of all the warehouse activities, including receiving, storing, assembling, kitting, picking and the despatching of customers'/users' orders. The warehouse is therefore able to consolidate, break bulk, cross-dock and provide value added services.

STRATEGIC ASPECTS OF WAREHOUSING

Warehouse management is often thought of as being just an operational day-to-day job. However, it should also be involved in the longer strategic aspects of the business. Warehousing has a critical part to play in supply chain management and it can only play this part if it is involved in the strategic aspects of the business. This will involve being aware of the expected development of the business in terms of the future:

- production
- product
- suppliers
- customers
- and all the associated product volumes and throughputs.

Strategic questions on warehousing

- Do you need a warehouse?
- Is it in the right place for the supply/demand balance, transport, labour, and all other services needed?
- Are all the future supply and demand requirements known?
- Is the labour force stable?
- Is absenteeism above the national average?
- Are communications good?
- Is accuracy 100%?
- What is the real time visibility of information for inventory, productivity, cost and service?
- What is the shortest response time for customer orders?
- What are the levels of productivity and how do we know they are 'world class'?
- When did you last plan an ideal 'layout'?

By answering these questions, warehouse management is able to proactively assess situations and make important contributions to the decision-making process.

THINKING POINT

Who takes such a strategic view of warehousing for your company?

CUSTOMERS

We have mentioned earlier the importance of the customer order, as it is only the order from the customer that triggers all the activity in the supply chain, logistics or distribution processes. Without a customer order, none of these process or activities is required. The customer may be interested in buying products, but is really more interested in buying delivered products. Additionally, the time scale from ordering to receiving the delivery has in recent years often been shortened. A normal expectation in the UK, for example, is for next day delivery with many products, with some suppliers (for example, of stationery) offering the same day delivery to major national locations for orders received before noon.

This clearly puts pressure on the warehouse pick/pack/despatch operations, as well as on the transport operations, but it also shows a response to market requirements/expectations and one that offers a competitive advantage to the first company to deliver such a service.

Customer service levels are therefore variable and each customer service variable (such as same day delivery) has an associated cost. The relationship between cost and service is rarely a straight line, but is more of an exponential curve. So, a 10% increase in service may mean a cost increase of 15 or over 50%.

Customer value

Customers will place a value of many aspects of the total service offering. Value is also placed by customers against quality, the cycle lead time and the cost and the service levels. As perception is reality, customers can see these as being interrelated or may view them independently. It is therefore important for a business to understand the specific reality as seen by the customer.

The following are the aspects of the four customer value criteria:

1. Quality is 'performing right first time every time' and involves:
   - meeting requirements
   - fitness for purpose
   - minimum variance

- elimination of waste
- continuous improvement culture.

2. Service, is about 'continually meeting customer needs as the market changes', and involves:
   - support available
   - product availability
   - flexibility
   - reliability
   - consistency.

3. Cost, is about knowing what the costs really are and then looking at how to reduce them. This involves the:
   - design of product
   - manufacturing process
   - distribution process
   - administration process
   - stock levels.

4. Cycle lead time is about knowing what the lead times really are and then looking for ways to reduce them. This involves considering:
   - time to market
   - time from order placement to time available with the customer
   - response to market forces
   - days of stock cover.

A business, therefore, ideally will try to improve its quality and service, while reducing cost and lead times. All of the aspects are interrelated and connected and, for example, it doesn't matter to the majority of customers whether the goods are transported by road, rail, sea, air or multimodal or intermodal means, or whether they are stored, kitted or cross-docked in warehouses. The four factors above are what they really value. The method of distribution is purely a means to these ends and outcomes.

CHALLENGE

Find out how your customers rate the above quality, service, cost and lead-time factors

THE VALUE CHAIN

Michael Porter of Harvard Business School in his book *Gaining Competitive Advantage* introduced this concept in 1985. From Figure 1.2 you will see that this has significant implications for logistics/supply chain/distribution.

The value chain divides into primary and support activities as follows:

- Primary activities
  - Inbound logistics covering stores, warehousing, handling and stock control.
  - Operations covering production and packing and all activities that transfer inputs into outputs.
  - Outbound logistics include transport and warehouse networks to get products to customers.
  - Marketing and sales cover the methods by which customers know about and purchase products.
  - Service includes the support for all activities such as installation or returns.

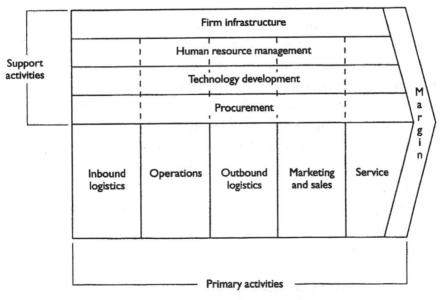

Figure 1.2 *The value chain*

Reproduced with permission from Cheltenham Tutorial College

- Support activities
  - Procurement includes the buying and purchasing of products as well as all other resources.
  - Technology covers such items as information and communications technology (ICT) and research and development (R&D).
  - Human resource management covers all aspects concerned with personnel.
  - Infrastructure covers finance, legal and other general management activities.

Porter then expanded this concept of a value chain into a *value system*. This consists of a series of linked value chains. By this joining together of value chains into a value system, in effect we create a supply chain. Where the value actually is, according to Porter, is dependent on the way a customer uses the product and not just totally on the costs incurred in buying, making and moving it. These costs, including all the raw materials and activities that create the product, then represent its value. But it is only when the product is purchased that this value can be measured; and, finally, it is not until the product reaches the final customer/consumer that the real value is to be found.

Part of the difficulty here is that each individual organisation in the supply chain will attempt to define value by looking only at its own profitability. Each company will in turn carry on this definition to their suppliers and as the definition of value moves back up the chain, it will become distorted. Indeed, one of the reasons for companies to try to work together more closely with suppliers and customers is to have a constant view of value throughout the supply/value chain.

Therefore, we have seen that costs are added during the buying, making and moving activities and that ultimate/real value is only found when the product is with the customer. Meanwhile, value has been added by improving the product, by changing its form, moving it to a different place and all this has occurred over time. Therefore, we can see that value is added by:

- making it faster by changing the form
- moving it faster to the place required
- doing it faster by time changes

and that

• ultimate value comes after the movement to the customer.

Figure 1.3 shows how cost and value are added in the supply chain process.

Clearly, this diagram shows that goods being stored are incurring cost and are not adding value. Indeed, one challenging definition of a warehouse is that, in supply chain terms, a warehouse is an admission of defeat as we are planning to stop the flow of goods and materials and, therefore, are increasing cost and not adding value. While it will generally be the case that stored goods will not increase in value, this may apply to a very limited range of products, such as with bullion in non-inflation times and with works of art. The diagram, however, emphasises that movement to the customer as quickly as possible while accounting for associated cost levels is what really counts in adding value.

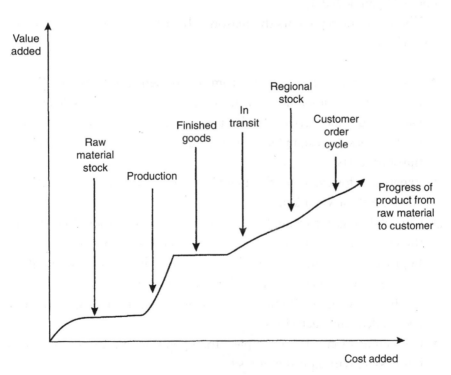

Figure 1.3 *Cost and value adders in the supply chain*
Reproduced with permission from Cheltenham Tutorial College

THINKING POINT

How can you add value to your company's customer offering?

WAREHOUSE LOCATION

The location of the warehouse(s) can be a critical decision. Clearly for a business that is involved in manufacturing, its raw materials stores are likely to be the production sites, and the stores location is therefore determined by the location variables of the production sites. However, this is not an absolute and, for example, the Nissan car factory based at Washington, Tyne and Wear, holds little raw material stock on site as it follows a synchronised just in time (JIT) system with its suppliers (mainly located in the West Midlands), so that raw materials are received and the line is fed immediately.

The following represents the reasons why it may be necessary to move a warehouse:

- Financial savings: for example, from government grants. Hopefully this involves full trade-off decision-making, including for example any impacts to customer service levels and resultant financial implications.
- Cost savings: for example, by being closer to customers and saving in transport costs.
- Expansion: for example, the need to hold more product lines due to entries into new markets.
- Consolidating: for example, the closing down of regional centres or the consolidation of separate local sites into one location.
- Improve performance: old buildings may be difficult to convert to allow the use of more modern, up-to-date activities and systems.
- Facilitate change in operations or organization: for example, to conduct added value activities.
- Communications: for example, incorporating all of a company's business activities on the one site.
- Image: for example, to a 'showcase' site.
- Expiry of current lease.

In making the move, the following need to be considered:

- Impact to workforce: for example, potential redundancies of existing staff and recruitment of new staff.
- Recruitment opportunities: for example, availability with the possible attendant need for medium-term training.
- Proximity to the transport network: for example, locations in Northamptonshire and Leicestershire are popular warehouse areas due to the M1/M6/M69 and A1/A14 intersection road network and their central location with the UK population; that is, the source location of demand/where people live who buy things.
- Availability of social, recreational and cultural amenities: for example, a 'new town' may not have a source of supply.
- Housing for staff and personnel.
- Tax breaks: for example, when buying new assets.
- Real estate values: for example, regional variations are high, with London Heathrow being the most expensive.
- Neighbouring property development: for example, compatibility.
- Environmental impacts: for example, planning permission may not allow high rise structures.
- Local authorities: for example, warehouses are frowned upon in some areas as they are seen to take up a high amount of land for proportionally low employment.
- Customer perception: for example, how will they see the change?
- Customer reactions: for example, will they be concerned about service disruptions?
- Disruption to service: for example, coordinating with the supply/inbound stock to the existing location and the stock build-up in the new location before going 'live'.

When moving, surveys reveal that employees' preferences are in the following ranked order:

- near to public transport
- a safe area
- near to shops
- pleasant surroundings
- close to cafés, pubs and restaurants.

Meanwhile the employers' preferences, in ranked order, were:

- the quality of the workforce
- the access to road networks
- low overhead costs
- quality of the local environment
- local economic conditions
- competitive wage levels.

MODERN WAREHOUSE OPERATIONS

The supply chain:
Temperature-controlled distribution

To illustrate the nature of modern warehouse operations in the supply chain, we look in this chapter at a specific operation of handling temperature-controlled food items. These are products that everyone in the UK will use, but the majority of people will understandably have no idea of what happens to ensure that quality is maintained. It will illustrate some of the detailed aspects of what is involved in warehousing.

Deterioration and climate

The aim of temperature-controlled distribution may be described as to create a micro controlled climate within the total supply/distribution chain. The object of this controlled climate is to prevent deterioration of the commodities being handled.

Commodities deteriorate more quickly in hotter and humid climates. Consequently the total design of the temperature-controlled distribution system needs to be undertaken carefully, and then run and controlled strictly.

System design

Important factors to consider in the design and operation of a temperature-controlled distribution system for food commodities are summarised below:

- Climatic hazards
  - Humidity
  - Temperature
  - Rain
  - Light (ultra violet)
- Biological hazards
  - Insects/mites/rodents/birds
  - Moulds
  - Bacteria
- Product composition
- Mechanical hazards
  - Handling process
  - Transport process
  - Sampling process
- Other hazards
  - Design of vehicles/warehouses
  - Pilferage
  - Working practices

If the system is to maintain product hygiene durability, then the reliability of operations (on mechanical and other hazards) and the reliability of control over climatic and biological hazards are of paramount importance.

Types of temperature control

Various types of temperature control are needed and these may be summarised as shown in Table 1.1.

A temperature-controlled distribution system therefore operates in a wide range of controlled conditions. The technical 'hardware' and the management 'software' needed to maintain such 'internal' conditions within a varying range of 'external' ambient temperatures will be explored further.

Cool/cold storage (−1 to +15 °C)

This temperature band prevents the rapid spoilage that is found when products are handled under ambient temperature conditions. While

Table 1.1   Types of temperature control

Type	Temperature	Product examples
Frozen	−30° to −10 °C	Meat, fish
Chilled	−5° to 0 °C	Fresh meat, fish, poultry
Cool	−1° to 5 °C	Dairy produce
Cold	5° to +15 °C below ambient	Citrus produce

microbiological spoilage is not completely prevented, the respiration rates in fresh fruit and vegetables are considerably reduced. Biochemical changes are therefore slowed down and the storage life is increased. For these reasons, preserved foods also benefit from cool or cold storage. For example, the storage life of canned foods can be doubled; dried foods can be stored 4–6 times longer.

When storing and handling food, it is necessary to specify the optimum conditions of temperature and the relative humidity. The optimum relative humidity arrived at is often a trade-off between the conditions that cause excessive drying and those that favour the development of micro-organisms.

Chilled/frozen storage (−30 to 0 °C)

In general terms, fresh foods of high moisture content have a freezing point 0 to 5 °C. However, with certain foods such as milk powders and some dry foods, the moisture content will not freeze. During the freezing process, ice crystals are formed within the food. This may have damaging effects on its texture and appearance and, to this extent, it is therefore possible to forecast the effect of subzero storage temperatures by considering the freezing point of the particular foodstuff. However, the rate at which heat is removed during freezing also affects the extent of possible damage.

While chilled storage does not provide indefinite protection against microbial spoilage, it does give a degree of rigidity to, say, animal carcasses, which aids handling and avoids tissue disruption.

With frozen storage, food materials may dry out unless protected by packaging. Drying in the frozen state causes a porous 'corky' appearance.

This condition, known as 'freezer burn', is caused when food is stored very close to the cooling surfaces.

Storage conditions

Temperature-controlled vehicles and warehouses are both very expensive to build and maintain. The cost of building a cold store, for example, is about three times that of an ambient store. Additionally, the storage temperatures required considerably affect the running costs of the distribution system. These running costs need to be balanced against the need to preserve the product.

Handling conditions

It is critical upon first receiving products into the system, to establish fully the required storage conditions under which the product is to be handled.

Next, it is critical to establish the match of the 'required' condition with the current condition of the product. The highest possible standards of quality control are needed. This is done by visual checking and by test probing and/or sampling the condition of the goods. Where a mismatch occurs, appropriate remedial action will be needed and must be fully documented. At each step within a distribution system, matching the condition between the actual and required states is a necessary and a critical job function. For example, reliance on the fridge vehicle to pull down temperature in transit is a hazard to avoid.

A product being stored needs to be handled in such a way as to ensure that adequate air circulation occurs around the product. Accordingly, product stacking methods and procedures need to be identified and followed.

Monitoring of the temperature conditions during storage and transportation need to be undertaken at regular intervals. This monitoring becomes especially important during the transportation as products are typically in the care of one individual – the vehicle driver. The driver needs to regularly monitor and undertake remedial manual defrosting and frosting as required. Within the very narrow temperature bands for chilled and cold cargos, this is not a task that can be easily dismissed.

Condensation damage

When goods are exchanged between low temperature and ambient conditions, it is probable that condensation will form on the exposed surface. For example, vehicle loading of frozen or chilled loads, in ambient conditions, can cause condensation to form on the product. Four courses of action are possible to prevent excessive condensation:

1. Ensure that distribution from the refrigerated storage is in small lots for immediate consumption.
2. Provide a series of 'tempering chambers' in which goods can be brought back to ambient temperatures in stages under conditions of low relative humidity.
3. Arrange immediate protection by moisture-proof covers.
4. Ensure that the removal from cold stores occurs at night when ambient temperatures are low.

The best course of action will depend upon actual circumstances and the specific requirements involved.

Service levels

As varying types of products are often handled in a temperature-controlled distribution system, these products will probably require varying rates of delivery into retail outlets. These varying delivery rates are due to the mix of service levels required, according to the product life cycle. For example, the requirements given in Table 1.2 may hold. Goods with a short shelf life may be moved in and out of a chill store in hours, whereas with a frozen store, the time scale may be weeks or years. The chilled and cold products are the most critical and, therefore, require stricter operational controls.

To illustrate some of the above aspects in practice, the following example of frozen food will be used.

Table 1.2 Service levels

Type	Examples	Typical deliveries
Frozen	Meat	2/3 times a week; 48-hour order cycle
Chilled	Fresh meat	Daily/3 times a week; 24/48-hour order cycle
Cold/cool	Dairy produce, Citrus produce	2/3 times a week; 48-hour order cycle

CASE STUDY 1.1: FOOD FREEZE PLC

The Company

Food Freeze plc (FF) are a UK based frozen food manufacturer/packer and have a major share of the European frozen food market dealing with all major and minor retailers and wholesalers. Whilst new product development is an important part of their business, they are relatively stabilised with around a constant of 500 SKU's at any one time.

They have three factories based in the East Anglia/Lincolnshire agricultural producing areas with another factory based in the Northwest in a former re-development area.

Distribution

The following flows of goods and materials are involved:

- Raw materials (such as packaging and ingredients) into the factories
- Finished goods from the factories to customers (either as full trailer pallet loads or as single pallets of one SKU).

FF deliver to customers on average 120 000 pallets per month but as a result of seasonality, the range is from a low of 90 000 to a high of 180 000 pallets per month.

Problems

Delivering direct from different factories to the same major retail
ers forced an examination of the physical distribution network.

Solution

A National Distribution Centre (NDC) was located in the Midlands,
effectively a 'factory product mixer'. This meant that products from
each factory could be combined into one customer load.

All finished goods are moved from each factory to the NDC for
storage/re-sorting and because of the throughput and not storage
nature of the product, a holding/storage capacity of one week's
stock, in peak (45000 pallets) was planned for.

The NDC was fitted with automated unloading/loading docks to
connect with the automated loading roller bed floor equipment in
the transport trailers. Once on the dock, a loading/unloading time
of less than three minutes per trailer is achieved; product is then
moved into the automated high bay warehouse.

Linked with the NDC is a dedicated core transport fleet of 30
tractors and 60 trailers, these being supplemented when required.
The transport operations are co-ordinated closely with customer
orders, and the collection of raw material supplies.

Both NDC and transport operations were outsourced to a third-
party contractor on a cost plus open book arrangement.

Results and key aspects

- Customer order lead time fell from 4 days to 1/2 days
- On time in full delivery to customers (OTIF) increased from 83%
  to 97%
- Raw material delivery costs were reduced
- FF only need a very small core central team of supply chain planners, stock control and QC staff. The 3PL undertake the day-to-
  day order management, replenishment and delivery (based at the
  NDC), with additional 3PL planners based in the factories to liaise
  on production raw materials/finished goods availability.

- Communication is enabled by one daily conference call planning meeting and regular fixed weekly, monthly and quarterly meetings to discuss and review and improve operations.
- The cost plus contract arrangement gives cost transparency. Back-load savings are shared 50/50.
- Relatively paper free operations with EDI customer orders into the FF SAP system. This then links to the 3PL WMS and Transport systems.
- Each point where goods are transferred has automated temperature readings and the transport trailers are fitted with GPS equipment for traceability and control purposes
- Transport fleet is well utilised, for example, full trailer from NDC to a retailer RDC, from that retailer's RDC to a store of the retailers that is located near to a raw material/ingredient supplier, collection from there to a factory, and then finally from the factory and return to the NDC
- Demonstrates complete transport and warehouse integration with the FF activities of buying/purchasing and selling/customer demand.

WORLD-CLASS WAREHOUSING

The following are the basic points to which everyone involved in managing warehouse must be alert. Unfortunately, many of these basics do often seem to get lost in the search for new technology, in implementing new ERP systems or in embracing e-commerce. These potential 'new flavours of the month' can divert from and override the 'basics'; for example, if the writer had £10 for every time he has been asked 'How can I get a computer package that will do all the basic detail for me?' then, he would be a rich man.

1. Do you need each warehouse?

Networks can grow without examination and looking at them overall in terms of a supply chain is needed. Inventory levels will generally grow as more warehouses are added. This topic has already been partly examined above.

2. How can each item be packed?

Product-handling groups are useful to show and to determine package sizes. The issue pack needs to account for marketing concerns; customer order policies, inventory levels, and operational activities.

3. What products should be kept?

The common problem is keeping too much stock (the warehouse may be a place where buyers are keeping their mistakes). An ABC Analysis can be very revealing and help to determine which SKUs should be carried. It can then be determined how they flow through the supply chain; for example, some can bypass, and some can be cross-docked. These above two topics are covered in Chapters 2 and 3.

4. How many times do you handle products?

Reducing handling increases productivity and lowers costs. It should be noted that handling twice only occurs for direct delivery from supplier to customers. Putting product into store and picking from store will generally be handled from supplier to customers, 12 times.

5. Do you store products in relation to the flow/rate of movement?

Not all products have the same demand. An ABC Analysis will show which products have fast/medium/slow movement, and help to better organise operations to minimise the time and the distance travelled in the warehouse.

6. Do you know exactly where each product is located?

Zoning in the warehouse will be needed.

Topics 4 to 6 above are covered in Chapters 4 and 5.

7. Is the layout optimal?

Organising the warehouse for flow works; however, things change and so a regular review of the layout is needed.

Warehouse layout is fully covered in Chapters 4 and 5 and Chapter 7 examines the regulation involved in warehouses, it being of no use for example, to have an optimal warehouse layout if, for example, it contravenes health and safety legislation.

8. What are the operational standards?

'You cannot manage it, unless you measure it.' Are the following included in the warehouse management?:

- Costs and utilisation of resources for each activity in the warehouse: for example, space and time.
- Performance of activities: for example, receipts and picking rates.
- Accuracy of activities: for example, full complete orders despatched.
- Lead times for activities: for example, time from receipt of order to time ready for despatch.
- Safety: for example, accidents.
- Morale and motivation: for example, absence levels.

Chapter 8 looks fully at these issues, with Chapter 6 looking at how standards may be recorded with ICT.

9. Should you outsource or manage warehouses yourself?

Assuming you know which warehouses are needed, the next step is to decide how they are operated. Some questions to ask are:

- Is warehousing a core competency?
- Can third parties be more efficient?
- What will be customers' reactions?

Chapter 9 examines this outsourcing topic.

10. *Do you have a multiskilled work force?*

Rarely are activities flat, but peaks and troughs are normal. Being able to move people between activities in the warehouse, or between warehouses in a network, will help to flatten out the peaks/troughs. Managing people correctly is critical, and is examined in Chapter 10.

CONCLUSION

Warehousing clearly has a critical part to play in all aspects of supply chain management. It also needs to be involved in the strategic aspects of a business and this will involve being aware of the development of the business in terms of the future production, product, suppliers, customers and all the associated product volumes and throughputs.

2

Inventory, Stock Analysis and Classifying Products

PRODUCT CLASSIFICATION

Product for stores and warehouses is received from a supplier and then, at some later time (perhaps within hours or years), it is despatched to meet a demand. The product being supplied will have resulted from the company inventory ordering policy. This will involve 'when to order' and 'how much to order' decisions. From a warehousing perspective this supply cycle will have implications for:

- the receipts area (goods inwards)
- the stock locations area/cube.

The product being despatched will be dependent upon the demand patterns arising from the customer orders. In turn the despatch of customers' orders will give rise to replenishment and the supply cycle starts once again. This demand cycle has implications for the warehouse as follows:

- Stock location area/cube
- Picking area/cube
- Despatch area/cube (goods outwards).

It will often be the case that the supply cycle will be more controllable than the demand cycle. This assumes that the demand patterns are generally more random and independent, therefore creating more uncertainty. Analysis of demand is therefore important as it is the demand that 'kick starts' the entire warehousing and supply chain process.

DEMAND ANALYSIS

To undertake this correctly, every individual line/product/stock-keeping unit (SKU) will need to be examined. This exercise, often typically undertaken by inventory managers, helps to determine product requirements from a stockholding point of view. This, in turn, reflects the supply and demand cycle with the goods inwards and goods outwards operations of the warehouse.

Demand is found in two basic forms (see Table 2.1):

Table 2.1 Comparisons of dependent and independent demand

Feature	Dependent demand	Independent demand
Replenishment method	MRP	ROP/ROL
Orientation	Product components	All individual parts/items
Demand patterns	Lumpy and discrete patterns	More continuous patterns
Order signal	Time phased	ROP/ROL
Time perspective	Future production/sales	Historic demand often will greatly help to predict the future
Forecasts	Forecast is on the final end items only	Forecast on all items
Safety stock	Safety stock is carried for the end items	Safety stock is carried

- *Independent* or *random* demand is that which is independent of all other products; e.g. tyre manufacturer with tyres needed for puncture repairs. It is the classic consumer-driven demand for 'end use' products or services and therefore is more random with uncertainty being found. It uses re-order point/level (ROP/ROL) systems for inventory management/replenishment.
- *Dependent* or *predictive* demand is that derived from consumer demand which produces 'end use' products or services – e.g. tyre manufacturer for new cars; this is driven by the derived requirement for new cars and planned for by the car assembler based on that company's view of the independent demand from consumers. Dependent demand is therefore found commonly in manufacturing or kitting environments where a plan (such as a Master Production Schedule) has already been established on the basis of a forecast. With dependent demand, this means that the previous event has to happen first and that subsequent events will then depend on the events preceding them. Dependent demand is therefore more certain for the upstream suppliers, enabling some degree of anticipation – for example, the tyre manufacturer obtains from the car assemblers their forward planning on production. It uses requirement/resource planning systems (MRP).

Patterns of demand

As a first step, the following patterns are being looked for in demand analysis:

- Random or independent demand. This does not have a consistent pattern and may have high or low volumes.
- Predictive or dependent demand is more consistent, there being some degree of certainty about orders.
- Stable demand is relatively fixed and steady.
- Lumpy demand is not at all consistent and displays limited demand patterns. However, generally, no zero demands are found.
- Trend demand can be either upwards/positive/rising (for example, following a successful promotion where demand per period is increasing), or downwards/negative/falling (for example, at the end of a product's life cycle where demand per period is decreasing).

- Fast movement has a relatively consistent high volume and the average demand rate, and variation, is stable.
- Slow movement is relatively consistent, but with low volume that may fall to zero. Average demand is low.
- High or low product value.
- Frequency of demand can follow a normal distribution curve for the most fast moving to medium moving products. With slow-moving products that have many zero demands, a Poisson distribution may be needed; this deals with low probability events.
- Obsolescence is where there is no demand over a long period, typically over one year. This may be due to technical changes, spoilage or defects, although it can be because the item is no longer required. This latter event should, of course, ideally have been pre-notified so that stock levels could have been objectively reduced. While some long-time stockholding may be objectively necessary for some obsolete items – for example, with product that is being held as critical spares – often no real examination is carried out on all the obsolete items and they are therefore not declared as dead stock. There is often a natural reluctance to admit that items need disposal, due to the subsequent perceived lack of availability to service any future 'rogue' demand and to writing off the money that has been spent. The best approach is a continuous review of obsolete inventory, with scheduled write-offs in small amounts on a regular basis.

Other complications that are found with demand patterns are from seasonality, promotions and a product's life cycle:

- Seasonality is where the average demand is repeated over time, which can be: annually, like the Christmas period or like lemons for the English Pancake Tuesday; monthly, following consumers' pay time; and weekly, like Sunday shopping.
- Promotions typically will give a sharp increase in demand. This is then followed by a sharp decrease in demand, as re-orders are delayed until the promotional items have been used/consumed.
- Product life cycle – for example, new products being launched and promoted need higher levels of stock than products that are declining and diminishing.

Demand must also critically be related to the service levels (the availability from the stockholding) – for example, on the amount of stock being held to give availability, where, say, a 70% stock cover may be held for slow-moving and less critical items, and 95% for fast-moving and critical line items.

Any given product can be categorised against each of the above. Taking, as an example, entertainment music CDs, then the following may be found on a daily to weekly basis:

- Random/predictive demand: the old top 20/the current top 20. It can be argued that the current top 20 is also random in terms of sales; however, it perhaps has more predictive elements due to the marketing push that is undertaken by the music industry.
- Stable/seasonal demand: the current top 20/Christmas carols.
- Fast/slow demand: the current top 20/Christmas carols (which will however be fast during Christmas weeks).
- High value/low value: box sets/budget labels.
- Product life cycle – launching: the forecast top 20.
- Product life cycle – diminishing: the current/old top 20.
- Low service level/high service level: the old top 20/the new top 20.

It will be seen that on a weekly time period the current top 20 has a predictive and stable demand with a diminishing product life cycle; whereas the old top 20 is random demand, with slow demand and a diminishing product life cycle requiring a low service level. Clearly with such a dynamic and changing product, the position changes very frequently (daily/weekly) and, of course, this is on an item by item basis.

As a contrast with a fast-moving grocery product range, the following may be found over a monthly time period:

- Random/predictive demand: baked beans with taco flavoured sauce/staple items like baked beans, bread, pet food, milk.
- Stable/seasonal demand: the staple items/Jiffy lemons for Pancake Tuesday and tinned soups in winter.
- Fast/slow demand: the staple items/baked beans with taco sauce.
- High value/low value: baked beans with taco sauce/budget-priced items and the staple items that will most likely be very competitively priced to attract shoppers into the store.

- Product life cycle – launching: 'fashion products' like Alco pops of the mid-1990s and increasingly smaller sized mobile phones in the 2000s.
- Product life cycle – diminishing: 'mild' beer and the older larger mobile phones.
- Low service level/high service level: beans with taco sauce/the staple items.

It will be seen here that the staple items like baked beans, bread, milk, pet food are the fast movers, having predictive and stable demand requiring high service levels but with a low value. Meanwhile slow movers are more random but have a higher value and lower service level. However, these distinctions on the slow movers are not absolute as each 'unique' and different product will have different patterns and can also be viewed differently by different companies; for example, high-value items may have a high profit margin and mean that high stock levels are required in order to ensure a high availability and profitability.

A critical point here is that each company will have its own specific and continually updated categorisations, especially for consumer/demand cycle-driven stocks. With more of a supply cycle-driven business, then stocks may, for example, be categorised as shown in Table 2.2.

The point to be appreciated with demand analysis is that, to be effective, each company must undertake its own demand analysis.

ABC ANALYSIS

A useful step to undertake is to analyse the products in terms of fast/slow movers by conducting an ABC analysis. This involves the classic Pareto analysis named after the Italian economist who, in 1906, reckoned that 80% of the wealth lay in the hands of 20% of the population. An alternative name for this type of analysis is the 80/20 rule, where a high incidence in one set of variables equates to a smaller incidence in a corresponding set of variables. The best way to demonstrate this is by a simple exercise.

Exercise: Conduct an ABC analysis on the following demand volume information:

300, 40, 25, 15, 8, 5, 4, 3, 2, 225, 30, 15, 10, 150, 6, 5, 25, 4, 3, 125

Table 2.2 Supply cycle-driven stocks

Category	Description	Demand characteristics
Maintenance repair and overhaul (MRO) items	Spares, etc., and daily used consumables (such as office supplies)	↑
Maintenance items	Non-time critical and dependent demand	Mainly slow-moving with a few fast-moving items. Mainly independent demand but some dependent demand for scheduled maintenance, e.g. shutdowns
Repair items (for breakdowns)	Time critical and independent demand	
Operating items	Non-time critical and independent demand	↓
Project materials	Specific items, e.g. for a new manufacturing plant	One-off usually phased in with building/ construction schedules. Dependent demand
'Insurance' items	Critical spares and items that are held in case of a need where the costs of non-availability are high, e.g. chemicals for a LNG plant	Used only in exceptional cases. Watch for obsolescence. Independent demand
Surplus	Have no foreseeable use	Use as substitutes, move to salvage/'scrap'
Programme materials	Support normal work programmes, e.g. drilling sequence in oil exploration	Planned and predictable. Dependent demand
Direct charge	Acquired for specific and immediate use and charged directly to revenue account	Ad hoc, may be call-offs from suppliers

Method: By ranking in high to low demand order we can make the calculations shown in Table 2.3

It will be seen that this simple exercise comes out classically at 80/20. In reality there would be much more volume demand information, but the calculations would be same. However, where the lines would be drawn between 'A' and 'B' and 'C' items is arbitrary and is a matter of judgement.

Table 2.3   Calculations for an ABC analysis

	Volume high to low	Cumulative volume	% of cumulative volume	No. of items	% of items
A items	300	300	30	1	5
	225	525	52.5	2	10
	150	675	67.5	3	15
	125	800	80	4	20
B items	40	840	84	5	25
	30	870	87	6	30
	25	895	89.5	7	35
	25	920	92	8	40
	15	935	93.5	9	45
	15	950	95	10	50
C items	10	960	96.0	11	55
	8	968	96.8	12	60
	6	974	97.4	13	65
	5	979	97.9	14	70
	5	984	98.4	15	75
	4	988	98.8	16	80
	4	992	99.2	17	85
	3	995	99.5	18	90
	3	998	99.8	19	95
	2	1000	100	20	100

Indeed, it could be possible to make the breakdown into, say, around 10 item categories, such as AAA, AA and A items (very fast, fast, not so fast), three B items, etc. When graphed, the relationship shown in Figure 2.1 is found. In this example the ABC analysis has been undertaken on product values and shows that:

A   10% of items represent 70% of consumption value
B   25% of items represent a further 20% of consumption value
C   65% of items represent only 10% of consumption value

Whatever method of categorising is used, the principle is the same: a high percentage of, for example, volume movement is found from a small number of lines (the A items above, the fast movers), and the converse, that the slow movers (the C items above), will account for a high number of lines for a low percentage of volume movement. Thus, to summarise:

- A items (fast movers) = high volume, few lines
- B items (medium movers) = medium volume, medium lines
- C items (slow movers) = low volume, many lines

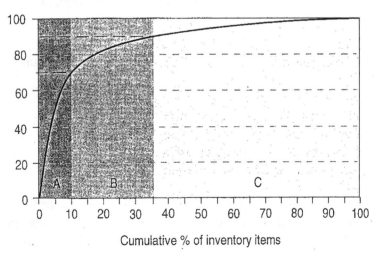

Figure 2.1   ABC analysis on value

As we shall see in Chapters 4 and 8, this is important for the positioning of stock in the warehouse and also, therefore, for the overall warehouse layout, costs and productivity. This will be especially so when a large amount of manual picking/selection is undertaken in the warehouse.

PRODUCT CODING

Each company will have a method of identifying products through the use of some form of coding system. The coding system maybe unique (for example, the Materials and Equipment Standards and Codes (MESC) 10-number coding used worldwide within the Shell group) or, it may be a coding system that conforms to industry standards (for example, the UK food industry bar code labelling of products). Whatever coding method is used, the reasons for it are universal:

- Provides a unique identifier per product line/item.
- Prevents duplication of stocks: for example, by ensuring that coding is used by all suppliers and can be identified by all customers and users.
- Provides standardisation: for example, coding a 'new' product for the first time can identify that similar products already exist and therefore possible duplication is avoided.
- Simplifies product identification for all suppliers, customers and users.
- Can help in determining stock locations: for example, within a store holding engineering items where all those products in one main coding category are kept together.
- Assists in pricing and costing: for example, with food supermarkets' EPOS systems

PRODUCT HANDLING GROUPS

As the demand analysis picture builds up, it then becomes possible to construct a matrix that will indicate all the different types of product being handled. A matrix can be constructed to show the different products with their individual characteristics, for example, as shown in Table 2.4.

Table 2.4 Matrix can be constructed to show the different products with their individual characteristics

Product identifier or code	F/M/S	Volume in/out per week	In/ receipts	Put away	Select/ pick	Out/ despatch method
001	F	5000 cases	100 cases per UK pallet	On UK pallet	By case	Roll cage
101	M	3000 cases	80 cases per UK pallet	On UK pallet	On UK pallet	On UK pallet
515	S	1000 cases	10 cases per Euro pallet	On UK pallet	By case	Roll cage

The matrix could also be extended to account for any specific product characteristics, for example:

- temperature control: needing separation and zoning
- security: needing specific lockable/safe areas
- hazard rating: needing segregation and possible temperature control and special fire protection
- any other requirements that mean that products cannot be kept together.

INVENTORY MANAGEMENT: WHY HOLD STOCK?

Inventory management is an approach to manage the product flow in a supply chain, to achieve the required service level at an acceptable cost. Movement and product flow are key concepts in inventory management (and also in the whole supply chain), as when the flow stops, then cost will be added (unless the stored product is one that appreciates in value over time). If product flow is important, why then should we be holding stock in the warehouse? The following is a summary of the reasons:

- *To decouple supply and demand.* Warehouses actually 'sit' between supply and demand where the following examples of stock may be found:
  - from the supply of raw materials to establish production
  - from work in progress and semi-assembled items, perhaps awaiting customised products
  - finished goods stock, for immediate demand order filling.

- **As *safety/protection*:** for example,
  - to protect against supplier uncertainty
  - to cover for non-forecasted demand
  - provided physically, by the warehouse.

- **In *anticipation of demand*:** for example,
  - promotional or seasonal build-up
  - bulk supply price discounts.

- **To *provide service to customers (internal and external)*:** for example,
  - cycle stocks of finished goods
  - availability from safety stock for non-forecasted demand.

Although it may not be a reason for holding stock in the warehouse, there may, in addition to the above, be a pipeline inventory in the supply chain. This would be stock in transit either from suppliers and/or to customers. This time may be considerable if goods are undergoing a long sea journey.

In financial accounting, stock improves the company balance sheet. Stock is therefore an asset in financial terms. However, holding stock also carries costs (as we shall see later), which will appear in the financial profit and loss accounts. The turnover of inventory will also mean sales and profits to a trading business; therefore, the faster the inventory turns, the greater will be the profitability. Thus, the key aspects to be considered in inventory management are:

- Determining the products to stock and the location in which to stock them.

- Maintaining the level of stock needed to satisfy the demand (by forecasting of demand).
- Maintaining the supply.
- Determining when to order (the timing).
- Determining how much to order (the quantity).

These key aspects involve the consideration of such issues as demand forecasting, supply lead times (SLT) and replenishment methods, all of which we shall be examining later.

INVENTORY COSTS AND SERVICE

The aim of inventory management is therefore to achieve the required service level at an acceptable cost. This is a question of finding the balance between cost of holding stock and the cost of providing the required service at the level desired by the customer or consumer. If there is too much stock then there is a high service cost; if too little stock is held, then both low cost and low service result. The ideal aim, therefore, is low cost with high service. Inventory replenishment methods, that we shall look at later, attempt to do this.

A key aspect in inventory management is dealing with uncertainty, not only with the supply and the customer or consumer demand, but also in asking whether the uncertainty is 'real' (and is definitely caused by the dynamic aspects of the supply chain), or is it caused by institutionalised and out-dated/ill-informed procedures and lack of communication?

With independent demand, for example, which is driven by, say, random and unpredictable consumer behaviour, this demand travels down the supply chain. This independent demand in the supply chain is based on responding to the random independent demand orders placed by one level to the next highest level in the supply chain. By being viewed by the separate players as independent demand, this can cause fluctuations and dependencies that can limit subsequent events occurring, as these depend on the last event and are therefore being influenced by the fluctuations of the preceding events. Where the supply chain is long with no end to end visibility, the accumulation of fluctuations in turn increases, involving higher inventory carrying and slower movement as each player in the supply chain 'struggles' to undertake its activities due to the fluctuations. They 'struggle' as the supply capacity and the demand are not in balance. Long and 'unconnected' supply chains like this will therefore, over time, increase inventory holding, increase carrying costs and have a delayed and slower product flow.

The following case study shows the so-called 'Forrester Effect' that can result when institutionalised demand distorts the real demand as it passes down a supply chain.

CASE STUDY 2.1: SUPPLY CHAINS AND THE FORRESTER EFFECT

In this case, the information ripples backward through the delivery process to create havoc at the production end of the chain.

Megadrug is a well-established pharmaceutical company. It has a wide range of products distributed over the world. One of its newer products is a homeopathic drug, Homeocold, to stop colds from evolving into real nastiness. Megadrug supplies retail shops from various regional centres. In March last year, at the end of the winter season, orders from retailers unexpectedly started to pour in. The regional centres serviced the shops and ordered the plant for more Homeocold. Unfortunately, the production line at the plant had already been switched to another 'summer' drug, and it would take at least a week before Homeocold could be produced again.

As the regional centres stocked out, the retailers were frantically ordering more Homeocold. Megadrug's management team realised then that a media-triggered 'poisonous drugs' scare had resulted in millions of customers switching from traditional drugs to homeopathic alternatives. After a crisis meeting, they decided to switch production back to Homeocold in order to service the increasing backlog with the regional centres. Even at full production for one month, they would not be able to catch up; but one thing Megadrug could not afford was a reputation for unreliability with retailers and customers.

Weeks later, the regional centres finally started servicing the retailers again. To their surprise, they were greeted with relief at first, but, as the weeks went by, with embarrassment. Retailers started cancelling orders, faster and faster. The regional centres, watching piles of Homeocold accumulate in their warehouses, started screaming at the plant to stop producing and shipping Homeocold.

The plant director was pulling out his last remaining strands of hair. He was now asked to stop producing Homeocold and to catch up with the summer production that had got way behind schedule. The management team was too busy blaming each other to notice that Homeocold was still selling steadily more than usual and decided to delay production next year to get rid of the stocks at the regional centres. By increasing expectations and ignoring the obvious delays involved, the company faced a 'Forrester Effect'. Minor market changes at the end of the supply chain accumulated to cause great havoc with production planning. Once again, not reacting would have been safer than over-reacting.

Source: Michael Balle, *Managing with Systems Thinking*, McGraw-Hill (1994). Reproduced by permission of Michael Balle.

Inventory costs

These are caused by many aspects (consider, for example, the costs that result from the Forester Effect), and the cause of these costs is from many different activities and departments of a company. This can mean that many of the costs may be hidden from view, and the following cost items could be involved:

- Capital investment:
  - value of stockholding
  - warehouse investment
  - warehouse equipment investment
  - ICT systems investments

- *Plus* . . . product holding costs, such as
  - storage/handling (if not in above)
  - obsolescence
  - deterioration/damages to stock
  - insurance

- *Plus* . . . ordering costs, such as
  - purchasing
  - warehouse receiving
  - finance payments.

All the above give the total cost of inventory, which can be calculated as follows:

Total capital investment = Cost of borrowing money per annum
+ Holding total costs per annum
+ Ordering costs per annum
+ Any other specific, annual costs

A large multinational oil company indicates the following percentage costs of its inventory value per annum:

Physical storage	3–5%
Deterioration/obsolescence	2%
Opportunity cost (cost of capital tied up)	12–23%
Total inventory costs	**17–30%**

Inventory service

In providing a service with inventory, this centres around the level needed (the availability) to satisfy demand. This will usually be a strategic decision of the business, but it also can be a decision taken at a lower level, and one being taken to provide cover against complaints and 'noise' factors. Inventory is a dynamic and interactive process, so such low-level decision-making can be a reflection that inventory is not fully understood and that suboptimal decision-making is occurring in the business.

The levels of stock being held to satisfy demand should be a company policy decision based upon an objective view of the requirements of users and customers. In a market situation, what the competition is offering will also have an input into the strategic decisions.

A summary of cost/service balance is presented in Table 2.5.

Table 2.5 A summary of the cost/service balance

Activity	Reduces cost of holding	Improves service availability
Increase holding	No	Yes
Reduce supply lead time (SLT) and supply lead time variability (SLTV)	Yes	Yes
Reduced demand variability/more accurate forecasting	Yes	Yes

LEAD TIME

Lead time (LT) is a critical component in making inventory decisions, as the following simple example illustrates:

If 70 items are used per week and the supply LT is 2 weeks, then the quantity to order to cover the demand during the supply LT (called the lead time demand) is 140 items.

But if the supply LT is variable by +/− one week, then the maximum order is 210 items and the minimum order is 70 items. But we may 'play it safe' and order 210 items. This is not the best decision but may be an understandable one for those who are left to base replenishment decisions on protecting against personal 'noise' factors when past stock-outs have occurred. In such cases, then clearly inventory management is also not understood or involved both strategically and operationally in the business.

Lead time covers many aspects and a comprehensive view of lead time is given below.

Types of lead time

The various types of lead time are listed in Table 2.6. The supply lead time used in inventory calculations is not the same as the supplier lead time mentioned above. The supply lead time is the total time taken from the decision to order to the time the item is available for issue. It is therefore made up of many parts both 'internally' within the business (for example, the pre-order planning, procurement and the receivers' stages) and 'externally' with the supplier lead time. These 'parts' are shown in Table 2.7.

Parts of lead times

These lead times need to be examined using real examples and ensuring, however, that all appropriate stages and steps are included. There may even be some additional stages on, for example, imports and the customs clearance lead time.

After each stage has been quantified, it will then need to be analysed to see if there is a better way to do things. By first understanding the processes and then rationalising them, lead time can be dramatically

Table 2.6   Types of lead time

Lead time	Action	By
Pre-order Planning	User	Customer
Procurement	Order placing	Customer to supplier
Supplier	Order despatching	Supplier
Production	Making to order	Supplier
Warehouse	Supplying from stock	Supplier
Transit	Transporting	Supplier
Receivers	Receiving	Customer
Payment	Paying	Customer to supplier

Table 2.7   Parts of lead time

Lead time	Lead time stage	Steps, by date
Pre-order planning	User need	Analysing status to determining need to order
	User requisition	Need to order to date of order requisition
Procurement	Order preparation	Order requisition to order release date
	Order confirmation	Order release to date of confirmation
Supplier (see also the production and warehouse lead times; the supplier lead time is *not* the supply lead time)	All the stages here are in the production and warehouse lead times	Confirmation to order despatched date
Production (e.g. made to order)	Order processing	Date of order receipt to date order accepted/confirmed
	Preparation	Order accepted to date manufacture starts
	Manufacture (Queue time, set up, machine/operator time/inspect/put away times)	Start of manufacture to date it finishes
	Pack/load (to the warehouse or to transit LT)	Finished manufacture to date order despatched

Table 2.7   Continued

Lead time	Lead time stage	Steps, by date
Warehouse (e.g. available ex-stock)	In stock	Date goods arrived to date of order receipt
	Order processing	Order receipt to date order is accepted or confirmed
	Picking	Date order accepted to date order is available/picked
	Pack/load (to warehouse or to transit LT)	Order available to date order despatched
Transit		Date despatched to date order received
Receiving		Date order received to date available for issue/use
Payment	Credit	Date invoice received or of other 'trigger', to date payment received
	Payment processing	Date payment received to date cash available for use

reduced. Such reductions in lead time will often come from the information flows and not from the goods flows in the supply chain.

As already mentioned, the supply lead time used in inventory management should not be confused with the above-mentioned supplier lead time. The supply lead time is actually the total of all the above lead times, excluding the payment lead times. Effectively, therefore, the supply lead time is from the pre-order planning lead time (from analysis of the order status/determining the need to order), right through all the above steps and stages to the receiving lead time (date order received to date available for use/issue). It is therefore undertaken by many different parties, including the supplier and the customer.

The problem of lead time variability

The main issue to be resolved with lead time is not its length of time but the uncertainty and variability that can occur. Consider the following example:

If lead time (LT) is halved from 12 to 6 weeks but the lead time variability (LTV) stays the same at 4 weeks, then

	Current LT				*New LT*		
	LTV	LT	LTV		LTV	LT	LTV
	–4	12	+4		–4	6	+4
Total LT	= 8 to 16 weeks				= 2 to 10 weeks		
	(Index 100 to 200)				(Index 100 to 500)		

So, if LTV stays the same and only LT is reduced, then there is a higher disruption factor.

While we shall be looking at inventory improvements later, the following are some ways to reduce demand and supply lead time variability:

- Demand LTV
  - Predictable orders/size/make up
  - Predictable order times
  - Data accuracy on what customers want/when/price
  - Is it 'end' demand or institutional/'Forrester' demand?

- Supply LTV
  - Predictable LT
  - Get correct quantity first time
  - Get correct quality first time
  - Data accuracy on what is supplied/price.

DEMAND FORECASTING

When demand levels are not known exactly, as with independent demand, then forecasting proactively aims to give the best estimate of future demand and to predict changes. Forecasting also aims, reactively, to minimise errors in previous forecasts (i.e. the difference between the forecast and what actually happened).

Methods used are basically *subjective* or *objective*. It can be important to distinguish between these two methods, as the common language used is 'forecasting', which does not distinguish between the two quite varied and different ways.

The subjective method, often called sales forecasts or market intelligence, may be educated guesses by experienced forecast people or purely more 'crystal ball gazing' or 'blue skying'. This is not to say that these subjective methods have no value; they clearly do have value when they are undertaken by experienced people – for example, by marketing taking a considered view of a new product launch or a promotional activity. Customers are not always going to be predictable but customer intentions can come from 'feel', from competitor activity that has just 'appeared' and needs reacting to, and from external events like weather. All of these will have effects that have to be subjectively determined.

Objective methods will, however, involve a mathematical statistical analysis of past demand to predict the future. From the inventory management view of forecasting, this is exactly what forecasting is. Inventory managers should therefore take care when being involved in subjective sales forecasting – for example, when launching a brand new product that has no history of past demand, such launches should more directly involve the stock level decision of, say, marketing, with perhaps inventory managers assisting with the details for any past similar product launches.

It is often, however, the combination of subjective and objective forecasting methods that gives the best prediction. For example, objective methods with statistics are a good basis, using history to predict the future, providing nothing else changes. However, in dynamic consumer situations this will often not be the case, for example, a strong belief that 20%

more will be sold in the next period due to the expected collapse of a competitor.

- Demand forecasting will therefore be easier when a product:
  - is old and established
  - is a consumer product where the end demand is more visible
  - has a stable demand
  - has a short time period.

- Demand forecasting will be more difficult when the product:
  - is new and being launched
  - is a part/assembly of a consumer product and may therefore suffer from 'Forrester Effects'
  - has an erratic demand, for example due to new competitor activity that is taking away sales or due to short-term weather pattern changes
  - has a time period that is far into the future, as projected forecasts have higher errors than forecasts for tomorrow.

Inventory demand forecasting uses varied statistical analysis:

- simple average on stable, no trend items
- moving average which extends the simple average method with previous periods
- weighted average on trend items and emphasis is put on more recent periods
- exponential smoothing is similar to weighted average but is more 'statistically correct'.

With seasonality, where the level of average demand alters over different periods of time, inventory demand forecasting uses two common statistical measures:

- Seasonal indices for when seasonal pattern is repeated over time are built up from averages of demands from many cycles as are available from the product history. It is widely used in the fast-moving consumer goods (FMCG) sector.
- Base series methods allow for short-term seasonality which uses smoothed demand/trend/constant.

It has been said that there are only two things about forecasts that are correct. One is that they will be wrong; the second is that it will be known by how much it was wrong. This 'planned/actual comparison' is known as forecast error and the aim of measuring this is to minimise errors in forecasts (i.e. the difference between the forecast and what actually happened). The statistical basis for this method of forecasting uses 'tracking signals', which take measures from past forecasting errors and whose value indicates the degrees of statistical confidence when the system fails to change. Measuring forecasting errors therefore gives important learning information towards making improvements. It should not be systematically used for blame!

INVENTORY AND STATISTICS

Inventory management involves the manipulation of historic data by statistical analysis to give objective information on which decisions can be made. It is not the purpose of this chapter to explain the rationale behind the statistics but to mention the statistics that are used, so that these may be verified and checked out fully if needed. Where computer systems undertake the calculations, it should be appreciated that, by default, the system may not always use the 'correct' statistics. It is therefore important to realise that there are different statistics that can be used more appropriately.

Statistics involve questions of probability that an event will happen, so inventory management statistics are therefore a classic application of the techniques. Normal distribution is often used which describes the frequency of occurrences with some probability of an occurrence, which, if graphed, follows a bell-shaped curve. It is defined by two parameters, the mean or average on the vertical axis and the standard deviation or the spread on the horizontal axis. Standard deviation is therefore used to describe the spread of the numbers and the difference from the average, or mean and is defined as 'the square root, of the difference from the average, of the squared deviations'.

For those who do not wish to use calculators or computers, the standard deviation is calculated as follows:

1. Determine the mean (average) of the numbers.
2 Determine the differences between each number and the mean.
3. Square these differences.
4. Calculate the average of these squared differences.
5. The square root of that average = the standard deviation.

In demand management replenishment forecasting, the forecast is the basis for ordering or for manufacturing, taking into account the existing inventory levels. It is always hoped that, over a number of time periods, the forecast will be more or less correct in aggregate. However, in any particular period there will be errors and the magnitude of these errors is also measured by the standard deviation. In determining the safety stock required, this takes into account the required service level and the manufacturing or supply lead time. In inventory management for random demand, and when calculating safety stock, the curve represents the service level factor. Table 2.8 shows the relationship between the standard deviation (SD) and the service level factor for availability of stock.

What is critical about this is the effect on the level of safety stock required to satisfy random demand. For example, note that the increase from 95 to 98% (plus 3%) means a 25% increase in the standard deviation/the extra stock to be carried.

Increasing service levels therefore gives an exponential curve relationship in the extra safety stock required. The relationship between the stock held and the service level is not therefore a straight line, as for example a 3% increase in stock does not equal a 3% increase in the extra stock required.

It will also be seen that there is a huge increase of 226.8% when moving from 95% towards the mythical 100% (or 99.99% in statistics, as there is always a probability factor). Higher service levels for stock availability with random demand mean that proportionately far higher levels of stock are carried, as shown Figure 2.2.

Table 2.8   The relationship between the service level factor and the standard deviation

Service level (%)	SD factor	Service level (%)	SD factor	Service level (%)	SD factor
50.00	0.00	85.00	1.04	96.00	1.75
55.00	0.13	86.00	1.08	97.00	1.88
60.00	0.25	87.00	1.13	98.00	2.05
65.00	0.39	88.00	1.17	99.00	2.33
70.00	0.52	89.00	1.23	99.50	2.58
75.00	0.67	90.00	1.28	99.60	2.65
80.00	0.84	91.00	1.34	99.70	2.75
81.00	0.88	92.00	1.41	99.80	2.88
82.00	0.92	93.00	1.48	99.90	3.09
83.00	0.95	94.00	1.55	99.99	3.72
84.00	0.99	95.00	1.64		

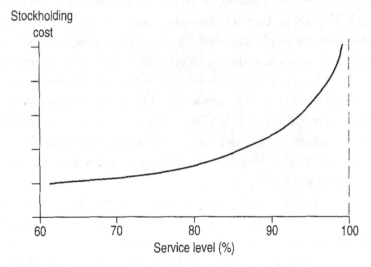

Figure 2.2   *Random demand, stock levels and service factor*

The subjective 100% availability, which is commonly stated as a requirement, is a myth for random demand. This is worth remembering by warehouse managers when space is at a premium. It is also worth while for all people in the company to know about and then to make a critically objective assessment.

Of course, the idea of setting, say, a 90% service level for stock availability is fraught with problems both for customers and for sales/marketing departments. All they rightly expect is 100% service and levels below this will mean little to them. The key aspect here, however, is that customers will always get their demand requirements satisfied and how we deal with the other, say, 10% influences how the level is set in the first place, what the extra costs are for maintaining higher levels of stock and also how the supply chain is being operated. For example, with an acceptance of back-ordering, this will often provide an acceptable service for non-stocks with a firm date for delivery.

In many companies the majority of profit will come from a relatively small number of lines; the 80/20 rule again. So here safety stock levels can be set to minimise the value that may be on back-order and minimises the cost to the company. While lost sales are extremely difficult to analyse, some companies do have the view that it is better to let a competitor have such sales, as this prevents the high cost of stocking and relatively slow-moving low-profit lines.

HOW MUCH STOCK SHOULD BE HELD?

Looking at this simply, there are three basic aspects to be considered:

1. If decoupling supply/demand, then we need enough to cover for the difference between the input and output rates. This is called the bulk or the quantity (Q) stock. It is the inventory to be used for routine demand consumption. If we have constant demand and supply lead times, then the position is as shown in Figure 2.3.

   The re-order level (ROL) is fixed here at a quantity of 200 and the re-order point (ROP) is fixed at a time period of 10 days; the level being dictated by the demand and supply lead times.
2. If there is some uncertainty with supply, we need to have cover for the expected use during the supply lead time. This is called safety stock (SS) and is held to cover the supply.
3. If there is some uncertainty with demand, we need enough to provide availability until the next delivery. This is also called safety stock, being held to cover the demand.

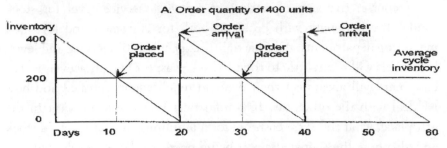

Figure 2.3   *Constant demand and supply lead times*

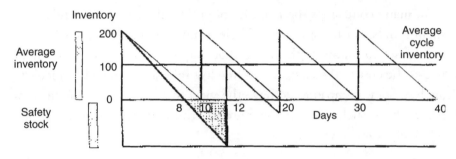

Figure 2.4   *Safety stocks guide*

When we have some uncertainty with demand or with lead time, then safety stocks are carried, as illustrated in Figure 2.4.

Any one or all of the above situations may be involved. This also illustrates the two types of stock that are found:

- *Cycle stock* (or replenishment or lot size stocks). These are held as a result of in and out movements and involve decisions on order quantity and frequency.
- *Safety stock* (or buffer or fluctuation stocks). These are held as a 'cushion' between supply and demand (for either or for both) and involve decisions on supply lead time (SLT), supply lead time variability (SLTV) and the amount of demand that will occur during the SLT/SLTV.

It should be appreciated that these two types of stock are not held separately, but are only separated out (as we shall see later) in the calculations for when and how much stock to order. 'Working stock' is the name used by some people for the cycle and safety stock together – the name illustrating its purpose.

Another way to think about stock is with the analogy of a car fuel gauge. When the tank is full, we do not worry about supply. When it falls to 50%, we may then start to think about when we need to get some petrol (the 'how much' to order and 'when' inventory decisions). We may wait to do this until the warning light flashes, which causes us to think: 'Where can I get a supply of petrol and how much will I be using before I can get a new supply?'

This illustrates the need to plan the time to order. While we can always wait until we run out of petrol, this is not really best practice as it will incur time penalties, extra cost, inconvenience, etc.

When we properly plan the time to order, then we will consider the options of:

- a variable time, for example, whenever we might pass a filling station or when the warning light flashes (VOT or variable order time)
- a fixed time, as we will plan to go to the filling station, say every Friday (FOT or fixed order time).

When we then get to a filling station, and assuming that stock is available, we have then to decide how much to order. The options here are:

- fill to top, therefore we get variable order quantity (VOQ) each time we order.
- fill with, say, £10 worth; therefore we place a fixed order quantity (FOQ).

This analogy introduces us to the reality that the 'when' and 'how much' to order decisions can have a fixed or variable time to order with a fixed or variable order quantity. Table 2.9 shows the possibilities, with some 'realities'.

This introduces us to the main inventory replenishment methods of continuous review (FOQ/VOT) and periodic review (FOT/VOQ). There are some other variations on these two: minimum–maximum and two bin methods for inventory replenishment, and we shall look at these issues shortly.

Table 2.9   The main inventory replenishment methods of continuous review (FOQ/VOT) and periodic review (FOT/VOQ)

Option	Meaning	Comments
FOQ/FOT	£10 every Friday	May run out before the FOT, but can be acceptable if constant demand and lead times (as in the basic EOQ method).
FOQ/VOT	£10 when pass a filling station, or, after the warning light has flashed	Needs a continual review of stock
FOT/VOQ	Check every Friday and then fill up the tank if needed	Needs a periodic review of stock at the fixed order time interval (e.g. Friday)
VOT/VOQ	Fill up when pass a filling station or, after the warning light has flashed	Too many orders are being placed and virtually a full tank is being maintained

REPLENISHMENT METHODS

Before considering further the 'how much' and 'when' to order decisions, it will be recalled that demand is found in two basic forms:

- *Independent or random demand.* This is independent of all other products, e.g. tyre manufacturer for puncture repairs. As it is end consumer driven and random, it therefore has more uncertainty. Independent demand uses re-order point/level systems for inventory management.
- *Dependent or predictive demand.* This is due to demand elsewhere, e.g. tyre manufacturer for new cars (OE). It is more driven by the derived demand of supplier/customer ordering enabling more anticipation and

more certainty than is found with end product consumer buying. Dependent demand uses requirement/resource planning systems (MRP/MRPII).

Replenishment for independent demand: the 'when to order' decision

This will be simply 'when stocks are at a level that is able to satisfy demand, and until the replenishment order is available'.

This in turn requires the following questions to be asked:

- How much demand is expected during the supply lead time?
- How long will replenishment (the supply lead time) take?

There are two methods that can be used to check to see if an order should be placed:

1. At a specific time period (ROP). This is called periodic review but it is also called the periodic inventory time-based method, the order up to level system and the fixed order interval method. This has a fixed order time period (FOT); e.g. weekly at the time trigger; at that 'point in time'.
2. At a specified remaining level of stock (ROL). This is called continuous review and is also called the perpetual inventory action level method and the fixed order quantity method. This has a variable order time period (VOT); e.g. when at the ROL of the 'trigger' of the quantity in stock.

Therefore, when making replenishment decisions, the following will need to be considered:

- Supply LT (SLT) is the time that follows from determining the need, deciding to place an order, up to the time it is available for issue. Accuracy of data is needed and the SLT involves many different steps (as was earlier shown by the explanations on lead time). SLT includes the external suppliers' lead times, plus the internal steps of the requiring/

ordering between customer/user and the receiving/available for issue lead times. It is surprising that many companies do not know objectively what their SLTs are. This therefore means that they are simply not effectively controlling their inventory.

- Supply LT Variability (SLTV), if applicable. This is also usually poorly dealt with; SLT must be measured on a continual basis to identify any variability.
- Average demand (Av.D), or the forecasted demand, during the supply lead time. This is sometimes called the lead time demand, but is more correctly called the demand during the supply lead time.
- Demand variability (DV), if applicable. This is the difference between the average demand and the actual demand over time and is measured by the standard deviation.
- Required service level (S/L). This ensures that the correct stock level is held and is available to service requirements to cover against any supply and/or demand uncertainty.

Where demand and supply lead times are certain, predictable and known, the calculations are easier. Known and fixed supply lead times with known and fixed demand create for simpler decisions; for example:

Fixed demand: 50 units per week
Supply LT: 2 weeks
Then one order option is 100 units ordered every two weeks.

The keys to having such predictability are found, for example, where:

- historic demand and supply lead time are good proxies for the future
- there are long, mature product life cycles
- there is no promotional product activity.

However, for most companies, such certainty is not the real world and conditions of uncertainty are normal. For example, the marketplace works against certainty with demand volatility and increased product variety by introducing new products and competition. Reduced and shorter product life cycles limit the value of historic data and, additionally, wider global supply bases cause complications for supply lead times. All of these changes to demand and supply lead times mean that greater safety stocks are required.

The following illustrates the calculations needed to cover against the 'probability' that we will be dealing with uncertainty:

1. Average demand   50 units per week
   SLT   2 weeks
   Demand variability   12 units
   Service level   95% (1.64 standard deviations)
2. Then 50×2 =   100   (cycle stock)
        $12 \times 1.64 \times \sqrt{2}$ =   28   (safety stock)
                   ROL   128

So the overall formula is:

Av.D × SLT for the cycle stock/demand lead time, plus
DV × S/L × √SLT for the safety stock.

3. To illustrate again the concept of variability, if we have SLT variability of 1 week, then
        50×3 = 150   (100 cycle + 50 safety stock)
        $12 \times 1.64 \times \sqrt{3}$ =   34   (safety stock)
                   ROL   184

Here the 'extra' for the variability is the extra 50 and the extra 6 (28 + 6) giving a total of 50 plus 34.

Some important conclusions are possible from this example:

• The longer the lead time, the more safety stock is required
• LTV is critical.

Replenishment for independent demand: the 'how much to order' decision

From our earlier example of filling a car with petrol, we saw that the options were as follows:

• Fill to top, therefore we get variable order quantity each time we order (VOQ)
• Fill with, say, £10 worth, therefore we place a fixed order quantity (FOQ).

So looking first at the fixed/constant order quantity (FOQ)/continuous review-variable order time (VOT) interval options first, we find that:

- Each time there is an issue/withdrawal from stock, the stock position is reviewed to see if a replenishment order is needed.
- The same quantity is ordered each time, but it is ordered and delivered at varied times, e.g. 10 tonnes in weeks 1, 3 and 4. Suppliers are therefore expected to deliver, when needed, with any quantity required.
- The quantity to be ordered can use the economic order quantity (EOQ), less the free stock. EOQ finds the optimum order quantity, at the balance between the cost of placing and the cost of holding an order. EOQ is explained below, as is free stock.
- The decision on whether to order is triggered by the ROL. The ROL is calculated from the demand lead time (Average of demand × Supply lead time), plus the safety stock calculation (DV × S/L × √SLT).

With the variable order quantity (VOQ) /period review-fixed/constant order cycle time (FOT) interval, we find that:

- The stock position is reviewed at a fixed time to see if a replenishment order is needed. As this is at a fixed time, it can then facilitate more regular deliveries from suppliers.
- A variable quantity (VOQ) for each order is placed at the same time, e.g. 1, 3, 5 tonnes ordered every Friday to 'top up' to the targeted maximum inventory level required.
- The time period (FOT) setting can be influenced by EOQ (for example, the annual demand quantity is divided by the EOQ to give the number of orders per annum), with the high annual usage items being ordered more frequently.
- The maximum level for more stable demand/SLT can be determined by the EOQ. For more uncertain demand/SLT, the maximum level is determined by the Average of demand × Supply lead time, plus the safety stock (DV × S/L × √SLT), plus, an additional allowance of Average demand × Review period (for demand before the next review period).
- The quantity ordered (VOQ), i.e. the 'up to level', is the maximum stock level, less the free stock.

There are some other simplified variations for inventory replenishment with independent demand; the 'minimum–maximum' and the 'two-bin' methods.

The *two-bin* method is a simple form of the continuous review method that starts with the holding of two identical quantities of maximum stock, the maximum stock being that needed to cover the supply lead time. One 'bin' lot is then used to satisfy demand, and when this bin is empty (the ROP) the second bin is used and an order placed to replenish the empty bin. The order quantity is therefore fixed at one bin (FOQ) and is placed at a variable time (VOT) as the usage will vary before reaching the ROP/ROL. The two-bin method is useful for low-cost, high-demand items that have large order quantities. So if a new order has a SLT of two weeks and the usage is 10 items per day per full week, then 140 items is the ROL and ROP.

The *minimum–maximum* method is a form of the periodic review that has a maximum level set, for example, at the EOQ plus the ROL. The minimum level becomes the ROL and this is set by the average demand, the supply lead time and safety stock. When the ROL is reached (at a VOT), then orders are placed at the required quantity to return to the maximum level, therefore giving a variable order quantity (VOQ). Similar to the basic EOQ model, minimum–maximum however has more varied order amounts. It is analogous to the thermostat on a heating system where, when the temperature gets below a minimum, the boiler operates and supplies heat at a rate dependent on how much the temperature has fallen, and how much heat is being consumed during the lead time required to restore the room temperature to the required level.

Economic order quantity

This is a simple way to determine the economic order quantity (EOQ) and size of an order. It is found at the balance between the cost of placing an order and the cost of holding it. EOQ makes assumptions that there will be no stock-outs, zero lead times and that we can 'safely' order when at zero stocks. This is not realistic when faced with uncertain demand, the need for variable order quantities and supply lead times with variability. However, where repetitive ordering occurs, EOQ can be considered, for example, in 'make to order', when purchasing for stockholding (such as wholesalers) and with stable maintenance, repair and overhaul (MRO) items.

As it is essentially an accounting formula, EOQ requires much data, which may not be readily available, such as the holding and order costs, the different line items, the demand and the product unit costs.

Although EOQ will not apply in every situation, it does however give indications for re-order levels and points; it also emphasises the importance of calculating order costs (Figure 2.5).

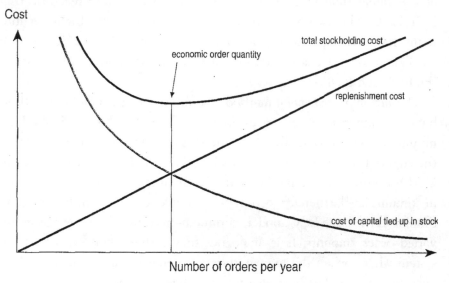

Figure 2.5   *EOQ model*

The order (or inventory or cost of capital tied up) costs fall with the number of orders, whereas the holding (or carrying or replenishment) costs rise with the number of orders. The formula is as follows:

$$EOQ = \frac{\sqrt{(2RS)}}{CI}$$

where R = Annual demand   say 3000
          S = Order cost   say £20
          C = Product unit cost   say £12
          I = Holding cost   say 25% of C

Therefore

$$EOQ = \frac{\sqrt{(2 \times 3000 \times 20)}}{12 \times 0.25} = 200\,units$$

The above figures used are for illustration only as each company will need to verify its own figures. Benchmark figures on order costs found in literature can be dangerous, for example the writer has seen quoted figures of £5–£15 at the lower end and £50–£75 at the higher end: quite a variation for alleged standard order cost benchmark figures!

Exaggerated costs are a common mistake when using EOQ, whereas in reality small variations will generally have little effect. However, critical costs must always be calculated by each company and be re-evaluated at least once a year. The critical costs are the order cost and the holding cost. It may not always be appropriate, for example, to include all the costs incurred in purchasing/ordering and warehousing/holding, as is shown below.

For *order costs*, if repetitive and regular ordering is undertaken, the fixed order costs are lower than when a long tendering process for, say, capital equipment is involved. For purchasing externally, the order costs would include the cost to enter orders, any procurement process approvals and also the processing after receipt, such as quality checking, invoice checking and payment. With internal ordering, such as requisitions from stores, the order costs represent the time to make the work order, together with selection/picking/issuing and inspections.

To calculate the order costs it can be more effective to determine the percentage of time spent performing the specific activities and multiply this by the total labour costs for a time period, typically a month. This should then be divided by the units processed in the time period.

Order costs, therefore, are mainly the cost of people in processing orders, but it may also include communication costs.

On the *holding* or *carrying costs*, these represent the cost of having inventory on hand, such as the storage costs and the investment costs. The investment costs are calculated as the value multiplied by the interest rate and the insurance charge (which is related to the value of inventory).

The storage costs are frequently mistaken. These should be the variable costs based on storing stock/inventory and should not be based on all of the fixed and variable costs of running the warehouse. The deciding factor is: are the costs directly affected by the inventory levels? If yes, then include the costs.

The cost per pallet stored is useful here, but then care is still needed as average values can be misleading: one pallet could contain £100 000 or £100 value of product. As the costs are applied in the formula as a percentage of the inventory value, then the inventory needs to be classified on the basis of the ratio of the storage space to the value. For example, the pallets of high-valued products are allowed for separately from the pallets of low-valued products.

Meanwhile, the conclusion from purely an EOQ point of view is to order the high annually used items often, and the low annually used items less often. When being used to determine a specific order quantity, EOQ can be useful for minor stock items of low value with known steady prices, demands and supply lead times. Where there is demand variability, such as seasonality, EOQ can still be calculated but using shorter time periods, ensuring that the usage and holding/carrying costs are also based on the same time period. EOQ is not really appropriate where there is random erratic demand with price fluctuations and variable supply lead times.

The comparisons between (a) the continuous and periodic review replenishment methods (Table 2.10) and (b) managing the inventory by value and volume (Table 2.11) illustrate the main differences. Both of these tables can be found in the Appendix to Chapter 2 on page 72–74.

Replenishment for dependent demand: Materials planning (MRP/MRPII)

It will be recalled that this is due to demand elsewhere; e.g. tyre manufacturer for supplying tyres to new cars (original equipment, OE). This is a more direct customer-driven decision which enables more anticipation and more certainty. It uses materials requirement planning (MRP) systems which are integrated computer systems planning tools used in production/manufacturing that determine the following:

- What input materials are required?
- How many?
- When needed?

Another method is manufacturing resource planning (MRPII) which follows on from MRP but adds in production capacity calculations. MRP is also one the parts of ERP (enterprise resource planning) systems such as SAP.

The basics of the MRP system are shown in Figure 2.6. The MRP has the following basic principles:

- Demand information goes into the master production schedule (MPS) which covers a specific time period and allocates the demand for each product into time buckets of days or weeks.
- The component structure for each product is held in the bills of materials file (BOM), which is the menu of parts and subassemblies item by item.
- From the top level of the BOM the MRP calculates the gross requirements needed. It then accounts for quantities in stock or already on

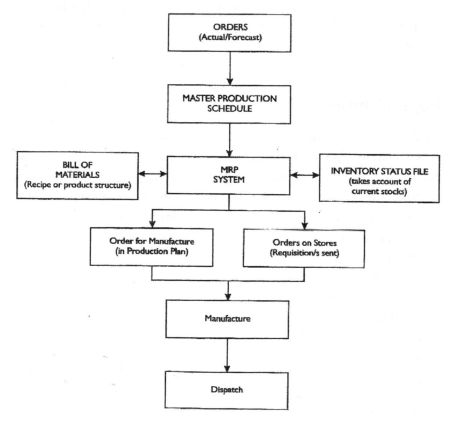

Figure 2.6 *The basics of an MRP system*

order and calculates the net requirements for the item. If there are any batching needs, such as a minimum order of 100 items, these are allowed for. Finally the MRP logic calculates against the lead times for supply and brings forward order dates accordingly. It then goes on to the next level of items until the lowest level of the BOM is reached.

- The output from the MRP is a set of time-phased materials requirements showing how much and when each item should be purchased.

To be effective, the MRP needs accurate forecasting and well-defined product structures in the bills of materials files (BOMs), along with known and reliable supply lead times. A common error however in some MRP applications is the reality of unreliable supply lead times and also that the default original lead time settings have never been reviewed to reflect subsequent changes. Therefore, wrong decisions are going to be made by the MRP application.

From the stores perspective, MRP systems will, in theory, give known and predictable receiving times for stocks, these stocks being only held for a short time. Indeed, MRP applications should foster cross-docking activities in stores and warehouses.

Replenishment for Spares

Generally these are not fast-moving stocks but may be held in stock to give instant availability for emergencies and breakdowns – a classic independent demand. The volumes held are frequently very low, so the use of replenishment techniques for fast-moving items is not really suitable. An option is therefore to use the original supplier who has an efficient spares support service; then hold one (or the appropriate number to cover the worse expected use during the supply lead time) and re-order immediately from the original supplier.

Spare parts for routine and scheduled service maintenance are more predictable as these are dependent demand. They therefore can be ordered in advance of the service maintenance, maybe using a MRP system.

Replenishment, free stock and current stock balance

The above discussion has considered the time at which an order point trigger can be calculated. Of course, it is more than likely that stock is on hand and this must therefore be allowed for.

The current stock balance will be recorded, allowing for issues, receipts, orders placed, etc. What is needed, however, is the measurement against the order point trigger, the so-called 'free stock' position. This is an adjustment to the current balance that allows for any of the following conditions:

- Addition of stock already ordered.
- Addition of stock in transit (if not recorded in the stock already ordered).
- Subtraction of stock already allocated to customers from the current stock balance.
- Subtraction of stock in hand being retained for any special purposes.

QUESTIONS ABOUT INVENTORY

Having studied the above, warehouse managers are now able to have a better view of the stock held in their stores and warehouses. This can mean that they become more proactive on the management issue of inventory. The following questions can be used to ensure that this is undertaken; it should be noted, however, that the division of questions is somewhat arbitrary.

Strategic aspects

- Why do you have inventory?
- What drives the present level of inventory?
- How are inventory levels set?
- How current is the decision on the inventory levels?
- How often are inventory decisions reviewed?
- In what direction is inventory being driven, and why?

- What are the actual service requirements of customers?
- How do the direction and/or change in inventory compare with the direction and/or change in sales?
- How much of the inventory reflects safety stock?
- Who is responsible for setting and for managing inventory levels?
- Are they the same person/department or not?
- How are excess inventories, and their cost, reflected in management responsibilities?
- How is the alternative inventory stock-outs, and their costs, reflected in management responsibilities?
- How are ICT system algorithms and underlying assumptions reviewed?
- Is customer input used?

Demand and forecast aspects

- How variable is demand?
- How is forecasting done?
- Is forecast accuracy regularly measured?
- How accurate is it, at the item/SKU level?
- How timely is it prepared and submitted?
- How does purchasing and manufacturing handle the forecast inaccuracies?
- Do they overbuy or overbuild to compensate for doubts about the forecast?
- Is inventory forecast to the distribution centre level so that the right inventory at the right quantity is carried at each facility?
- Or, is the forecast at a macro level with no direction on what inventory, how much inventory and where inventory should be positioned?

Lead time and methods aspects

- How variable are supplier lead times?
- How are the total lead times, including in transit stock lead times and internationally sourced items, incorporated in the system?
- How accurate are the free stock inventories that are used in the resulting production planning and sourcing?

- How are supplier reliability and lead times reflected in inventory planning and management?
- Are additional inventories factored in to buffer for each of these issues?
- How are these aspects factored into supplier selection decisions?
- Does purchasing have purchase order visibility with suppliers to control ordered items at the SKU level?
- Do suppliers understand and collaborate with the inventory philosophy and approach?
- Do purchased products flow to keep inventory in the supply chain or are they irregular, aggregated?
- How are transportation reliability and transit times reflected in inventory planning and management?
- Are additional inventories factored in to buffer for each of these issues?

Warehousing aspects

- Where is inventory stored and why?
- How many distribution centres are used and why? (Each distribution centre means that additional safety stock will be carried.)
- Are they in the right locations?
- How much obsolete/dead, old promotions and very slow-moving dead inventory is there?
- What is the storage cost for such 'dead' inventory?
- Is inventory often transferred between distribution centres to provide inventory to fill orders? (That is inefficient use of transportation, not good customer service and resulting from wrong forecasting allocation.)

Finally, in this look at inventory, stock and product classification, the following summaries will illustrate how inventory management can be better planned.

Seven rules for inventory

1. All inventories should be justified and minimised, with the target being zero inventory.
2. Staff needs training and motivating to identify, locate and count all inventory correctly.

3. Safety stock should only be held to protect variable demand to give customer service, or, against variable supply.
4. Orders should only be placed when a stock-out is anticipated.
5. Re-order just enough to cover demand, until the next receipt is due.
6. Focus effort on the few important items and not on the trivial many.
7. ICT can help and take away the 'number crunching', but manual checks and reviews are still needed.

Model for planning inventory

1. Establish whether current performance is cost or service driven.
2. Conduct an ABC analysis and demand analysis, for example:
   • focus on the important few not the trivial many.
3. Consider reducing order quantity options, for example:
   • re-order only enough to cover demand until next receipt
   • increase order frequency consistent with EOQ.
4. Measure and consider reducing safety stock, for example:
   • hold only when protects service against variable demand
   • SLT and SLTV
   • check that service levels are needed
   • reviews
   • measure and improve forecast accuracy
   • reduce the number of stockholding locations.
5. Reduce finished goods stocks, for example:
   • move towards make/assemble to order
   • reduce variations, obsoletes, low sale items
   • make smaller batches.
6. Review and check parameters manually and regularly, the target being zero inventories, for example:
   • analysis at item level
   • order more frequently at item level.
7. Aim for short fixed lead times with accurate demand forecasting.

ACTION TIME 2.1: ENTERTAINMENT UK, DEMAND AND WAREHOUSING

Entertainment UK is the UK's largest wholesale distributor of home entertainment products, supplying many of Britain's best-known retailers with nearly a quarter of the UK music and video industry's entire output. With the ability to unite the interests of suppliers and retailers, it makes it attractive, simple and profitable for them to do business together.

Founded in 1966 as Record Merchandisers Limited, the company achieved rapid growth to become the largest wholesale distributor in the UK. Following Record Merchandisers Limited's rebirth as Entertainment UK in 1988, the company has concentrated on building the systems to become entirely responsive to the commercial and operational needs of individual customers and suppliers.

Specialises

Entertainment UK is a wholly owned subsidiary of the Woolworth's Group plc which specialises in delivering a range of entertainment, home and family products, through its retail, distribution and publishing arms. Entertainment UK's clients include Tesco, Woolworth's, MVC, Safeway, Comet, Waitrose and Makro.

Last year its turnover was over £750 million and, with business growing at about 10% a year, Entertainment UK has installed an integrated materials handling system at its new distribution centre. The £114 million system, which has been designed and installed by Vanderlande Industries, uses a mix of picking techniques and automated handling systems to deliver exceptional 99.9% order accuracy.

The project is part of Entertainment UK's development of a new 200 000 sq.ft distribution centre in Greenford, Middlesex, that will work alongside three existing facilities in the London area. To handle the rapid growth in Entertainment UK's business, the new system has been designed to provide a flexible expansion path to accommodate a throughput of up to 120 million items a year, while supporting an increase in the number of SKUs from the current level of 25 000.

The entertainment industry is unusual in having a very large number of both suppliers and products, with the most popular 10% of titles accounting for more than 95% of throughput. This 10% is, however, extremely dynamic, with around 200 changes each week, and new items ('chart toppers') frequently coming in with an exceptionally pronounced volume spike.

'The broad mix of products and throughputs made this a very challenging project,' commented Alan Faulding, development manager at Entertainment UK. 'Inventory is a major part of our costs, so order accuracy, product protection and the accuracy of our stock management are all critical factors in our business improvement.'

Reliable

The solution, developed jointly by Vanderlande Industries and Mr Faulding's team at Entertainment UK, provides reliable, efficient movement and tracking of product from receipt, through appropriate storage and picking systems, to sortation and despatch.

Of the eight companies originally approached, Vanderlande's proposal was slightly more capital intensive but was able to provide substantially greater operational benefits and a preferred operating philosophy.

To meet the business requirements efficiently, Vanderlande used automated conveyor systems to integrate storage and picking operations that are optimised for four different levels of throughput. Super-fast items are held in a four-crane high-bay then order picked off pallets in full-tray quantities. Fast and medium movers are batch picked (using a pick to light system) from totes held in a miniload system.

Slow-moving items are picked from flow racking or shelving. Product from these three areas is held in the miniload system and sorted for despatch in a two-hour wave. Very slow-moving items are order picked directly into cartons. The eight miniload cranes are thought to be the first in Europe to be fitted with four individual handling devices, allowing up to four totes to be stored or retrieved in each pass.

Each Tilt Tray Sorter is fed by fully automatic high-speed induction units incorporating a combination of state of the art inline labelling and security tagging machines.

Gentle

The tilt-tray sortation system has been optimised for gentle handling of small single items and incorporates sophisticated flow control to ensure that even small products are accurately placed.

'We were impressed by the overall quality of the Vanderlande organisation and the rigour they applied to ensure the system delivers the best possible performance,' says Mr Folding. 'It was commissioned within the agreed budget and timescales and is proving very accurate.'

TASK

Explain how demand influences the warehouse processes.

Source: Distribution Business, December 2002.

APPENDIX

Table 2.10 Comparisons on replenishment for independent demand: continuous and periodic review

Parameter	Continuous review FOQ–VOT	Periodic review VOQ–FOT
How much to order, plus, need to allow for the free stock position: The stock on hand, plus any stock expected, less any stock allocated or being kept for special use	A fixed order quantity (FOQ) when at the ROL. Typically the EOQ is ordered	A variable order quantity (VOQ): dependent upon what has been used since the last fixed time check and what is now needed, if any, to bring stock back to the required level. Allow for Av.D × SLT, plus Av.D × Review Period, plus the safety stock calculation
When to order	When at the ROL, therefore a variable order time (VOT). The ROL is calculated by Av.D × SLT plus the safety stock calculation	Fixed order cycle (FOT), as there is a predetermined time when to order. The time is influenced by the EOQ (annual demand quantity, divided by the EOQ, giving the number of orders per annum)
EOQ	Amount to consider ordering when at ROP	Helps in setting the review period frequency of when to order

Table 2.10 Continued

Parameter	Continuous review FOQ–VOT	Periodic review VOQ–FOT
Assumes/Prefers	Certainty with constant demand, lead times and prices throughout a period. Suppliers have to deliver at any time	Can deal better with uncertainty. Suppliers can make regular deliveries
Stable demand	Lower safety stocks	Higher safety stocks as protecting over a longer time period
Seasonal/variable demand	Higher stocks due to big demand swings	Lower stocks
Control	Needs continual/ perpetual monitoring of inventory levels, therefore is more responsive	Checked at the review period only
Usage	Most common for low-value items and infrequently ordered 'C' items. Used by industrial manufacturers	Most common for high valued and critical 'A' items. Used by FMCG industry as it gives a rhythm for checking whether to place an order or not

Table 2.11 Comparisons on replenishment for independent demand: managing inventory by value and volume

	Low volume	Medium volume	High volume
High value	1 for 1, Poisson distribution	PR: 7 to 14 days	PR: 1 to 7 days with fixed lead times
	Average periods forecasts	Exponential smoothing forecasts with seasonal, trend and error tracking	Exponential smoothing forecasts with seasonal, trend and error tracking
	Parameters reviewed every 3/6 months	Parameters by tracking signals reviewed 4 times per year	Parameters by tracking signals reviewed monthly
Medium value	CR	CR: Q on EOQ, ROP on av.D + SS	PR: 14 to 28 days
	Average demand forecasts, plan for seasonality	Average demand forecasts	Exponential smoothing forecasts with seasonal, trend and error tracking
	Parameters reviewed every 3/6 months	Parameters reviewed every 1/3 months	Parameters by tracking signals reviewed 1/3 months
Low Value	Two Bin	CR: Q on 6–8 orders p.a. ROP on av.D + SS	CR: Q on EOQ, ROP on av.D + SS
	Average demand forecasts	Average demand forecasts	Average demand forecasts
	Parameters reviewed every 6/9 months	Parameters reviewed every 1/3 months	Parameters reviewed every 1/3 months

3

Stock Control

Stockholding represents capital tied up in the business and is therefore subject to financial controls. Indeed, from a purely financial point of view, stock is viewed as an asset as it is capable of generating income and revenue to the business. Stock control checking is therefore undertaken for the following reasons:

- To verify the value tied up
- To identify the costs of holding stocks
- To respond to non-conformance
- To check for loss or fraud of stock
- To show where mistakes are being made so that they can be rectified
- As part of the management control system.

STOCK INACCURACY

Stock therefore needs to be controlled and a careful watch should be undertaken on the physical stock being stored. If stock records are not accurate, then the following are some of the consequences of inaccuracy:

- Unforeseen stock-outs; for example, this usually happen when an important order is required to be fulfilled!
- Informal stockpiling; for example, 'squirrel' stores by internal users.

- Excess stockholding; for example, by over-ordering, as the stock actually there is not visible to users.
- Informal stock recording; for example, through an inefficient recording system.
- Purchasing direct; for example, as users do not believe the stores records.
- Pickers get frustrated; for example, by having to 'search' for goods the documents say are there, but are not to be found.
- Orders are not met.

The causes of stock inaccuracy can be varied and many and the following are some of the possible reasons for this:

- Data input errors; for example, from manual keying in, or from scanning the wrong items.
- Incorrect recording; for example, incorrect product identification.
- Processing delays on documents; for example, delays in entering into the system receipts or despatches or internal damages/ write-offs.
- Loss of documents; for example, making issues without documents, meaning non-recording.
- Mismatch between the 'actual' and the documents; for example, the shortfall is not recorded.
- Identifying receipts incorrectly; for example, with a different set of supplier invoices.
- Identifying returns correctly; for example, incorrect allocation to the original customer.
- Poor stock check reconciliation procedures; a topic which we will cover shortly.
- Wrong locations; for example, the goods found in a location are not the correct goods for that location but they are recorded as being the correct goods.
- Theft, for example, by internal personnel or from external 'break- ins' people or a combination of both.
- Poor packing/labelling; for example, wrong identification.

To minimise inaccuracy, there is a need to create a climate of high expectations, for example, by giving the clear goal that only total accuracy will be acceptable. Training can also be of help by giving not only knowledge of product and processes, but also training on the wider aspects of the company and the impacts of 'getting it wrong'. Performance monitoring is often of value by measuring accuracy by section/department and then publishing the figures and giving feedback for improvement.

Inaccuracy can also be minimised by limiting access to goods and materials, and by monitoring systems, investigating and eliminating errors. For example, by reviewing checking process, recoding and analysing errors, investigating, giving feedback and correcting mistakes. Automation with associated bar coding/scanning/auto identification is often found to be valuable in reducing stock inaccuracies, providing the 'integrity' of the labelling is correct.

CONTINUOUS OR PERIODIC STOCK CHECKING

There are two basic methods of undertaking stock checking: the continuous or perpetual methods and the periodic check methods.

Continuous/perpetual stock checking

This is used in larger operations and involves a continuous check through the year. Workload is therefore more evenly distributed with, for example, every item checked at least once per year. The checking can be manual or automated, with the principle that the scheduling is done secretly and by segmenting the actual counting/checking.

ABC analysis can be used to do the segmenting and the following is the principle used:

- A lines: Fast-moving lines, or higher value lines are counted more, with a lower (1%) tolerance for error.
- B lines: Medium movers or medium value lines are counted less, with a lower (2–5%) tolerance level.
- C lines: Slow movers or low-value lines are counted even less; with an even lower (5–10%) tolerance level.

An example of this is as follows:

- A lines: 2000 items counted 6 times p.a. = 12 000 counts
- B lines: 3000 items counted 3 times p.a. = 9000 counts
- C lines: 4000 items counted twice p.a.   = 8000 counts
- D lines (non-movers): 500 items counted = 500 counts
  once p.a.

Total = 29 500 counts p.a.

So, if 230 days are available in the year, then 128 counts per day are needed. This may also fit well with the standard for stock checkers, which is commonly around 100–130 counts per day.

Continuous/perpetual stock checking enables the checking to be an ongoing activity and enables all other stores/warehouse operations to continue 'as normal'. It is not subjected to the 'shutdowns' that will often be found when undertaking periodic stock checking.

Periodic stock checking

This is found in smaller companies and usually means a 'shutdown' period. This, in turn, means that there is a known time for stock checking, accordingly any discrepancies in the year can be covered up before the stock check. Additionally with periodic stock checking, often untrained people are used due to the need to 'get it over as quickly as possible'; errors therefore are more commonly found with periodic stock checking.

Spot checking

This can be used with either of the above methods, the main feature being that it is undertaken unannounced. No one knows when it will happen. Spot checks may also be undertaken on just specific lines/items and can also be undertaken for security reasons. One useful and ideal way to spot check is when the systems say there are zero items. This means that the checking will be undertaken at low cost with high accuracy, and as zero stocks take little time to count, there should be no errors in counting. Alternatively, counting at the re-order point can also bring similar counting benefits.

STOCK CONTROL

Some key questions to ask on stock control are listed below.

Users and customers

- How do stock levels move in relation to sales?
- What is the control information for customer service and stock levels?
- Do we have slow-moving or redundant stocks? How are these dealt with?
- Are we always running out of items? If so, why?
- Is the availability of our finished stock reduced by stock reservations for customers?

Forecasting

- Do new product proposals explore the implications of additional stock and their effect on cash flow?
- Do we have cash flow forecasts?
- Is sales forecasting taken seriously?
- Do we fully use historic demand data?

Suppliers

- Are our terms of credit compatible with our suppliers' payment terms?
- Do our suppliers frequently put us on 'stop'? If so, why?
- Can our suppliers help us, e.g. supplier stockholding, vendor managed inventory?
- Can we hold part-processed stocks that can be customised to order and, therefore, reduce finished inventory levels?

Methods

- Do we set meaningful stock level targets?
- Are our stock records accurate?
- Is our system a burden or an aid?
- Is the computer working for us or against us?
- Do we invest in practical training for our staff?

- Are we making use of techniques that will help us, such as EOQ, exponential smoothing for sales forecasts, etc.?

Responsibilities

- Who is responsible for balancing the conflicting issues of stock, customer service and suppliers, production or purchasing performance?
- Are there regular inspections by senior management of our warehouses?
- Are our housekeeping standards high at all times, or just for VIP visits?
- Have we fully explored variety reduction?
- Do we have exception reporting techniques?

Adding new products/items to stock

It can be all too easy for business functions to add new products to the company's catalogue and this may lead to a proliferation of raw materials or finished products. Therefore, before embarking on an action that will lead to an increase in the variety of products, the following questions (adapted from *Stock Control*, IPS, 1991, reproduced by permission of CIPS) need to be answered:

- Do we really need this item?
- Do we need it now?
- What will be the effect on cash flow?
- Do we have the storage space?
- Can we use a proprietary item?
- Do we need so many sizes, colours, and shapes?
- Can we replace, not add?
- If this replaces, what is the effect on existing stock and raw materials?
- Can we use multi-language descriptions?
- Can we hold part-processed stocks, and then adapt them to our customers' needs only when they order?
- What is the development lead-time? Will we miss the market?
- Will this new item change/reduce demand for any of our existing products?
- Is there a shelf life problem?
- Do we have 'feet on the ground' forecasts?
- Can this new item be supplied in the quantities we need?

- Does this fit in with our long-term plans?
- Can we adapt existing tooling?
- Do all the departments in our organisation know about this?
- Has it been safety-tested?
- What assumptions have been made? Have they been tested?
- Can we get this from another division or from a competitor?
- Can this design replace two or more of our existing designs?
- Can we utilise existing raw materials or components?

SECURITY AND PREVENTING LOSS

Most people, when considering this topic, think only of having to prevent break-ins from outside: so-called external theft. While such prevention is certainly needed, warehouse security must concentrate more on the reality that most theft is internal – and is often undertaken by 'trusted' employees. This can be hard to accept and certainly can be a most unpleasant business, but internal theft is both the most concealed and prevalent form of theft. The evidence for this is very clear and indeed some security experts reckon that the 80/20 rules applies, with 80% of theft from internal sources and 20% from external sources.

Despite this knowledge, it is reckoned that over 80% of prevention measures are directed towards preventing external theft.

Actual figures and values of theft are always going to be difficult to discover. However, some indications are available from the European FMCG retail sector, where their so-called 'shrinkage' problem (which includes theft/stock loss and damage) amounts to some 18 billion euros across Europe alone. If this were to be eliminated, then 1.7% is added straight to the bottom line profit.

To illustrate the scale of the problem in another way, for the 'average' theft, security experts reckon that five people are involved and the thefts have been taking place for six months. Government has also stated that approximately two-thirds of all staff steal from their employer (*source:* www.burtonsecurity.com).

Finally it can be noted that internal theft is reckoned to be valued at 10 times more than all 'external' street crimes (which includes far more than just external theft from warehouses).

Some trouble signs to look for in a warehouse

- Figures changed on order documentation
- Missing documents
- Authorisation stamps missing
- Decline in employee purchases
- Discrepancies in records and stock checks
- Strange marking on packages
- Petty 'grazing' of product
- Partly opened product is visible
- Product stacked to prevent the view path of closed circuit television (CCTV) systems
- Window guards having screws missing
- Emergency doors have cardboard wedged in the lock
- Excessive spending patterns of staff
- Checkers and pickers always take breaks together
- Product found in rubbish skips
- Skip contractor is friendly with certain staff
- Employees make frequent trips to their cars during work time
- Too frequent smoke breaks
- Product not in the right location
- Picking slips found in skip
- Product not checked against master documents when loading
- Drivers load their own vehicles
- Staff living above their means
- Receipts not double checked by authorised person
- Cleaning contractors staff related to company staff
- People seen wandering around without authority or being challenged.

Employers often model a culture of acceptance on employee theft; those who are caught are rarely prosecuted – the lack of prosecution being seemingly due to fears over bad publicity and the fear of not being able to prove the theft which, in turn, may demonstrate an inability to ensure that the correct summary dismissal procedures are undertaken. Summary dismissal is allowed for proven theft within the UK Employment Legislation.

As an example of the continued failure in detecting and preventing theft, the theft of alcohol rises four-fold in the months before Christmas yet these 'statistics' happen year after year.

Management can therefore all too easily become complacent with a false sense of security and have a view that 'it never happens here as my people would never steal'. Regrettably the evidence does not support such an understandable view and overlooking the human element of theft can be fatal. After all, it will need people to catch people. This will only happen if management and other people are prepared, but meanwhile the thief already is.

Some employees see theft as providing informal 'perks of the job' as, in addition to goods, cash and time are commonly pilfered. Cash and time theft, for example, can happen when an employee who is fit and well makes sure that sickness entitlement with pay is taken fully each year; it is seen as a 'holiday perk'.

The goods that are regularly stolen from warehouses and stores include 'mundane' items like packaging and wooden pallets. In excess of £100 million per annum is one estimate of the value of wooden pallets that go 'missing'. These are commonly neither reported nor regarded as theft, with the loss being sometimes largely due to poor control systems.

There is much in business that cannot be controlled such as inflation and market conditions, but warehouse internal security can almost always be kept in better control.

Management needs to recognise that any potential thief (internal and external) must have knowledge of the products, access, opportunity, time and the market to sell to. Clearly, the internal employee is well placed on many of these points, but the following lists some ways in which internal thefts can be prevented.

- Install security systems and internal controls for all people entering/leaving premises, including all grades of management and every visitor, including customers and suppliers.
- Install good lighting and eliminate blind spots.
- Keep the warehouse congestion free and ordered, ensuring if possible, as the work flows through the warehouse, that there is an automatic check by the next link in the flow.

- In recruitment and selection, use valid integrity tests and be alert to the real fact that there are people who seek employment purely to have an opportunity to steal, after which they leave and move on to another job before they are caught.
- Conduct background checks, as thoroughly as is allowed by legal requirements.
- Review and revise information that is made available to employees, and restrict access if appropriate.
- Carry out spot stock control checks.
- Establish audit trails with accurate and timely reporting systems.
- Stress the importance of honesty, integrity and the costs and consequences of being caught stealing.
- Model honesty in the company.
- Counsel 'troubled employees' out of the company.
- Improve the working environment and eliminate discontent, and create bonds between employees and the company (people management will be covered fully in Chapter 10).

Meanwhile, on external theft prevention, the following can help:

- Fit burglar alarms to cover all doors and all other openings.
- Fit foils on windows, infrared beam system, motion detectors, CCTV.
- Ensure that alarms are connected to a security company/police station.
- Conduct security patrols, both internal and external
- Build a secure perimeter fence, over 7 feet (2.2 metres)
- Consider fitting exterior perimeter lighting.
- Fit a modern people access control system. (Card/Keypad, etc.)

INFORMATION SECURITY

Security is also needed, not just for the product flows but also for the information. The UK Department of Trade and Industry has issued the following listing to draw attention to this increasing problem – a most critical aspect for every business in the twenty-first century:

- Does your organisation have an information security policy?
- Are staff members allocated specific security responsibilities, e.g. locking the building, allocating passwords?

- Are specific personnel measures, such as training users or including security in their job descriptions, taken with respect to security?
- Does your organisation have an information security policy?
- Do you know what your organisation's main assets are? Do you have a list of them, and does this list include information?
- Does your organisation take steps to prevent unauthorised access to your premises?
- Have you implemented operational controls and procedures to safeguard your information, e.g. use of back-ups, anti-virus software, firewalls?
- Do you control access to information through the effective use of user IDs and passwords; e.g. making sure users don't share passwords, write their passwords on post-it notes?
- Have steps been taken to ensure that security requirements are defined and incorporated during system development or met by packaged software solutions?
- Do you have any business continuity plans?
- Do you ensure that you meet all your legal requirements/obligations, e.g. licensing, copyright, data protection?

ACTION TIME 3.1: THE YOGURT COMPANY AND SECURITY

The following is a briefing note given to a security expert by the Yogurt Company which has a warehouse complex of 50 000 square feet located in London next to a railway line. Housing in the area is expensive. The perimeter has a chain fence around the premises and access is through one entrance only. Parking is allowed inside the premises as parking in the local area is not allowed. There are over 100 vehicle movements in and out per day. Goods are packed in cartons and are shrink wrapped onto Euro pallets.

A local small independent company based nearby handles the security. They work 24 hours a day. There is a CCTV system in the premises and there are two cameras watching externally. The monitor is situated in the traffic manager's office. Loads are recorded in and out of the premises.

A series of small-scale thefts have been going on for some time. In the months of October and November, the thefts have increased and more discarded cartons of yogurt can be seen in the warehouse. The claims from major supermarkets for short deliveries have also increased.

Tasks

1. Discuss the security implications.
2. Describe what you would do.

TRAINING TOPICS

It can be useful for a company engaged in managing stock to ensure that all concerned personnel have a common understanding of what is involved. The following is an example of the contents from one such training programme:

- The role of stock
  - Why hold stock?
  - Inventory costs and service variables
  - How much to order and when.

- Product classification
  - Supply and demand variables
  - ABC analysis to show where to concentrate limited resources
  - Product handling groups and classifying for effective operations
  - Checklists to help on the analysis.

- Stock coding
  - Different methods
  - Understanding of all involved
  - Checklists to help on deciding the best option.

- Stock recording
  - Separation of powers
  - Legal issues
  - How do we get inaccuracies?

- Stock checking
  - Roles and responsibilities
  - Requirements
  - Job descriptions
  - Authority levels
  - Tolerances and approvals
  - The programme
  - Options
  - Reconciliations/discrepancies.

- Security and loss
  - Internal theft
  - External theft
  - Preventative measures.

4

The Warehouse and Operational Principles

WAREHOUSE STRUCTURE

Not too many companies will have the chance or opportunity to move into a purpose-designed warehouse. Indeed, for most companies, they are 'stuck' with what they have, or if they do move they will usually inherit an existing warehouse building. The following points can be used to assess the warehouse structure:

Structure and site

- Are the walls constructed of concrete (preferred) or wood/non-metallic (least preferred)?
- Is the electrical wiring in good condition?
- Will you have sole occupancy? If not, are you clearly physically separated from other tenants?
- What products are any other tenants storing?
- Is the site free from yard storage/rubbish/vegetation?
- Is there a local history of flooding?
- What facilities are there for 'staff welfare'?

Fire safety

- What fire protection equipment is installed?
- Is the fire alarm connected to a place with 24 hour attendance?
- Are automatic sprinklers, smoke/heat detectors fitted?

- Is the no smoking policy effective?
- What are the procedures for supervising any hot work/cutting welding? (An important topic that is returned to later in Health and Safety in Chapter 6.)

Security

We have already covered this in Chapter 3 and noted there that most of warehouse theft is undertaken by the internal staff. The following measures therefore cover mainly external theft from break-ins, etc. and are repeated here for continuity.

- Is a burglar alarm installed?
- Will burglar alarms cover all doors and all other openings?
- Are the following fitted: foils on windows, infrared beam system, motion detectors, CCTV?
- Is the burglar alarm connected to a system in a police station?
- When was it last tested? What is the testing programme?
- What security patrols are there – internal and external?
- Is the perimeter fence secure and over 7 feet (2.2 metres)?
- Is exterior perimeter lighting fitted?
- What is the people access control system? (Card/Keypad, etc.)
- What are the stock management controls?

Loading Bay(s)

- Is there any broken brickwork beside doorway?
- Are the vehicles' turnaround times long?
- Is there sufficient space in the yard for manoeuvring of vehicles?
- Is the yard being used for unloading/loading?
- Are mobile ramps used?
- Is there 'weather' inside the building?
- How much time is spent resetting any dock leveller plates?
- Is there any damage to leveller plates and doors?
- Is there a bad match between warehouse floor levels and vehicles?
- Are any dock leveller platforms too short or steep, causing fork lift trucks to be grounded?

WAREHOUSE OPERATIONS

Warehouse operations and activity fall into the following activities:

- Goods in or receiving
- Put away into the storage area
- Order selection and picking/ packing
- Goods outward or despatch.

The key aspect to be considered in all these activities is the conflicting priority of maximising the use of the space allocated to each activity, while minimising the time taken to undertaken the activity. These activities will usually involve the use of equipment such as fork trucks, racking and ICT. Indeed it can be difficult to discuss warehouse operation without discussing equipment. While some reference to equipment is inevitably made in this chapter, it will be covered more fully in the next chapter.

The other key aspects involved here are the connections and links between the activities to prevent errors. So called 'pick-errors' and mistakes noticed by customers are not necessarily picking errors. For example, if the wrong goods were received but not checked fully, then these could be subsequently delivered to the customer and explained as a 'pick error'.

Errors can therefore come from the following aspects of warehouse operations:

- Receiving and product details; such as the packaging, labelling, incorrect contents, pack quantities, varied pack sizes, etc.
- Replenishment and storage; such as wrong locations being used, loose parts in bins getting mixed, ambiguous location labelling, etc.
- Picking process; such as time pressures, unclear instructions, etc.
- Transport delivery; such as to the wrong locations, proof of delivery signing, etc.
- Customers own sorting/checking processes; for example, product that has been received physically correctly, but is entered on the system wrongly.

The cost of errors noticed by customers is not therefore limited to the warehousing operations and a 1% customer delivery error can easily result in 10–30% extra cost to the supplier. This involves far more than just the warehousing re-picking costs, for example, customer service authorisations, credit note issuing, finance delayed payments, stock records corrections, transport return and re-delivery; plus those costs resultant from breakdowns in creditability and reliability factors.

Accuracy throughout all the warehouse activity is therefore needed and each of these activities has its own specialist considerations on, for example, goods inwards, checking, quality control and the structure/layout of the goods receiving areas. We will therefore look at each area in turn.

RECEIVING

There is a view that what happens in receiving sets the whole time beat, pace and tone for the total warehouse operation. Ultimately, mistakes made here will impact elsewhere in the warehouse/company and, even worse, with the customers/users.

Assessing when goods will actually be arriving and taking action to schedule receipts can help to improve the workload scheduling. Appointments and 'book-ins', which are then given priority, can work well in work scheduling for the warehouse, providing there is adequate coordination to prevent this being unhelpful and counter-productive. For example, standing time costs for road freight transport vehicles is a major cost item. Indeed, it is known that poor turnaround vehicle performance can feature in price negotiations by suppliers and, although rare, the writer has knowledge of penalties being paid by retailer RDCs to major suppliers if vehicle turnaround is not undertaken within agreed parameters.

Being able to 'flatten' out receipts over a shift can help to leverage resources and possibly have staff who, say, concentrate on receipts in the morning and switch to despatching in the afternoon.

Working with suppliers on receipts should be mutually beneficial; besides the vehicle turnaround time, aspects such as labelling, coding, marking and packing quantities can all help to give mutual advantage.

The following activities are involved with receipts:

- Establish the unloading area that is to be used, ensuring that it is safe and suitable for the operation.
- Record the arrival of the vehicle and note the seal(s) number(s).
- Break the seal(s) with the driver present.
- Check the order documentation and record each item against the consignment note.
- Ensure that the vehicle is safe before unloading.
- Unload the vehicle.
- Assemble the goods in the goods receipt area.
- Check the goods for quantity (use blind checking?), condition and possible damage.
- Carry out any required quality checks.
- Report any discrepancies and condition/quality at once.
- Finally, move the goods out of the goods receipt area as soon as possible to the appropriate destination:
  - location in the warehouse where goods are to be stored (see the later section on location)
  - the staging/holding area they are to be held in (such as quarantine)
  - any cross-docking activity (see below).

If the receipts activity is large enough, then separate physical receipts areas can be made for the internal destination areas. For example, if a large amount of returns is received requiring much checking, then these could be better handled completely separately from the new product receipts and cross-docked products could be kept nearer to the destination despatch areas.

The receiving operations and the despatch operations both act at the interface between the supply and demand requirements. In some supply chain operations receiving and despatching may occur almost simultaneously. This is often known as cross-docking as goods effectively move from the receipt dock area to the goods despatch dock areas, without incurring any long-term storage. Product also flows through the warehouse more quickly and more easily. There is therefore less movement and less cost incurred in the warehouse operations due to reduced lead times, minimised handling and no storage holding costs.

Cross-docking, however, requires that the following conditions are satisfied:

- Integration and coordination of the appropriate supplier/customer interfaces. EDI/email, scanning and bar code technologies can be most useful enablers.
- Destination is known, ideally before, but at the latest when the goods are received.
- Customer is ready to receive the goods.
- Product data recognition, to facilitate quick checking/verification.
- No long timescales for any quality control or checking on receipt.
- Good quality information (for example, with advanced knowledge and EDI/email).
- Cooperative supply chains.
- Disciplined deliveries.

Cross-docking will therefore be sensitive to the following:

- Non-receipt of suppliers' deliveries.
- Short receipt on suppliers' deliveries.
- Late arrivals of suppliers' vehicles, bad weather, road traffic delays.
- Last minute changes in customer orders.

The following case study gives an example of how the amount of stock held can be reduced by cross-docking.

CASE STUDY 4.1: STOCK REDUCTION BY CROSS-DOCKING

Company

- Retailer of apparel, household merchandise
- £500 million per annum turnover
- 3 RDCs
- Product sourced 50% overseas and 50% UK
- All products bar coded.

EDI with UK Suppliers

- Used with suppliers for order call-offs
- Suppliers give stock availability
- Call-offs given per RDC to supplier
- Tracked at key points
- UK stock is cross-docked

Supplier lead times

Day 1: Call off
Day 2: Schedules for collection
Day 3: Collection by retailer
Day 4: RDC
Day 5: Store.

Reasons for success

- Lead time disciplines clearly stated and agreed.
- Commitment of all involved.
- Multi-disciplined internal team of purchasing, store merchandising, logistics and store operation.

Dock levellers, when installed, will need to accommodate the following:

- Minimum 5/6 tonnes axle loading for normal fork lift equipment access
- Steel gauge strength
- Slope maximum 1 in 10 (gentler slopes, for example 1 in 12, will give power savings).

The various types of dock leveller are shown in Table 4.1, and the *loading bay design* of these levellers will need to consider the following features:

- Are all vehicle types and sizes/projections that will use the facility known?
- Can the end loads, at the back of the vehicle, be removed safely?
- Do any loading dock seal head curtains obstruct the top of loads?

Table 4.1   Various types of dock leveller

Feature/type	Speed	Cost	Other
Swing lip	Slower	Cheaper	Fixed
Telescopic lip	Quicker	Expensive	Adjustable
Mechanical	Slower	Cheaper	
Hydraulic	Quicker	Expensive	Safer

- Is the area well lit, including the inside of vehicles?
- Are the controls for the leveller door and seals all housed in one control box?
- Are the length and gradient of the dock leveller platforms appropriate?
- Will the leveller lip reach into all of the vehicles that will require access?
- Is there a safe waiting area for vehicles when all bays are busy?
- Are full instructions on dock operation sequences known and kept in the right place?
- Are the vehicle driver and dock operator clear about the signals or instruction that are used to allow the driver to pull away from the dock?

The right number of doors/docks will depend upon the operation being undertaken. For example, slow in/out movements for long-term storage warehouses will need fewer door/docks than those cross-docking high throughput warehouses and those transit sheds (like parcel sortation) depots. To assist in determining the number of doors/docks required, the following questions can be asked:

- How will the product be received (in cartons or cases, on pallets or slip sheets)?
- What quantity is received (small van loads or full trailer loads)?
- What are the frequency/velocity of receipts/despatches?
- What type of vehicles do we unload/load (rear or from side)?
- What material handling equipment (MHE) is required (pallet trucks, fork trucks, conveyor or handball).
- Will the MHE have high utilisation levels (can it be used elsewhere if necessary)?

- What are the timescales for the operations (fast cross-docking in and out or for long-term storage)?
- Are receipts and despatches better on the same side of the warehouse (giving flexibility between receipts and despatches) or better at opposite ends (giving a cross-dock/though flow activity)?
- What inside staging area is needed for receipt checking, etc., and for despatch load marshalling?
- To give future flexibility, when building a new warehouse, is it worth while to build in knock-out panels in the external structure to facilitate future extensions and therefore ease the joining of structures?

LOCATION METHODS IN THE WAREHOUSE

After the receiving of product and having determined its storage needs, products have to be put away and located in the warehouse. This means asking the question: Just where is the product to be kept? While reference to the earlier discussion on product handling groups will determine some of the location aspects (such as non-compatibilities like chilled/ frozen food products, products with an odour, hazardous products), we are concerned here with the principles behind the generalised location that is to be used in the warehouse.

This largely depends on whether we use a fixed or a random location system for the locations. A fixed location means that for a specific product group, a fixed and known location is given; random location means the location is generated randomly. The former is often used for pick face locations but can also be used for bulk stock storage. It does mean that space utilisation can be negatively impacted as space is available, in theory, for holding the maximum stock levels of the product. With random locations, however, the location is determined by predetermined algorithms and is usually ICT warehouse management system (WMS) controlled. Accordingly a better use of storage space is found, assuming that a correct algorithm has been set up by using correct logic and rules involving decisions on velocity and popularity (i.e. where an ABC analysis can assist). The WMS algorithm needs careful management input when being set up. It is not an automatic set-up process of the software

Table 4.2 The principal features of location

Method	Knowledge of the locations	Utilisation of storage space	Best use
Fixed location	Easy, as stays the same	Poor	Pick faces
Random location	Ideally WMS controls	Good	Bulk storage

and the default setting from the system's provider will need to be calibrated to the specific requirements.

After this has been done, the system will require regular monitoring and checking, especially if any of the requirements have changed. The principal features of location are noted in Table 4.2.

PICKING OPTIONS

Once orders have been received, the products will need to be picked or selected from the warehouse. This is often the critical activity in the warehouse as this is where customers' orders are made up. Also picking is, for many operations, a manual activity and so often represents the cost-critical activity. The following are the important features for picking operations:

- *Travel times.* For example, if manual walking picking is undertaken at 150 pieces per hour and the travelling involves four extra steps for each piece, then the extra travel is 12 000 feet (2 miles) per shift. Manual walking warehouse pickers should be lean and fit, as they will typically be walking many miles per working day; 5/6 miles per day is not uncommon in well-managed operations.
- *Product location.* Clearly the nearer it is to retrieve the product the less travel time is needed. So here an ABC analysis with fast/medium/slow product categorisation is important, with the fast movers, for example, located nearer to the despatch area. It should be noted that the ABC

categorisation used in demand analysis (Chapter 2) may not be suitable for picking as the ABC analysis for picking needs to use a correct indicator. For example, reducing the distance travelled means looking at the daily pick face visits and this may not be the same as an ABC analysis of the demand volume per annum.

- *Planning.* The pick run length is important, with the picker being routed the optimum way around the warehouse. 'Supermarket shopping trolley wandering' to locate what is required must be avoided. Again, WMS can be helpful here, and management determining and controlling is therefore important.

- *Service Level.* As picking will normally be undertaken after the order has been received, the speed in which it is undertaken is often an important aspect of the customers' perception of the service being provided. The timescale from ordering to receiving the delivery has shortened, with next day delivery being a normal expectation in the UK for many products. Indeed, some UK suppliers (for example, of stationery) offer the same day delivery to major national locations for orders that are received before noon; this clearly puts pressure on the warehouse pick/pack/despatch operations. The aim is to find the balance between the cost of providing the service, the speed of response needed and the type/size of order.

- *Accuracy.* Picking is often a large cause of customer complaints due to wrong products being picked and despatched to customers. This may not always be 'down to' picking – for example, if wrongly coded labelled carton outers from original suppliers are in the full carton pick area, the contents may only be 'discovered' as 'wrong', when the customer opens up the carton. A 1% pick error may however easily equate to a 20% or more increase in cost due to having to make returns, replacements, etc., as these all need more physical movement and extra time to correct the mistake.

It is probably correct to note that most companies do not actually know what their picking profiles are. Many do not analyse this activity to give a picture of the actual activity based on daily orders processed, products and lines/SKUs. What needs to be done on a given day is more indicative than any annualised throughput volumes. It will almost certainly be the case that a minority of the lines/SKUs will be activated on each day, and that 80–20 rule/ABC profiles will be found.

CUSTOMER ORDERS

This is another important aspect of the warehouse operation and therefore is one that is important to understand as customer orders will, for example, vary by industry. Orders can be picked individually from shelving, racking or live storage, with assistance from ICT equipment such as scanning, pick to light equipment and can involve automated carousels, sorters and conveyors. (Equipment is covered more fully in Chapter 5.) Orders can also be grouped/batched together so that each item/SKU is multiple picked and is then resorted to make up the order.

Retail stores, for example, are characterised by high lines per order, multiple items per line, few returns, and case picking into roll cages for despatch. Therefore, pick by case from pallets is undertaken at the pick face. This has a location based on an ABC basis or as a mirror image of the layout within the store receiving the goods. Goods are picked into roll cages, with the picker often using a powered pallet truck to speed up manual walking.

Mail order, as another example, is characterised by low lines per order, single items per line, many returns and single (sales item) picking for parcel despatch. The high-volume products are usually zone picked onto conveyors into a customer carton, which either passes through all the zones or is batch picked in bulk, then individually sorted per customer. Meanwhile, the low-volume products are held on shelves or in carton live storage. These are either multiple order picked (say 6 cartons each picking trolley, and items picked into each carton), or are batch picked and then 'pigeon hole' sorted.

Within these two examples are found all of the three basic forms of picking:

- *Item or piece picking* (also known as broken case picking). This is where individual items are required, which may be held in shelving or bins or require picking from a carton. Usually there is a high level of items/

SKUs, such as with centrally held spare parts for motor vehicles, meaning therefore small quantities per pick.

- *Carton or case picking.* This is where a full case is picked, often from a pallet; usually lower SKUs and higher levels of picks per SKU are found – for example 20 cases from a full pallet of 110 cases.
- *Full pallet picking.* This is where full pallets are despatched, and is the simplest of the three methods.

METHODS OF PICKING

As seen above, the methods of picking vary due to the interactions of number of lines/SKUs, picks per line/SKU, quantity required per pick, number of picks per orders, numbers of orders, product characteristics, as well as additional packing that may be required and any product customising/added value activity.

The key characteristics for picking methods with manual and automated options are discussed below.

Picking methods – mainly manual

- *Basic order picking* is where the picker travels to the goods in the warehouse. The warehouse can have wide aisle or narrower aisle racking, with appropriate handling equipment being used. (Please note that we shall be looking at warehouse equipment in more detail in the next chapter.) Important features are as follows:
  - The picker travels to the goods with one order and picks line by line from the product stored in racking. With low-level picking, the reserve stock is held above the pick faces; with high-level picking, only a small amount of reserve stock is held in the area (if at all).
  - The picking sequence at low level can be either, snake/U or switch/ star or zigzag patterns. The efficiencies will vary; for example, with snake picking the picker travels up one aisle and down the next aisle – effectively travelling in a U shape or 'snaking' around the warehouse. With switch picking, the picker moves from one side of the aisle racking to the other, effectively 'switching' or 'zigzagging'

sides or by moving in a 'star' formation from a central positioning point in the aisle.

– Clearly these options will have impacts on travel times. Again, a critical area and one to be determined by management, especially in an operation having a high activity of case picking. If management is not aware of such variations it is usually noticeable by observing the pickers as they will have found out naturally the best way to do the job, especially if 'job and finish' or other incentives work methods are being employed.

• *Batch picking or pick by line* is where multiple orders are grouped into small manageable batches. Pickers may either travel to pick all orders within the batch at one time using a HPT for example; here one picker would have all batched orders together and will then pick these from the warehouse, one line at a time, for subsequent resorting. Alternatively, bulk product that may be on pallets is brought to the picker for single case picking by line, from the varied bulk product lines that have been placed into the pick area. The picker will pick the individual orders from these pallets, and may place these into roll cages for each destination/user/customer.

• *Zone picking* is where the picking area is divided into zones with pickers allocated to zones. As one order is picked, it is passed to the next zone for completion, and so on, very similar to a car moving down the assembly line.

• *Wave picking* is where all zones are picked at the same time and the items later sorted into the individual customer orders.

The picking methods summarised in Table 4.3 are not mutually exclusive, as combinations are often found.

Picks per hour figures are used largely by companies as a productivity measure. While there is no such thing as 'industry standard' figures, as each operation is unique not only in terms of its product but also its throughput volume, location, layout, equipment, etc., a maximum of 300 pieces per hour per operator for manual basic picking would be expected in the 'easiest' of operations.

In theory it can be argued that as there are 3600 seconds per hour, and if a picker takes one second to step, one to pick, one to step back and one to place the item, then 900 picks per hour are possible. However, in

Table 4.3   Summary of picking methods

Picking method	Equipment	Picks per picker	Orders/pick density
Basic	HPT/PPT or MLPT*	Moderate to high	High number picks per order
Batch	HPT/PPT or MLPT	Low	Low number of picks per order
Zone	Plus possible conveyor for moving to next zone	Low to moderate	High number of orders and SKUs
Wave		Moderate to high	High number of orders and SKUs

* HPT/PPT/MLPT are abbreviations for hand pallet trucks, powered pallet trucks and multi-level riser picking trucks. We consider such equipment more fully in Chapter 5.

basic picking, the walking time must be added; we shall examine the timing of this activity more closely in Chapter 8.

The scheduling of picking can be either planned as discrete, where picking is undertaken at any time (for example, 'on demand' where the customer is 'waiting at the window for the spare part'), or planned throughout the day/shift, where picking is undertaken to a specific plan to optimise productivity.

Improving manual picking

As mentioned earlier, picking is often the critical cost area and it therefore directly affects the overall costs of running the warehouse. While we shall return later to warehousing improvements, the following can immediately be noted.

- Travel faster; for example, by using powered pallet trucks and by using only low-level picking as 'rising up' takes longer as vertical travel is slower than horizontal travel.

- Travel less: for example, fast, medium, slow movers' separations, the use of conveyors or by the use of live/flow, racking/shelving. All of these reduce the distance travelled.
- Pick several orders at once: for example, batch picking.
- Bring goods to the operator: for example, with carousels and conveyors (which are examined below).
- Simplify/remove paperwork: for example, with WMS, radio frequency, voice recognition, pick by light, finger scanning (which are all examined in Chapter 6).
- Motivated workforce: this is discussed more fully in Chapter 10.

Picking methods – mainly automated

These methods involve the use of mechanical equipment which is placed in a fixed/static position. There are varied types available and the following can be found:

- *Robotics*. This is similar in concept to the robotic manufacturing processes with moving robotic arms working on an assembly line. It has limited application in warehouse operations, although the following case study for Upper Crust plc gives an example that uses an overhead gantry.
- *Carousels*. Here, product with a high number of small uniform-sized items, such as slow-moving spare parts like nuts/bolts, are preloaded onto shelves and placed in a vertical carousel. Alternatively, with shuttle carousels, the shelves are placed in a lift shaft and a computer-controlled extracting system 'shuttles' up and down the shaft. The picker 'calls up' the product, removes it and places it into a despatch unit. This is often called 'Station Picking'. Carousels have relatively low levels of productivity, typically around 1–300 pieces per hour, but have good levels of accuracy.
- *Conveyor/Sorter*. Product here is preloaded into shelving. The picker travels through the shelving, as done with basic order picking, but places orders onto a conveyor belt. This runs into a sorter, which splits products into the individual orders via a chute. We will shortly examine sorters more fully, where it will be seen that they can have very high levels of productivity.

- *Auto Sortation.* Bulk loads of product of one line are loaded into the sorter. The sorter splits products into individual orders, which fall down a chute. This is followed by manual loading into, say, roll cages.

Upper Crust plc is an excellent example of the use of an overhead gantry system.

CAST STUDY 4.2: UPPER CRUST PLC

The Company

UC plc has a large share in the UK bread market. This is a highly competitive market as bread is often used as a 'loss leader' by supermarkets. They therefore look to buy it cheaply whilst retaining both high product quality and delivery performance.

Day one for day one is expected in this market, as there is also only a day product life cycle; yesterday's bread is not going to be purchased by consumers.

The distribution 'problem'

Delivery is undertaken direct to customers' stores/shops from bakeries. Product is packed into standard plastic trays; (these can often be observed, illegally, at car boot sales).

Due to the continued business requirement to reduce costs whilst maintaining service, efficiencies are continually being looked for.

With production a highly automated process, investigations to automate warehouse activities at the bakeries have been examined.

The solution

An overhead monorail gantry system from the production to the warehouse was installed. This system deposits the plastic trays in block stacks, therefore there are no aisles thus saving space. Traditionally large floor areas have been used.

(The system can be visualised as a being similar to straddle carriers used in container ports for moving 20/40 foot freight containers, however it is a fixed installation, with the 'straddle carrier' moving on fixed rails suspended from the roof.)

Product identification by tray was undertaken by automated bar code scanning. Consequently the location of every tray was instantly known, thus making the order selecting/picking highly accurate.

Results and key aspects

- Service level increased. Automation has 'forced' reliability and the certainty of supply. Customers knew that Upper Crust would deliver exactly what they said they would deliver. Customer orders were therefore more exact

- Production also benefited due to this reliability in customer ordering as this meant minimising excess production.

Automated picking methods using conveyors and sortation are on the increase in the West, mainly because of improvements in technology and lower costs, coupled to the rise in labour costs. The following represents a view of this growth in automated conveyers/sortation operations:

- Falling capital costs, as prices are 30% of what they were 10 years ago.
- Payback periods are extended from 2/3 years to more realistic 3/5 years.
- Labour costs have risen in recent years.
- The growth of constant sized and quality re-usable plastic tote box delivery boxes.
- Mechanical aspects are now simpler.
- 24/7 operation is enabled.
- More 'instant' customer demand drives the supply chain/delivery process, requiring 'new' ways.
- Cross-docking and links to WMS are both more readily facilitated.
- Can operate in 'hostile' environments (such as minus 30 degrees Fahrenheit).
- Sortation can handle varied weights, for example from 50 grams to 80 kilos.
- Flexible travel patterns, for example, up and down and round corners.

- Key issues are the fragility of products being handled, the possible need to have separate systems to cover varied products and whether to have one circular or two linear sorters for contingency purposes.

Various types of sorters are available, of which Table 4.4 gives some indication. The following case study shows one use of automation sortation.

Table 4.4   Various types of sorters

Type	Sort speeds*	Other points
Tilt trays/slats	18 000 per hour	Standard sizes/weights, like with parcel carriers
Swing arms	7500 per hour	Up to 80 kilos, one-sided tip
Pushers	2000 per hour	One-sided tip
Sliding shoe	12 000 per hour	Multi-sided, wide variety of sizes and weights
Bomb door or bucket	24 000 per hour	Flat pack small items, like books. Multi-levelled if needed
Cross belt	35 000 per hour	As above
Garment rail	9000 per hour	

*These are the theoretical design speeds. For practical operation sort speeds are much lower over, say, a 24-hour period due to the batching of products for sortation.
Source: *Logistics Europe*, November 2002, www.logisticse.com, reproduced by permission of UK Transport Press Ltd.

CASE STUDY 4.3: FANCY RAGS PLC

The Company
Fancy Rags plc are a major UK retailer of clothing and footwear and has 300 small/medium sized stores, averaging 8000 square feet.

Distribution

Fancy Rags operate from an NDC located in the north of England. This location is central to their traditional market base from Scotland to the Midlands.

They have had high growth in recent years. They also increasingly need high speed to market and fast turnaround of stock.

Solution

An automated case sortation was installed. This uses wave picking by store batches of between 15 and 25 stores per batch. At ground level is the carousel conveyor sorter that is fed from two areas:

- The bulk stock area. This is conventionally racked and holds orders for full case picking. Access is by reach trucks for replenishment and powered pallet trucks for case picking.
- The picking area. This is four levels of mezzanine shelving. This is for small orders, typically of one individual item. Access is by manual pickers using picking trolleys with plastic tote boxes.

For small order individual item picking, the order is made available to pickers by a barcode label placed on tote boxes. The picker manually picks from the shelving into the tote box, places a lid on the box and straps the box, which is then placed on a conveyor at each mezzanine level. The conveyor then transfers the tote boxes to the ground level carousel sorter.

For bulk order full case item picking, bar-coding and tote boxes are used with the case content being transferred into a tote box. These are then transferred to the ground level carousel sorter and the empty case placed into a waste area that is manually emptied and transferred to a re-cycling area.

At the carousel sorter, the totes are scanned and this then triggers the movement to the take off lanes that are arranged per store destination. The sorter can use more than one lane per store. This ensures the sorter works continually and is not delayed by any full take off lanes holding product still awaiting transfer to despatching vehicles.

Results and key aspects

- Increased efficiency
- Improved product visibility
- Lower costs
- Higher speed of throughput
- Faster turnaround of stock

Improving picking accuracy

Customer-reported errors can occur for many reasons, for example:

- the product itself, e.g. wrong product in the case
- the replenishment, e.g. wrong product in the location
- the picking process, e.g. wrong product selected
- the sorting and/or delivery process, e.g. wrongly delivered
- the receiving process of the customer, e.g. wrongly recorded/allocated
- customers ordering wrong products in the first place.

We have earlier commented on the costs involved when customers receive wrong products, and, as the above listing shows, this may not always be attributed to a picking error. However, it is useful to consider the accuracy issue here, and a survey reported by www.werc.org in the USA is a useful starting place in noting the following key factors:

- Order accuracy levels achieved was 94.2% for orders and 97.6% for cases.
- On average, four employees pick, check, pack and load each order.
- Every order was checked by 38% of companies, while 48% check sample orders and the balance 14% of companies were not checking at all.
- The most common picking error (41%) was selecting the wrong product, with 25% of errors resulting from customer errors in ordering.

In looking at the influencing factors, the following was found in the survey:

- Order accuracy levels did not differ between firms that checked orders and firms that did not check orders.
- Tracking errors by customers had higher order accuracy than when tracking by any other variable.
- Firms with picking incentives productivity schemes had worse accuracy than those that did not.
- Firms using fully functional WMS had higher levels of accuracy.
- Accuracy improved with the use of full pallet picking and decreased with full case picking.
- Methods of order picking had little difference in accuracy, apart from batch picking which had lower levels of accuracy.

If there are errors in the product itself, then there is little that may be done in the warehouse. Incorrect product identification can, however, cause warehouse inaccuracy and a more common problem is with pack quantities. For example, a previous supply is 30 pieces in a carton, the pack size is changed to a pack size of 40 without communication, and a picker is asked to pick 30 pieces and empties a complete carton into the customer tote box.

In replenishment, one aspect involved with accuracy is the storage locations ID with location labels incorporating check digits; paper post-it notes are not helpful on products or on locations. Replenishment also needs to be timed correctly so that the product is available when it is required. If the replenishment is late, then pickers cannot pick and a short order results.

Meanwhile, other aspects that militate against high-accuracy picking levels include unclear instructions, handling errors, sorting to wrong orders, incomplete orders, and incorrect quantity. The receiving process of the customer and those customers who order wrong products, are beyond the direct scope of the stores/warehouse, but they must still form part of the reporting and recording processes for a company.

Detecting errors at the time they occur enables instant correction, but detecting errors later will usually be too late. The following can be useful to improve the stores/warehouse order accuracy:

- Motivated workforce (see Chapter 10)
- Scanning technology at receipt, put away, pick, replenishment, despatch and delivery
- Weigh at time of pick
- Pick by light with push-button confirmation

DESPATCHING ACTIVITY

This activity is a reflection of the goods receipt/receiving area, for example with the loading bays and docks that we looked at earlier. Meanwhile for despatching specifically, the following is involved:

- Ensure that there is room available for any packing, loading into cages, stillages, pallets, etc.
- Assemble the goods in the goods loading/assembly areas (maybe using a template following the floor layout of delivery vehicle).
- Check the order documentation and record each item against the consignment note.
- Check the goods for condition, possible damage and carry out quality checks (carry out blind checking?).
- Report discrepancies and inferior condition/quality.
- Establish the correct loading area; ensure that it is safe and suitable for the operation.
- Ensure that the vehicle is safe before loading.
- Load the vehicle.
- Position/fix the security locking system, for example seal(s), with the driver present.
- Obtain the driver's signature.
- Record the departure of the vehicle and note the security locking seal(s) or number(s).

ORGANISING FOR FLOW

Having looked at each 'separate' activity in the warehouse, next we can usefully consider how to make sure that the operation takes place in an efficient and effective way where all the separate activities flow well together. While we return in Chapter 8 to productivity issues and warehouse layout, the following are the important principles for flow:

- Check the correct product handling group data and velocity throughput principles (see Chapter 2 on product handling groups).
- Check the levels of stock holding (see Chapter 2 on demand analysis).
- Minimise travel distances to save time and resources (see this chapter for each activity, in conjunction with equipment in Chapter 5).
- Check the trade-off between manual labour and mechanical handling (see Chapter 5 on equipment).
- Assess the impact of operational requirements and real-time information paperwork/automated systems (see Chapter 6).
- Check the trade-off needed between speed of access and the utilisation of available space by assessing the labour and equipment requirements, the costs and the key performance indicators (see Chapter 8 on productivity).
- When planning and simulating a 'new' warehouse layout, allow for adequate stock control/security and compliance with appropriate regulations (Chapters 2 and 7 respectively).

5

Equipment

Stores and warehouses will operate varied equipment and their selection should be determined from the products being handled and stored, coupled with an objective operational methodology. Warehouse equipment ranges from those used to move the products (such as mechanical handling equipment, like fork-lift trucks), and equipment used for the storage of products (such as racking and shelving). Clearly there is a relationship between the two as they both need to exist side by side and be compatible. Additionally, the correct choice of equipment for a specific/unique operation is involved – an important decision that will ensure both effective and efficient operations.

There is a wide range of standard equipment available from many competing suppliers and any specialised operation can always have bespoke equipment made for it. We shall, however, be looking here at the general and standard types of fork-lift trucks and racking equipment. Equipment such as dock levellers/bays and sorters/conveyors have already been discussed in earlier chapters.

FORK-LIFT TRUCKS

The fork-lift truck is the 'work horse' of most stores and warehouses. They are available in enormous variety, beyond their lift capacity and lift heights. In larger warehouses with large-scale operations, perhaps the choice is easier as specialised equipment is more readily available, for example, powered pallet, counter-balance, reach and narrow aisle trucks. But in smaller operations, multipurpose pieces of equipment such as hand pallet trucks or a counter-balance truck are perhaps the only options. Typical specifications for such equipment are given in Table 5.1.

The choice of fuel can be diesel, LPG or electric. Diesel and LPG fuel require internal combustion engines and therefore give out fumes – dirty visible smoke fumes with diesel and odorous invisible fumes with LPG. Both will require a tank of fuel stock nearby and are more ideally suited to outdoor operations, or well-ventilated indoor activities. Electric trucks are battery operated for indoor use and therefore require charging. This means having a special area that has fume extraction equipment, or adequate ventilation, for the volatile fumes produced during the charging process. The power options are summarised in Table 5.2.

Counter-balance trucks (CBTs) are the most common type of fork-lift truck and are available with any of the fuel options. Wide aisle widths are needed as the load is carried in front of the fork-lift truck on the fork blades, and therefore a wide turning circle is needed. The weight at the front when loaded being then counter-balanced literally by a counter weight built into the rear of the truck. *Reach trucks* (RTs) operate in narrower aisles and were specifically designed for pallet racking. They consist of out-riggers at the front with telescoping 'reaching' fork blades that allows the pick-up and the load is then retracted into the outriggers. As such the pallet is contained within the fork-lift truck, reducing its overall length and therefore allowing turning in narrower aisles. Generally, reach trucks are only available with battery power and are also only fitted with solid cushion tyres for indoor operation on level surfaces. They require a longer operative training period than with a CBT, as reach trucks have more complex controls and work in narrower, more confined spaces. *Narrow aisle trucks* (NATs) operate in very narrow aisles using battery power and are of two basic types:

- Swing mast trucks are like a standard reach truck but have a mast that swings through 90 degrees in one direction only, while the truck remains stationary.
- Turret trucks have an additional mast that turns through 90 degrees in either direction.

Table 5.1 Typical fork-lift truck specifications

Type	Lift capacity	Lift height	Maximum speed	Minimum aisle width	Application
CBT Counter-balanced truck	3 tonnes	7 metres	15 kph	3.0 metres	Indoor and outdoor
RT Reach truck	2 tonnes	11 metres	15 kph	2.1 metres	Indoor, within racking
NAT Narrow aisle truck	1.5 tonnes	15 metres	10 kph	1.3 metres	Indoor, within racking
HPT Hand pallet truck	1 tonne	Zero (8 cm)	Walking	1.3 metres	Indoor
PPT Powered pallet truck	3 tonnes	Zero (8 cm)	12 kph (rider)	1.3 metres	Indoor
MRPT Multi-riser picking truck	1.5 tonnes	10 metres	10 kph	1.3 metres	Indoor. Order picking from high level
AFT Articulated fork truck	2 tonnes	11 metres	15 kph	1.6 metres	Indoor and outdoor within racking

The above details are only what would 'typically' be expected. Any specific requirements must be checked. Note also that 'Minimum aisle width' assumes the use of 1 × 1.2 metre pallets and short-side pallet handling by the fork-lift truck.

Table 5.2 Types of fuel

Truck type	Advantages	Disadvantages
Battery	Clean, quiet and power efficient with low running costs; can be used in hazardous conditions; AC motor options allow for faster acceleration, lower maintenance and higher efficiency	Time required for charging; may require more than one battery; higher capital costs
Diesel	High lift; fast travel speeds; quick refuelling; long endurance	Noisy; soot emissions; need space for fuel tank storage; possible cold start problems
LPG	As above for diesel trucks plus cleaner engines, minimal fumes and reduced engine wear	Noisy; some fuel odour emissions; need space for fuel tank storage or for carrying out more expensive cylinder exchanges

Narrow aisle trucks usually require a guidance system in view of the tight tolerance levels while they are operating in the racking. This may be from chock side aisle rails or from wire guidance buried in the floor.

The difference in aisle widths is illustrated in Figure 5.1, where 'A' is a narrow aisle reach truck and 'B' is a reach truck that has to use the aisle for turning. A counter-balance truck would need a wider aisle.

Hand pallet trucks (HPTs) or pallet jacks, are well known; however, in the UK the battery motorised versions, *powered pallet trucks* (PPTs), are generally less used. They have no lifting capacity and can be rider mounted or walked like the HPT, but the PPT is fitted with a motor assistance. PPTs are fast and manoeuvrable with minimal controls and are ideal for 'traming' over long horizontal distances and for loading/

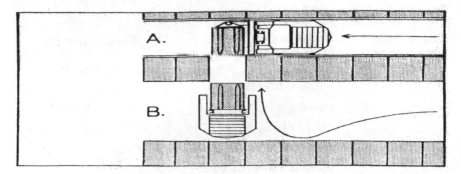

Figure 5.1   *Difference in aisle widths*

unloading transport vehicles. *Multi-level riser picking trucks* (MRPTs) or 'man-up' trucks are used in order selection and are specially designed for manual picking at varied levels of pallet racking. Working in very narrow aisles, they are similar to a NAT without a swinging or turning mast but with a caged platform instead of blades on the mast, from where the operator picks from the racking. *Articulated fork-lift trucks* (AFTs) or bendy trucks are a hybrid combining CBT/NAT applications. Powered by battery or LPG, the mast is fitted with ground wheels which are fixed to the main truck body by a swinging mechanism – hence the name 'articulated'. They can operate indoors or outdoors and by combining the characteristics of CBT and NAT equipment, AFTs can therefore avoid the operation of two separate pieces of equipment.

In addition to these basic types of fork-lift truck, a wide range of attachments and optional equipment can also be fitted. For example:

- Side shifts allow the fork carriage blades to slide left or right, enabling better positioning and engaging into the pallet/load being lifted/ carried.
- Double pallet handlers (two sets of fork blades in one), enabling two pallets to be lifted/moved at the same time. Widely used, for example, with high-frequency unloading/loading of pallets using CBTs from ground level access to the side of curtain-sided trailers
- Clamps of various types such as carton clamps, paper roll clamps, drum clamps; these 'clamp round' the product enabling a more secure, easier and faster handling.

- Prongs or spears for moving carpet rolls, rolled steel and wire spools.
- Slip sheet attachments, where a slip sheet (a sheet of cardboard or plastic) is used instead of a more expensive pallet. The attachment has a push/pull mechanism that fixes onto the slip sheet and pulls the load on the blade platform. The procedure is reversed for unloading. Slip sheets are very useful for closed circuit operations where both sender and receiver can gain, for example, in deep sea shipping of cartons in containers, saving the one-way pallet cost and also giving slight cubic gaining of space in the container.
- Fork extensions, which slide over existing forks enabling longer loads to be moved.
- Crane attachments to convert a CBT into a crane.

Selecting a fork-lift truck

It can be seen from the above that there are many aspects to consider, and the following questions can be asked to aid in the selection process:

- Are there any special products to be handled, e.g. are any special attachments needed, such as clamps?
- What are the characteristics of the collecting/delivery vehicles, e.g. lift height, floor loading, aperture, etc.?
- What about the premises, e.g. doors, corners, pipes?
- What about the racking, e.g. aisles and heights?
- Consider the environment, e.g. noise, fumes.
- What funding option should be used, e.g. new/used trucks, or hire/ buy/lease?
- Is the fork-lift truck to be used on public roads? If so, then FLTs need to be registered (and therefore carry number plates) and insured. If travelling beyond the immediate vicinity (defined as 1000 yards), they will also need transport vehicle construction and use or type approval. This will involve many additional requirements.
- Are any environmental regulations applicable?
- Do hazards or contamination rule out certain fuels?
- Is noise critical?

- Is the ventilation sufficient in closed areas?
- Is space available for recharging/storage?
- Is sufficient electric power available for recharging the batteries?
- Is there access for bulk delivery vehicles?
- Are there any local restrictions on fuel storage?
- How expensive are spare batteries and chargers?
- How expensive is (any) RF equipment?
- How intensely will the trucks be worked?
- What driver training is required?
- Are hydraulic attachments a factor?
- On how many shifts will the truck be operating?
- How much inside/outside usage will there be?
- Is there an extreme working environment for trucks?
- Is lifting equipment (for cylinders/batteries) available?
- Can any fixed set-up costs be met by the existing use of the fuel sources elsewhere on site?
- How will fuel be purchased efficiently?
- Would it be better to have a full maintenance contract?
- If own maintenance is envisaged, what skills exist on site?
- Are there any local benefits for a given type of fuel?
- Are parts, batteries and tyres common and compatible?
- What is the cost comparison based on fuel consumption?
- What are the travel distances covered in a typical work cycle?
- What is the length of any gradient, and the condition of the surface and the slope?
- Where will the truck be required? (Inside–outside, loading–unloading, putways, picking, private–public roads.)
- What is the warehouse environment? (Cold–ambient, abrasive–dusty, hazardous.)
- What are the work patterns? (Hours per shift, pallets in/out per shift, seasonality-peaks.)
- Who will professionally cost and manager the fleet?
- Are the trucks properly specified for the job in hand?
- Will any of the above factors change?

Meanwhile, the following criteria are those that users have ranked as important when selecting fork-lift trucks:

1. Reliability
2. Parts availability
3. Consistent servicing
4. Life expectancy of the truck
5. Price
6. Servicing intervals
7. Fuel source
8. Appearance of the truck
9. Brand name of the manufacturer.

RACKING/SHELVING

This equipment is used for storing products and goods. To illustrate the main aspects to be considered, we shall examine the common application for the storage of pallets. The principles involved here can then be applied to all other products requiring alternative forms of racking and shelving.

If pallet racking is not being used, then an alternative is block stacking of pallets, where each pallet is placed on top of others. Clearly there can be issues here on product crushing/damage and on access where, for example, in a large block stack of different products, the pallets in the middle of the block stack cannot be readily accessed.

Selecting racking

The following will have to be considered:

- Pallet (or for the product being stored):
  - size
  - type
  - construction
  - capacity
  - security
  - stability.

- Handling equipment:
  - type
  - maximum lifting height
  - dimensions/aisle width.

- Storage area:
  - dimensions
  - type and construction
  - floor loading, capacity
  - obstructions, exits, stairs, etc.
  - floor fixing facilities.

- Goods:
  - type
  - frequency of movement and access.

- Safety:
  - fire protection requirements
  - fire exits.

- Specialist requirements:
  - equipment
  - accessories
  - protective.

There are many different types of racking available, and the key features are given below and in Table 5.3.

Adjustable pallet racking (APR) is the most common type of racking. It is adjustable with the horizontal beams between the vertical uprights, the uprights being fixed securely to the floor. Accordingly, with APR, different pallet heights can be accommodated, but different length/width dimensions cannot be covered by adjustments to the beams as the length/width is determined by the floor area fixed upright positioning. Adjustments to the beams are not easily made, however, as the beams are solid structures held securely by pins that need to be manually moved and repositioned. Clearly the beams/racking must be empty while this is being done.

Table 5.3 Different types of racking available: key features

Feature	Adjustable pallet racking APR	Drive in racking DIR	Live racking and powered mobile racking PMR	High bay
Floor storage space utilisation: This can be critical as it reflects the use of the floor area/square metres, which is often a basis for charging of the warehouse structure	30–40%	80%	70%	70–90% (High bay warehouses can be built higher than other warehouses; subject to planning permissions)
Speed: Time is often a critical factor and the ease of access is involved here	Very good	Good (one way)	Very good (one way) but PMR can be slow due to time in moving the racks	Very good
Stock rotation	Easy	Very good (one way)	Very good (one way)	Easy
Stock visibility	Easy	Limited	Limited	Easy
Order picking access	Very good	Limited	Good	Very good
Mechanical handling equipment type: These are needed to access the racking	Standard	Standard	Specialised or bespoke	Bespoke

As stated above, with APR the floor space utilisation is low as APR needs relatively wider aisles to allow product access. This can be overcome by using *drive in racking* (DIR), which effectively can be thought of as block stacking with racking. DIR is a 'solution' for getting good floor space utilisation with no product crushing, but can still create problems for product access, as the product is 'in' the racking. The product has to be placed in/out of the racking by fork-lift trucks and a skilled positioning is needed as there are no wide aisle space tolerances.

One way to help to overcome this can be with *live racking* (so called as pallets move in the racking). After pallets are positioned at the end of the racking by, for example, a fork-lift truck, the movement in the racking is facilitated by having a structure that permits movement horizontally down the racking by incorporating rollers on which the pallet slides. The movement can be with gravity with, say, a 4% slope, or the pallets can be moved by powered rollers. The choice depends on individual company requirements and on safety requirements at a maximum speed of 0.3 metre per second. Live racking can be used to 'automatically' position pallets on a First in–First out basis and also position pallets in another part of the warehouse.

The following case study illustrates usage of live racking.

CASE STUDY 5.1: LIVE RACKING AT BMW

Pallet live, carton live and mobile line side live-storage are all features of the investment that will help the plant to achieve a 39 second cycle time for engines to support the BMW group's production network. The production of the engine requires a supply of 400 000 varied components to assembly lines every day.

Hams Hall is a pristine, state-of-the-art manufacturing and assembly facility for BMW's 1.6l.8 and 2 litre, four-cylinder 'Valuetronic' petrol engines, with highly automated operations that adhere to the principles of lean, JIT production.

'Our storage and component delivery systems have to support a truly 21st-century enterprise,' says Hughes of BMW, 'a floor plan was devised for our "small container supermarket" comprising nine aisles of pallet live storage, providing 110 pallet pick locations, each with a reserve pallet location and a single tier carton live storage, above the empty pallet return system services each bay for efficient pallet return, safety and minimal congestion at the pick face.'

The feed sides face on to wide aisles, replenished by electric fork-lift trucks operating from a conveyor feed from an auto store, while special commissioning vehicles operate in narrow aisles fronting the pick face.

'The components within the bays are positioned in such a way as to allow the components to be picked sequentially, exactly in the order that they will be required at the production line. There is no need for pick vehicles to back up or travel along the feed aisles,' says Hughes.

Inside the main assembly hall, engine sub-assemblies are delivered to work stations by AGV's (automated guided vehicles). At these stations, line side live units are an integral part of a pick-to-light system. Ergonomics are a key consideration and the minimal motion required of operators at each station is immediately noticeable.

'The main live storage installation services our slow moving com-ponents which on average draws between one and two boxes of a particular part number, per hour' explains Hughes. 'Fast moving components are delivered to the line by pallet-load.'

A consideration when specifying the project was that the storage system could keep pace with increasing complexity as various engine derivatives are introduced into the build schedule. The static carton live bays will eventually take many channels each and there is capacity to put at least 300 part numbers through the system, which should satisfy long-term projections for the plant.

Source: Industrial Handling and Storage, October/November 2001. Repro-duced by permission of Quartz Publishing and Exhibitions.

Powered mobile racking (PMR) is racking that is fitted onto rails in the floor. A whole rack is then powered along the rails and opens up access down the now opened aisle into the, effectively, normal pallet-racked areas. Once access has been made, that aisle of racking is closed. The advantage here is that within a given space, more pallet spaces can be fitted against the trade-off of a slower non-instant access to each aisle. There is also a cost impact as PMR requires an adequate power system with very precise installation.

The 'ultimate' racking is that found in *high bay* warehouses. Indeed, often the warehouse structure can be totally supported by the racking in a so-called 'rack-clad' structure. This form of high bay racking has fully automated access with automated fixed cranes. Effectively these are very sophisticated, narrow aisle multi-level riser/side movement fork-lift trucks which do not require any manual driver operation. Such operations are purposely designed and operate within tight tolerance clearances with bespoke equipment and ICT planning and controls.

Finally, a brief summary of the racking options available for palletised goods is given below. The main objective is to minimise pallet movement while maximising storage capacity.

For limited pallet access:
- Is block stacking feasible? (= low cost)
- Drive in/drive through racking?
- Live racking? (= higher cost)

For random access of pallets:
- APR? (= low cost)
- Powered mobile racking?
- High bay? (= higher cost)

Once the type of racking is determined, the next to be considered is the height and length of the row/run/racking. Consideration is given here to the lift heights of equipment, rack height limitations, building limitations and legislative aspects such as fire regulations and the health and safety requirements.

APR rack lengths of around 25 to 30 metres favour good flow movements with gaps as needed to give cross gangway access. Finally the direction of entry of fork-lift blades into pallets – the short side or the long side – will have to be agreed as this impacts on the turning circle in the aisles and, therefore, affects the aisle widths.

THE AISLE WIDTH DECISION

We noted earlier that fork trucks are restricted in the size of aisle widths in which they can operate. The minimum aisle widths for 1.2 metre pallets are given in Table 5.4. It is also important to check specific details as the table gives only 'typical' details and the minimum aisle widths assume the use of 1 × 1.2 meter pallets and short-side pallet handling by the fork-lift truck. Accordingly, if different sized pallets are being handled, then these need appropriate adjustments. The major problem with pallet sizes is where mixed pallet sizes are handled, for example, with Euro pallets of 1200 by 800 mm. Here the option taken is often one where the larger size of pallet being used will then determine the racking aisles width. Alternatively, separate areas for different sized pallets will be required. Should the UK ever fully adopt the Euro standard, then the vast majority of existing warehouse racking and equipment will need to be re-examined and potentially reconfigured.

With the space saving of narrow aisle/very narrow aisle (NA/VNA) equipment, it could be envisaged that all warehouses should have them. However, wider aisle options are still viable, especially in warehouses that require much movement. As the aisle widths narrow, then speed slows. Wide aisle trucks enable the picking of pallets from racking and loading to a trailer immediately, combined with fast travel speeds. They also operate at lower costs. So, wide aisles give more flexibility.

Moving to narrow aisles gives greater storage density. The varied capacities can be seen in the comparisons given in Table 5.5, which have been calculated using an identical normal rectangular open area sized warehouse with different internal racking types installed. These are figures for this specific warehouse only, but the principles are valid when assessing storage density.

Storage density

With narrower aisles, slower travel speeds with slower putways/pickup times are found. Additionally normal NA/VNA equipment cannot load trailers, although the hybrid articulated fork-lift trucks can. Additionally

Table 5.4   Aisle width options

Type	Minimum aisle width	Comments
CBT Counter-balanced truck	3.0 metres	Also called wide aisle trucks
RT Reach truck	2.1 metres	Can be also called narrow aisle trucks
NAT Narrow aisle truck	1.3 metres	Can also be called very narrow aisle trucks (VNAT)
HPT Hand pallet truck	1.3 metres	Also called jacks, pump trucks
PPT Powered pallet truck	1.3 metres	
MRPT Multi-riser picking truck	1.3 metres	
AFT Articulated fork-lift truck	1.6 metres	Hybrid CBT and RT

Table 5.5   Storage density

Racking type, and FLT type where appropriate	Pallet spaces/ storage density Index	Access to each pallet
PMR	100	100% pallet access, but slow
Block stack	85	Limited to the stack sides only
Drive in	75	Limited to the in/out area only
Live	65	Limited to the in/out area only
APR with NAT	60	100% pallet access
APR with CBT	50	100% pallet access

in narrower aisles, the tolerances are greater for level floors and racking fixtures. Guidance rails can also be required with VNA applications at additional cost.

The balance therefore has to be determined between the speed of operation, the storage density and the cost. It is often not a straightforward decision but should be one on which time is taken, before erecting relatively permanent fixed racking structures and perhaps also committing to semi-specialised and expensive handling equipment.

6

Warehouse Information Communication Technology

IMPORTANCE OF INFORMATION

Information and communication technology (ICT) enables the collection, analysis and evaluation of data and the transfer of information from one point to another. Information flows in warehouses and supply chains are as fundamental as the physical flows of goods and materials. Such information flows occur not only internally in companies, but also between external suppliers, contractors and customers. Consequently all the physical goods, people and material flows are triggered and paralleled by ICT. The whole warehouse and supply chain process is kept moving by communication and the supply of information.

The timing and quality of the information enables decision-making. Good information enables good decisions to be made. The opposite is also true and all parts of supply chains rely on ICT for planning, organising, operation and administration together with all the other management processes involved. When using any form of e-based communication, this will also include the customer interface.

Information flows not only from top to bottom but also internally and externally. For example, a warehouse order picker uses a pick list, which is generated from the (external) customer order. These picking operations, in turn, are part of decisions taken at the tactical warehouse planning level and the tactical inventory planning level. The information required by anyone at any level is therefore connected and is part of a complex set of data handling and communication. ICT will facilitate all these fundamental triggering, coordinating and controlling functions throughout the supply chain, including the warehouse. The introduction of XML (extensible markup language), which serves as protocol for data transfer between computers, enables more flexible and easier transfers and improves upon electronic data interchanges (EDI) methodology as it works over the internet and does not need dedicated networks. It can therefore open up the electronic world to smaller companies as the following benefits of web-visibility indicate:

- Real-time access to data for customer:
  - Incorporates status updates that have been received just seconds earlier
  - Gives users real-time access to information about multi-party events for informed business decisions
  - Customised report creation
  - Exception alerts that automatically notifies users of changes, problems, etc.
  - Monitors milestones like early/late arrival
  - Lets users find shipments and view associated status via their own information, such as PO number, sales order or waybill
  - Enables tracking and tracing and accommodates user's existing business process and info systems
  - Can be branded with logos, terminology, etc., as user organisation's own value-added visibility service.
- Supports selective data sharing with specified trading partners.
- Facilitates smoother inter-enterprise operations and supply chain management.
- Expanded service coverage (longer hours, wider area).
- Flexible communication methods.
- Expanded customer base:
  - access to new markets that requires web-visibility functionality
  - differentiation in a price-driven market.
- Enhanced company image and brand.
- Automation of operations such as shipment tracking.
- Automation of transactions such as order processing.
- Increased overall transactional and operational efficiency.

- Increased profit margin on services via value added proposition.
- Reduced transaction and customer service costs.

The following case study illustrates many of the benefits of ICT for distribution operations.

CASE STUDY 6.1: REED BOARDALL – FROZEN AND CHILLED FOODS DISTRIBUTION – ICT

Logistics requirements of frozen and chilled food distribution do not stop at getting products at the right place and the right time. They must get there at the right temperature and with the right paperwork and often with shorter lead times.

At its distribution centre at Boroughbridge, North Yorkshire, Reed Boardall has over 4000 SKUs of frozen and chilled foods consolidated for onward deliveries to the entire main supermarket regional distribution centres in the UK. The company is the only single site consolidator for the 'big six' supermarkets.

More than 1.5 million pallets are handled each year with a market value in excess of £1 billion. The company processes 260 000 orders a year. The challenge for its supply chain is to handle shorter production runs, achieve lower stocks with both manufacturers and retailers and provide shorter lead times – order to despatch – late day one for early day two.

With these kinds of figures and the challenges of cold distribution, Reed Boardall has looked to new technology to provide some interesting solutions. IT controls all in-store and traffic operations; orders are received on-line from customers and retailers via EDI 24 hours a day, seven days a week and customers can access live, on-line their stocks and movements.

Reed Boardall operates a fleet comprising 140 vehicles, all of which are under three years old and use a communication system and on-board temperature monitors with radio frequency download.

In addition to building the Boroughbridge NDC, other weapons in the company's strategy to meet its challenges include the development of a shared user network to achieve lower cost base; the provision of greater on-line links with the supplier and retailer and cooperating in partnership with retailers to facilitate faster stock-replenishment.

The technological advances the company has adopted include on-line order receipt and progress; live order fulfilment reports; live stock information available to supplier and retailer and on-line complete product traceability with audit trail.

Further technological developments for the future include a live load and trace system; increased capacity and versatility of reefer trailers and extending the use of radio frequency identification (RFID) from the tractors and trailers to the products – utilising the system for units that can be returned. The Reed Boardall management are very much interested in this system. The company, which has been operating a paper-based system, does not operate bar code-based data capture systems believing them to be almost passé and are keenly awaiting the time when RFID prices come down to the 5–10 pence range rather than 35 pence they are now.

The pick lists, clipboards and pencils have now been put away and replaced by the other significant technological development, as Reed Boardall has automated its picking team by adopting a speech recognition system for pick to voice.

The system is a real-time data interchange with the company's stock system. 'Human dialogue is the easiest and most productive way to keep hands free,' explains Keith Boardall. Used together with WMS the staffs receive spoken instructions direct from the WMS and issue vocal responses. This removes the need for truck-mounted or hand-held RF terminals with keyboards, scanners or RFID tags. With the headset on to receive instructions, the picker's hands are free to carry more boxes, which is an obvious benefit in a cold store. The headset is linked to a wearable computer inside the order picker's cold protection jacket. The picker logs on to the system verbally. A shift manager can also log on and have his own wearable unit enabling him to discretely listen to the dialogue of a picker which comes in useful if, for example, a new picker is being trained.

Source: Distribution, June 2001.

DECISION-MAKING AND ICT

Many of the techniques in supply chain management rely on the electronic gathering and manipulation of data. Electronic communication enables automatic decision-making, the modelling of proposed changes, automatic tracking control, and the automatic generation of performance monitoring and control. This means that faster and improved decision-making is possible as shown by the following examples:

- Stock re-ordering against pre-set levels and quantities. Here stock levels can be monitored against customer deliveries and once stock levels fall to a predetermined level, a re-order is triggered to the supplier so that stocks are replenished to the desired levels.
- Proposed changes to operations and networks can be modelled so that the effects can be assessed and decisions taken. Here a company may wish to change the way it schedules its warehouse operations. The company can model many and varied alternatives and options, which are then assessed and decisions taken on any changes that are needed to the current operations and layout.
- Automatic tracking control of equipment, products and assets (such as packing trays, roll cages, beer kegs). This enables constant visibility, which improves security and can enable real-time response to operations. Losing a record of, for example, the number of beer kegs can cost major brewers up to £10 million per annum and the loss of pallets nationally has been estimated at over £100 million per annum.
- Automatic generation of performance monitors and controls. Here, for example, all the physical operations can be monitored and any variations against the expected and planned performance can then be highlighted. For example, product can be planned to be delivered to customers within three days of receiving the order. By entering into the ICT system the time and date the order is received, along with all the subsequent steps of marketing (customer orders/service), inventory (stock availability), warehousing (picking) and transport (delivery), the actual and real-times and dates of all these operations are visible. This enables the actual performance to be compared with the planned performance expected.

Information is required for every stage and at every level in the supply chain and advances in developments of both ICT operating systems and computing power make it easier and cheaper to obtain this information. It is usually the case that information and communications technology reduce costs, which in turn means that the appropriate use of ICT can effectively bring increased profits.

IMPROVEMENTS WITH ICT

ICT has brought, and will continue to bring, improvements wherever the following are needed:

- Immediate access to information
- Cost savings
- Competitive advantage
- Accuracy
- Integration and coordination
- Lead time reductions
- Improved control
- Better service

ICT becomes a tool for integrating and coordinating logistics, supply chains and all the enterprises and companies involved in the processes. Warehouses are increasingly becoming more flexible, involving complex sorting operations instead of static storing operations. As stock has to be accessed without delay, bar-coded tracking systems are replacing paper-based manual methods. Mobile computing and laser scanning captures data with real-time wireless communication, giving real-time decision-making information.

While some of the application areas of ICT may be 'rocket science' to some companies, to others they are a day to day reality. Through automation, the movement of material in the warehouse is no longer a mainly manual operation but now includes automated storage and retrieval, and the control of all operations can be performed by a warehouse management system (WMS).

ICT has brought enormous and increased efficiency and effectiveness to supply chain management. Some people would indeed argue that it is mainly the developments in ICT that have advanced warehouse and supply chain management. For example, consider the following examples of ICT. How many of these are taken for granted and accepted as normal, yet they were all 'rocket science' at one time:

- Purchasing: Electronic data interchange (EDI) ordering, progress chasing and supplier payments.
- Production: Materials requirements planning (MRP) systems which enable rapid re-ordering, replenishment, stock management and production planning for known product ranges.
- Inventory: Stock control and stock-ordering systems.
- Warehousing: Warehouse management systems (WMS), automatic storage and retrieval systems (AS/RS), radio frequency (RF) internal communications, bar code scanning (which are all discussed below).
- Transport: fleet management, routeing and scheduling system.
- Marketing: order-processing systems.

WAREHOUSE ICT APPLICATIONS

Inventory management system

An inventory management system (IMS) can manage the information flows for all the stock items that pass through the warehouse. It can therefore advise on the following:

- Demand patterns, for example, average demands, standard deviations per SKU.
- Determine the methods of replenishment on what to order and how much to order – subject, of course, to being calibrated with appropriate decision-making rules by management.
- Monitor usage rates per SKU.
- Provide management data such as:
  - What items are being used?
  - When and how many?
  - How many items are on hand?
  - Where are they located in the warehouse and/or in the distribution network?

- Who is the supplier?
- What are the lead times?
- What is the cost per SKU?

Warehouse management system

A warehouse management system (WMS) can cover all handling operations in the warehouse, for example: receiving stock with receipt documentation and put away labels, generating pick lists, retrieving stock for pick faces, replenishing pick faces, etc. They therefore give enormous benefits, such as improved stock control, traceability, improved productivity levels, and better management reporting. Additionally they can be integrated with ordering systems, such as web systems relating to at-home catalogue shopping, and give direct links from the order receipt to picking and despatching operations, along with finance and credit control.

Table 6.1 presents some of the activities that can be undertaken by a warehouse management system, and in each of these activities, automated data collection gives built-in checking, which is arguably the most

Table 6.1   Activities that can be undertaken by WMS

Activity	Some possible WMS characteristics
Receiving	Automatic checking by scanning Paperless
Put away/storage	Automated locations generation giving space reductions
Picking	Product release prioritisation Batch and/or wave picking Real time pick confirmation Automated replenishment activation
Despatch	Load planning and sequencing Automatic checking by scanning Paperless

important aspect of a WMS. This gives 'built-in' cross-checks and vali-dations and therefore 'automatically' prevents those errors and mistakes that can be found with manual self-checking. For example, with picking accuracy, it has been demonstrated that there is little difference in accu-racy whether second count checks are undertaken or not before despatch, or whatever picking method is used; however, a main differentiator in the accuracy of order fulfilment is found to be dependent on when the WMS is being fully and correctly used.

However, it may not always be 'good news' with a WMS, as many basic packages are unable to cope with pallet/equipment control in a pool system, cannot handle booking-in information and may not deal well with all the dynamics of work scheduling. In looking to implement WMS software it will always be vital to define the problem areas by checking with all other 'users' on such issues as:

- Inventory accuracy
- Error reduction
- Productivity and resource management
- Customer service
- Paperwork reduction
- Information management and control.

It also means being able to fully understand the connections and inter-actions of the warehouse activity on a manual basis. It seems pointless to automate any status quo of confusion; unfortunately, this happens too reg-ularly and the system blamed, but the system will do what it has been told to do. WMS software will not, by default, produce the optimum.

A WMS is introduced at a cost, and the expected saving in each of the identified problem areas will need to be calculated. Once a view of the possible savings has been made, this can then be examined against: the price of the WMS; its features; its ability to meet future needs; how repairs and management will be carried out by the supplier; the supplier's knowledge and practice in the sector; and the support and upgrade options that will be available.

SELECTING A WAREHOUSE MANAGEMENT SYSTEM

The following checklist may be used:
- Summarise the requirement, simply (e.g. one sheet A4)
- Estimate the cost of not using a WMS
- Look forward 10 years
- Be prepared to only make small changes to standard packages (that will not compromise upgrades).

Find a supplier:
- who shares your views
- has expertise in your industry and your type of warehouse
- is warehouse and supply chain oriented
- has a strong team of former warehouse managers who lead the design with programmers
- has a 24/7 help desk
- has good references.

Check that the software package:
- is relatively new with a sound track record
- uses the latest technology and will be compatible with future technology
- is developed regularly and can be easily upgraded
- is not a 're-invention of the wheel'
- is well demonstrated, easy to use and accepted by all the users.

A WMS can evolve into the wider supply functions and contribute to the visibility and velocity of items in the extended supply chain by exchanging data with other supply chain systems, including enterprise resource planning (ERP) systems. ERP systems fit with the warehouse, via the order-picking data and links with sales and demand and post-picking, to the transport delivery and invoicing by accounts departments. A WMS can also be used with automated data collection to give warehouse operators higher accuracy, reduced labour costs and reduced cycle times. This will be further examined after looking at automated warehouses.

Automated equipment operating systems

These are available for handling and storage and result in tall warehouse buildings, over 15 metres high. These systems will definitely favour those warehouse operations that have a low product range with high throughput levels (minimum two shifts and over 60 pallets per hour), and operations where the following advantages can be exploited:

- has a 24/7 operational capability
- reduces high labour costs
- maximises the use of expensive 'footprint' rents per square metre
- uses fewer people and lowers the support costs for lighting and heating – for example, 100% 'in the dark' operations with no lighting (apart from occasions when emergency or maintenance access is required)
- improves security and reduces pilferage as people access is limited
- is useful for dangerous operating environments like chemicals (as they are practically operator free)
- reduces errors due to track/trace systems and less human intervention
- products have standardised dimensions and weights and product identification.

The disadvantages of automated warehouses can be summarised as:

- high initial capital costs and payback periods of 3–4 years minimum
- slow return on investment, which can be up to 7–10 years
- difficulty in getting planning permission in high population density areas as 'visually intrusive'
- difficult to rent out/resell
- relatively inflexible in terms of throughput, load size, operating patterns and future changing requirements
- vulnerable to software failures
- requires greater care in standardised packaging and bar codes/product identifications.

The following case study illustrates the warehouse automation in one organisation.

CASE STUDY 6.2: WILKINSON AND WAREHOUSE AUTOMATION

With a nationwide chain of more than 200 high street stores and enjoying a sustained period of 20 per cent annual growth, Wilkinson is undoubtedly one of the UK's retail success stories. Established in the 1930s, this family-owned business has, in recent years, developed from its original base in the East Midlands to serve a wide area of England and Wales. A fast-growing retail operation on this scale is always likely to represent a major challenge in terms of logistics, and for Wilkinson the equation is made even more complex by the truly diverse range it offers customers. Some 25 000 different product lines are stocked, encompassing hardware, toiletries, gardening, DIY, clothing, toys, household and electrical goods. Furthermore, the company's highly competitive pricing strategy ensures that minimising supply chain costs is an obvious priority.

Back in the early 1990s, the company developed a central distribution centre near Manton Wood in Nottinghamshire. At the time, virtually all the company's stores were concentrated in the Midlands and north of England, and Wilkinson turned to what was then Mannesmann Demag Material Handling (now Siemens Dematic) to design and implement an order-picking solution that could deliver industry leading performance while supporting ambitious expansion plans. By the late 1990s, the company's continued success meant that the Manton Wood distribution centre, which had already been extended, was effectively at full capacity in terms of the number of stores it could service. Furthermore, with two-thirds of Wilkinson's new stores being opened in locations in the south of England and Wales, transport costs were also becoming an issue. The decision was taken to build a second distribution centre, in Magor, near Newport, South Wales.

The choice of logistics system for the new distribution centre was a relatively straightforward one for Wilkinson. With several years of successful experience with the system at Manton Wood, it clearly made sense to repeat the formula at Magor. Despite rapid growth, the fundamentals of the company's logistics requirements had not changed since the Manton Wood system was designed. Furthermore, it had certainly proved very effective in helping Wilkinson to meet a number of key objectives: industry-leading figures for 'stock-turn' (essentially the length of time that stock is held before it is sold), a high degree of responsiveness to customers' buying patterns and reliable next day delivery of each store's order. Consequently, Wilkinson had no hesitation in awarding the contract for the Magor system to Siemens Dematic's Banbury-based logistics automation team.

The order-picking system now in operation at Magor is built around an 11 kilometre tote and carton conveyor network and two high-speed sliding shoe sorters. Not surprisingly, given the product range involved, the design is characterised by a number of different picking areas designed to handle products according to size and shape, speed of turnover and type of transit packaging used.

The 'eaches' area, for example, is dedicated to items that are picked individually into tote boxes, covering a total of four levels, staff work to picking lists that incorporate self-adhesive labels. Once an order is complete, the tote lid is closed and a despatch label indicating its final store destination is placed on top. The tote is then put onto a central conveyor line running between the two parallel pick faces to be carried onwards to the despatch sorter.

The 'case into tote' pick area follows a similar process but, as the name suggests, inner packs of 6 or 12 items rather than individual items are placed into pick totes. Cartons that have the right characteristics in terms of size and weight to be conveyed without a tote box also have their own dedicated, four-level picking area. The same picking principles apply, with staff applying the despatch label to the top surface of the carton.

Bulky and 'awkward' items – which includes a diverse array of garden furniture, mops and brooms, ironing boards and the like – represent a significant proportion of the Wilkinson product range. Unsuitable for conveying, some are managed in a ground floor picking zone next to the goods-in area. Here products are picked directly into roll cages and taken straight to despatch. There is also a four-level bulky item picking area where staff pick from pallets into roll cages. These are subsequently taken to ground level by a lift and on to the appropriate despatch bay.

In terms of stock replenishment, the 'eaches' pick area is served by the smaller of the two sliding shoe sorters. This automatically diverts totes carrying replenishment stock into the right lane and level. They are then placed into the appropriate pick location (which consists of gravity flow racking) by staff. Narrow aisle trucks are used to replenish other picking areas.

Alongside these picking zones, the new distribution centre has a dedicated goods-in area along one side of the building. Incoming goods that are not destined immediately for pick zone replenishment may be held either in a bulk pallet store, or sent to a repack area responsible for transferring goods into tote boxes for the 'eaches' pick zone.

Ultimately, all the conveyable picked items – cartons and totes – are routed to the despatch sorter. Given the sheer scale of the picking operation, this involves a considerable process of merging, with 36 conveyor lanes first reduced to nine, then into a single line that combines cartons and totes prior to sorter induction. At this point, all items on the conveyor are spaced before passing under an overhead barcode scanner. This information is used by the scanner to direct the tote or carton automatically into the appropriate despatch lane.

As the name suggests, the sliding shoe sorter incorporates a series of low profile plastic shoes that travel across the width of the conveyor to divert goods into despatch lanes. The number of shoes which are used to do this is automatically adjusted to match the length of the tote or carton in question; the low impact nature of the divert ensures that there is virtually no risk of product damage. Furthermore, the 'omni-directional' scanner provides an excellent standard of barcode readability at high speed, helping to achieve a maximum throughput in the region of 180 items per minute, while still maintaining excellent reliability.

A total of 21 despatch lanes descend from the sorter to the despatch area. This incorporates 33 loading bays, each of which is dedicated to two or three particular stores. Picking is organised in a series of 'waves' throughout the day, with each one encompassing orders for a relatively small number of stores. This ensures that, by and large, each despatch lane is only handling orders for one store at any given time. Staff at the bottom of these despatch lanes transfer totes and cartons into roll cages, which are marshalled, together with any bulky items, ready for loading onto the correct vehicle.

The Magor distribution centre soon reached a high standard of operational efficiency. Indeed the success of both the Manton Wood and Magor systems reflects not just the good sense in sticking with a proven system and supplier partnership, but also the high priority the company places on the logistics function. According to Gordon Brown, managing director of Wilkinson, there is certainly no question of contracting out this side of the business: 'Logistics is a critical element of our business and by maintaining direct control we enjoy a level of responsiveness to customer requirements that simply wouldn't be possible through a third party.'

Wilkinson's approach also demonstrates that the right logistics system is really only the starting point to an efficient supply chain. At Magor, the company has not only replicated the technology, but also the operating techniques it has developed at Manton Wood. Ultimately, these are what continue to provide Wilkinson with a real commercial advantage and a sound basis for continued success on the high street.

Source: Storage Handling and Distribution, March 2003. Reproduced by permission of Quartz Publishing and Exhibitions.

Automated data collection

Bar codes are usually read by either fixed 'pass by' readers (such as those found on a belt past which the product moves) or by manual hand gun readers. Increasingly these manually pointed hand guns are being replaced by smaller and compact finger scanners which carry out the same procedures, but are effectively hands free. The scanner works by finger pointing with the reader screen being strapped onto the lower arm. The hands-free wearable scanners communicate by radio frequency and pass data to the WMS system, which in turn, can communicate back with information on the next work cycle needed. The wearable units are often allocated to certain individuals who take ownership of the equipment and are responsible for charging the battery and maintenance of their own unit. Users are often keen to use such equipment as it gives them direct ownership of the work and they can visibly see and compare what they do on a shift basis. Also, management information is available in real time on performance and accuracy; additionally, jobs can be easily allocated on a priority basis and therefore remove feelings of favouritism or nepotism in the work allocation.

Such communications are also possible with handling equipment. For example, manually driven fork-lift trucks can be directed immediately to the next job required; therefore after, say, a put away, they do not have to return empty to find out the next job that is required; empty returns and inefficient working can therefore be removed.

A variant of the above bar code scanning is using voice communications. Here a headset and microphone are worn as well as a small control unit on the waist that transmits via radio frequency (RF). Text-based instructions from either a PC or from WMS-held programmed instructions at 'command centre' are converted into speech commands with the user confirming that the command has been carried out by speaking into the microphone on the headset. For example, with order picking, after the conversion of computer data into voice commands, the picker is verbally instructed where to move to make the first pick. The picker confirms the location by stating the random check digits at the pick location and, if these match, the system informs the picker of the quantity to pick; the picker then confirms that the quantity has been picked by confirming the number picked.

Radio frequency identification (RFID) is a system and not just a single component, like the fixing of tagging transponders that transmit data. The system involves the identification of physical objects, following their scanning by radio waves. The RFID devices range from large to small, such as those found in tagging – for example, the use of RFID with plastic tote tray/boxes enabling real-time track and trace of these assets. RFID tags do not require line of sight contacts to be read, as is the case with bar codes. RFID can hold more data than bar codes and they can act as passive tracking devices by sending out signals when they pass near a special scanner.

RFID systems involve three main components:

- A transponder, which is the memory chip and antenna and is powered by battery or the radio waves and transmits data from the chip.
- A scanner or reader, which captures the returned data.
- Software, which converts the data into information. This software will often cost far more than the physical transponders; additionally, the systems integration must be handled with great care and with attention to detail.

Another variant is with 'pick to light' communications that have been available since the early 1980s. These are designed for split case picks in case flow racking or conveyors (for example, from a case of audio CDs, where only one is required). The picker picks an order by responding to a light that indicates the location and the quantity. When the product has been picked, the picker pushes a button to signal completion and then looks for the next location to light up. Pick to light is, however, a less flexible system than a picker's 'structured roaming' of the warehouse using scanning equipment or voice recognition, as pick to light requires fixed equipment such as flow racking or conveyors, along with the hardware, to light up each location. As such, pick to light will favour operation where there are very high levels of picking per line/SKU.

RF communications systems will help in the following situations:

- locating where the inventory is in real time
- immediate access to data to enable informed decisions
- preventing people physically looking for inventory
- giving control performance information when linked to a WMS
- improving accuracy.

The following case study illustrates RF communications.

CASE STUDY 6.3: UNWINS & WMS/RF

Introducing radio frequency (RF) terminals for use with its advanced Chess Logistics Technology warehouse management system (WMS) has led to significant improvements in stock control efficiency and accuracy for Unwins, the UK's largest independent wine merchant. Since the RF equipment was installed in 2001 Unwins has boosted order accuracy to almost 100 per cent, with a 44 per cent reduction in stock over-delivery and a 32 per cent reduction in under-deliveries. The company has also eliminated the need for labour intensive pre-delivery checks and redeployed staff dedicated to this task to more productive duties.

Unwins estimates that it has reduced warehouse costs by over £500000 through its programme of continuous improvement including enhancements to its WMS.

The 110000 square foot, 9500 pallet location Dartford warehouse operated by UDS – the distribution subsidiary of Unwins Wine Group Ltd – supplies 419 Unwins retail outlets and the 300 customers of its Phillips Newman wholesale business. The Chess WMS controls stock for both while ensuring that items can only be assigned to the correct part of the business. Some of the 1800 product lines are available to both operations and can be treated as common to each, but certain items are reserved for Philips Newman customers. The warehouse despatches over 120 million units (a single can or bottle) each year, equivalent to 2.3 million units or 150000 cases a week.

Orders range from a single bottle to a full pallet, although 70 per cent of the lines ordered are split case picking. Order picking and stock control must be carefully managed to reflect the complexity of the distribution operation and high value of some products. The warehouse is like any other but there are some special considerations due to the nature of the products. For example, weight can be an issue and when assembling orders it makes sense to place canned beer at the bottom of a stack with wine and spirits on top for increased load stability and to reduce the risk of breakages.

Wines in particular need careful handling and should not be exposed to major temperature fluctuations.

When Unwins originally installed its Chess WMS in 1995 the operation was paper-driven. This performed well and allowed Unwins to manage its stock effectively but as the business grew the company recognised it needed greater sophistication. The decision to introduce RF equipment to interlace with the WMS was taken as part of an operational review that led to a number of changes in the warehouse.

RF terminals allowing staff to interact directly with the warehouse management system offered a number of potential benefits. They enable real-time stock control by allowing staff to enter and retrieve up-to-date information as they move around the warehouse, increase data accuracy by confirming and providing automatic checks for all handling operations, improve productivity by simplifying tasks and reducing time spent checking information and eliminate the need for paper picking lists and other documentation by presenting information on-screen as it is required.

Unwins selected 65 hand-held RF terminals with built in barcode scanners from Psion-Teklogix. These were chosen because they are robust to cope with prolonged use in a busy warehouse and offered a simple upgrade path to scan-based operations if Unwins needs this in the future. The terminals have a shoulder strap so that staff can carry them around and still use both hands when working.

Warehouse staff collect an RF terminal at the start of their shift and must enter their PIN and password before they can start work. They are then allocated an order to pick and given a set of pallet labels to attach to the completed load when it is assembled.

'Some people thought the scanners would be difficult to use but they are really just like mobile phones,' says Kevin Harris, Late Shift Manager at Unwins. 'The trick was designing a system with as few keystrokes as possible.'

The Chess WMS presents the full picking list to the operator on screen with information including the product, its location and the number of units to pick. Operators have some flexibility in how they work but must pick beer lines first followed by wines and then spirits. At the correct location the operator makes the pick and confirms its completion using the terminal to respond to an on-screen prompt and by entering a check digit found on the racking. The WMS asks the operator to reconfirm the pick if there is a discrepancy or allows them to move on to the next item if all is correct. The combination of RF and WMS ensures complete data accuracy, minimises the amount of time spent retrieving and responding to information and eliminates the need to look through paper picking lists.

In the past beer and wine were picked separately but they are now worked as a single order. This makes the process more efficient and means there is less chance of missing an item because one person is responsible for the entire order. Picking is carried out at first and, for some spirits, second level using low level order pickers. Higher level storage accommodates palletised loads that can be handled into picking locations at any time using reach trucks when authorised by the WMS. Once the order is completed it is taken to the marshalling area where pallets are wrapped ready for loading onto delivery vehicles. The Chess system takes care of stock rotation so that the oldest available products are picked first. In the case of products with a best before date Chess controls rotation using the best before date.

'Truck drivers and order pickers no longer have piles of paper to wade through,' says Kevin Harris. 'It used to take all afternoon to print the papers for the warehouse but we don't do this now. All we do is print and attach the pallet labels. If you told anyone here we were going back to paper they wouldn't be happy.'

The Chess system ensures that a smooth flow of products is maintained. Unwins can set a range of simple task priorities within the system that change in real time so that the task with the highest priority is always the one that is given to the first available lift truck operator or order picker.

The most obvious benefit of the new RF system has been in accuracy of delivery. This measures how closely deliveries match orders from the retailer or wholesale customer. Before RF, delivery accuracy was 99.39% for retail and 99.86% for wholesale, an overall rate of 99.62%. The difference reflects that wholesale trade tends to involve more full case deliveries where there is less obvious potential for errors. With RF, accuracy has risen to 99.7% retail, 99.92% wholesale and 99.81% overall.

'These small percentage increases equate to large numbers of items,' says David Harrold. 'The impact is a massive reduction in the cost of errors and correcting them. We have reduced stock over-delivery by 44.40% and under-delivery by 32%. We have also reduced break-in-transit by 51% which, while not down to RF, is indicative of the improvements in working practices. This means that more items are ending up where they are supposed to be at the right time.'

Before the RF system each order was checked prior to loading onto delivery vehicles by one of a team of 12 people. Order accuracy is now so high that this check is no longer required and 11 of the team have been redeployed to more productive tasks. Marshalling is now carried out by a single person supplemented at busy periods in the afternoon by one additional member of staff with a significant associated cost saving.

The increase in accuracy has a major impact on the way that retail managers and wholesale customers perceive the service they receive. Drivers encounter fewer disgruntled customers at the point of delivery and more stock is retained in the warehouse and is available for picking, another long-term Unwins objective.

The combination of Chess WMS and RF has had dramatic effects in other parts of the business. Stock checks are easier and more accurate, allowing Unwins to reduce the number from four to two each year. Stock rotation is better organised and more efficient and the number of annual turns has risen from 11 to 13.4. This means Unwins is using the available space more effectively and there is less demand for additional capacity even though business has increased. David Harrold, managing director of UDS, estimates that operating costs have been cut by £500 000 as a result of the changes, including the introduction of the RF technology. But there is still room for improvement.

'We know that the stock control is working properly so now we can concentrate on errors in the warehouse and who is making them,' says David Harrold. 'We can monitor picking efficiency and see how each operator is performing. Regular reviews with individuals help identify areas for improvement. We don't scan at present but have the capability if we want it, for example for high-value products or to introduce additional monitoring on specific lines or operators.'

Source: Storage Handling and Distribution, June 2004. Reproduced by permission of Quartz Publishing and Exhibitions.
www.chess.uk.com/www.psionteklogix.com

SYSTEM IMPLEMENTATION

The success will usually depend on the following basic points:

- Identifying systems technology that will fit the needs of the business with a correct definition of objectives. Any form of ICT should not be just a system 'fix'. Detailed handling and operations analysis are needed, with definite user requirements that are fully specified and agreed, followed by cost/benefit analysis of the options, with simulation if appropriate.
- Hard work will be required, with investment in time to address all the operational, facilities, system and training activities. Failures often occur; because of under-estimating the magnitude of such needed investments.
- The operational and the people aspects need close attention at the design stage, so they are then 'eased' at the implementation. Being honest with people – by sharing business objectives, explaining openly what the impacts are and not having hidden agendas – works. Letting people see it working elsewhere with a multi-level team can bring 'champions' who then become keen to 'get on with it'. Implementation is also not the time to realise that users have no knowledge of the system. Purely software functionality is not the only requirement which should be involved in implementation.

- Unknown factors can still arise, often due to the complexity of issues and the constant moving changes that may have occurred since the initial investigations to the implementation; therefore, the risks/costs need to be assessed against the planned gains/credits. All aspects of the interfaces/impacts with customers are critical aspects to be considered here. Top management visible support will be needed. Additionally a full change management programme may be required to overcome people's uncertainty and anxiety.

- Besides the software location, there will be effects on other facilities such as new MHE, reconfiguring layouts, bar code labels, etc., as well as the requirement for user training which will be needed well before the 'live' date.

- Project planning with realistic timescales needs to be internally managed and not left to an external software provider, who really has no idea of the fine complex details of the user's business. It is the user after all, who needs to get the implementation right first time. Allocation of adequate resources to undertake this is needed

- Be prepared for things to go wrong, such as key people leaving, hardware failures and exceptions occurring to the normal activity. Contingency plans will be needed along with flexible mindsets, followed by responsive clear direction and action.

- Testing and trailing before going live must be undertaken by users who need to subject the system to specific operational flows and activity with a clear view to bring the system 'down'. Learning and modifications can then be safely made and testing carried out again.

- Ownership by the user is paramount. Software providers need to be met half way and it should be recalled that, at some stage, they will not be there.

- Sufficient support personnel should be available once the system has gone live.

The consequences of wrong systems implementation can be dramatic. Only in late 2004 two major UK blue chip companies (Sainsbury and MFI) both issued profit warnings due to implementation problems with SAP/ERP systems, and both specifically mentioned supply chain problems as the major issue. How far these are just dramatic 'teething troubles' remains to be seen.

Meanwhile, the following item examines a successful implementation.

HEALTHY SUPPLY CHAIN DISTRIBUTION LIMITED

The Company

Healthy Supply Chain Distribution Limited (HSCD) is a third-party company specialising in delivering pharmaceuticals and healthcare products to NHS hospitals and wholesalers. Its customers are the major pharmaceutical companies, health care manufacturers, and many other smaller suppliers.

Warehouse operations

HSCD operate from an NDC in Northampton. It is 14000 square metres and stores 20000 pallets in 10 high narrow aisle racking. A 200-transport vehicle fleet covers the national daily delivery to the NHS and the wholesalers.

Receipts are notified in advance, using mainly EDI links with the major customers. Standard products are catalogued with package weights and dimensions. Any new and 'first time received' products are manually checked and entered into the catalogue for future reference.

Products are checked by individual scanning the cartons/package outers that are then input into the WMS. This then generates a bar code label per pallet of product.

Pallets are transferred by reach truck into the **storage** area and locations are generated from pre-set algorithms. These are reviewed monthly to ensure optimising of the time/access trade off. Each pallet location is bar coded and this, with the pallet bar code is scanned at put-away.

The **picking** area is arranged with:

- Slow movers for carton live racking and arranged in a horseshoe shape to facilitate replenishment from the outside.
- Fast movers in double deep pallet live racking.

Full case picking is on powered pallet trucks with roll cages and radio data terminals (RDT). The picker keys in their individual PIN and is then given instructions on where and what to pick. The picking routes are designed to ensure optimum roll cage fill. Split case picking is also undertaken by PPT/roll cages/RDT but uses pick labels and plastic tote boxes. Both full case and split case picking involve scanning and RDTs. There are varied order waving picking options: by client, by warehouse area and by time of departure.

The roll cages are then assembled for **despatch** at pre-assigned lanes for each delivery area, these areas being postcode based.

Key Aspects

- High use of ICT for visibility, traceability and accuracy.
- Algorithms for storage locations are reviewed monthly to ensure optimising of the time/access trade off
- Varied picking activity related to product fast/slow movement, package sizes/weights
- The picking routes are designed to ensure optimum roll cage fill.

7

Regulations

The stores, warehousing and distribution industries are potentially dangerous places in which to work. For example, large vehicles, mechanical equipment and people come together, working at speed and often under pressure. It is essential, therefore, that management plans for safety to minimise the risk of accident and injury. The law has recognised the key role played by employers in controlling health and safety at work. Important obligations and restrictions have been placed on employers by legislation, originating in the UK parliament and in the EU. These are examined in the following sections under 'Health and Safety at Work', adapted with permission, from the Institute of Logistics and Transport Open Learning materials covering the Introductory Certificate in Logistics.

HEALTH AND SAFETY AT WORK

The Health and Safety at Work etc. Act 1974 (HASWA) is primary legislation defining principles and objectives. It is very general in its scope, and places responsibility for the health and safety of workers into three categories, namely:

- the responsibility of the employer
- the responsibility of the employee
- the responsibility of manufacturers.

HASWA clearly states that it is the responsibility of employers to maintain the health, safety and welfare of all employees, including provision of a statement of health and safety policy, safety equipment and training staff. HASWA also states that employees have an obligation to the employer to undertake the training when provided, to use equipment provided for safety as trained, to report any unsafe practices and not to misuse safety equipment. The manufacturer of equipment has a specific responsibility under HASWA to ensure that the product is safe to use in the environment it was designed for in normal circumstances and is fit for its purpose.

All managers need to be aware of their obligations under HASWA, which may mean undertaking specialist training or liaising with an appointed health and safety manager. It is prudent for managers, when assessing any operation or new development, to liaise with a suitably qualified health and safety professional to ensure compliance with the legislation. More specifically, to aid managers in their dealings with health and safety issues in the workplace, there is a wealth of supporting approved codes of practice (ACOP) and other regulations which are all legally binding and underpin HASWA.

MANAGEMENT OF HEALTH AND SAFETY

The Management of Health and Safety at Work Regulations 1999 support managers in fostering a proactive approach towards building a health and safety culture within the organisation. In the past some employers merely responded to unsafe practices in order to limit damage, minimising the impact on production, sales and direct costs. Under these regulations organisations are encouraged to be proactive in their approach to accidents and unsafe practices, which means that the logistics manager must ensure that systems are in place for planning, organising, monitoring and reviewing operations with regard to the health and safety of staff at work. (In other words, all employers have to have at least one competent person to assist in carrying out the health and safety obligations.)

Display screen equipment

The Health and Safety (Display Screen Equipment) Regulations 1992 apply to visual display units (VDUs) for computers or microfiche, in that the risks associated with the use of VDUs – mainly eyestrain, backache and limb pain – are minimised by providing staff with suitable training and equipment that can be adjusted for each individual at that workstation. This includes the ergonomics of the workstation layout.

Personal protective equipment

The Personal Protective Equipment Regulations 2002 state that employers are required to provide PPE to employees where there are risks to their health and safety which cannot be controlled by other means, e.g. mechanisation. PPE is described as being any equipment designed to be worn or held by the person to protect them from one or more risks. This could be simply gloves and goggles or warm clothing or heated cabs on MHE for use in temperature controlled warehouses.

Provision of equipment

The Provision and Use of Work Equipment Regulations 1998 (PUWER) require employers to ensure that equipment provided for use at work complies with the regulations (for example, MHE, staple guns, wrapping or weighing machines). Work equipment must be:

- suitable for intended purpose
- assessed for risks associated with use
- subject to a recorded inspection
- maintained in efficient working order.

Reporting injuries

The Reporting of Injuries, Diseases and Dangerous Occurrences Regulations 1995 (RIDDOR) require employers to notify the Health and Safety Executive of fatal and major workplace accidents and those causing more than three days incapacity, work related diseases and any dangerous occurrence, whether or not anybody is injured. In the case where an accident occurs to an employee away from the normal place of work, e.g. delivery drivers, the Health and Safety Executive suggests that the occupier of the premises where the incident occurs should advise the person's employer as soon as possible.

Workplace regulations

The Workplace (Health, Safety and Welfare) Regulations 1992 deal with preventing hazards that result from poor housekeeping and include cleanliness and waste materials. Waste materials should not accumulate, creating slipping or tripping hazards or obstructions to fire exits and fire doors. In addition, these regulations impose requirements on management for the maintenance of the fabric of the workplace, ventilation, lighting, space planning and provision of washing facilities and changing rooms.

Risk management

For managers, the role of the risk assessment is to assess what is probable, and not what is possible. This means making an informed judgement based on the balance between the needs of the business, the operation and the customer. Risk assessment requires the employer to ensure that assessments are undertaken and the findings acted upon, recorded, and communicated to employees. The control measures introduced as a result of assessment must be monitored and reviewed to ensure that they are effective. Risks may include:

- slips, trips and falls
- pedestrian and vehicle movement
- objects falling
- fire
- power failure
- eating, drinking or smoking in the workplace.

Handling of loads

Handling of loads applies to both mechanical and manual handling (Manual Handling Operations Regulations 1992). The Health and Safety

Executive publish specific guidance notes for the safe operation of mechanical handling equipment.

More recently, employees are turning to litigation for damages as a result of manual handling incidents. Therefore managers must be confident that all staff have been adequately trained in the correct lifting and carrying techniques, commensurate with the operation in which they are working.

A risk assessment might imply that a manual handling operation should be replaced by mechanical handling. If the logistics manager cannot eliminate the hazard, there is a responsibility to reduce the hazard by providing aids (e.g. scissor lift or hand pallet transporters) to reduce the risk of injury, or reduce employee exposure (for example, by reducing the distance or the frequency the load has to be carried).

Hazardous goods

The Control of Substances Hazardous to Health (COSHH) Regulations 2002 are designed to further protect the health and safety of people at work and place additional responsibilities on employers to assess the risks to employees working with hazardous substances. Again, this involves logistics managers assessing the risk of exposure to chemical hazards and taking steps to minimise any such exposure. Managers must inform employees of risks that exist and provide training in safety procedures and monitor the working environment. Options to reduce risks include removing employees from exposure risk and mechanising the process or contracting out the process to a specialist organisation.

In addition, manufacturers and suppliers of hazardous goods are required to classify, package and provide information on substances listed in the Chemical (Hazard Information and Packaging for Supply) Regulations 2002 (CHIP 3). The Transport of Dangerous Goods (Safety Advisers) Regulations 1999 stipulate the requirements for movement of dangerous goods by road, rail and inland waterway. It makes employers responsible for loading, transport and unloading of dangerous goods and requires employers to have a sufficient number of qualified safety advisers to sign off and supervise the loading and unloading of dangerous goods.

HEALTH AND SAFETY ARRANGEMENTS

It can be seen from the above section on HASWA, and its sub-sections, that the employer must therefore have arrangements in place to cover health and safety, and that these arrangements must include:

- planning to eliminate risks
- a suitable organisation structure
- control systems to ensure decisions are implemented
- monitoring and review procedures.

Health surveillance

If the risk assessment shows the likelihood of employees, etc., being exposed to disease or adverse health conditions, the employer must introduce appropriate health surveillance.

Information for employees

The employer must provide employees with comprehensive and relevant information on matters such as:

- the risks to health and safety identified in the assessment
- the preventive and protective measures
- the identity of the people nominated to assist in this safety work.

Training

All employers must ensure that their employees are provided with adequate health and safety training. This should begin at recruitment, be supplemented whenever an employee is exposed to a new risk, and be 'topped-up' by means of refresher training.

Working environment

The Workplace (Health, Safety and Welfare) Regulations 1992 replaced many of the requirements previously laid down in the Factories Act 1961 and the Offices, Shops and Railway Premises Act 1963. The major provisions contained in the regulations are backed by approved codes of practice and deal with: ventilation, falling objects, temperature, windows and skylights, lighting, toilet and washing facilities, cleanliness, drinking water, room dimensions and space, clothing and changing rooms, workstations and seating, meals and rest, and floors.

Administration and enforcement of health and safety legislation

The Health and Safety at Work etc. Act 1974 set up three bodies:

- *The Health and Safety Commission*. This advises the Government on future health and safety policy, and on strategy. It also helps to prepare new regulations.
- *The Health and Safety Executive*. This carries out policies and is responsible for the Health and Safety Inspectorate.
- *The Health and Safety Inspectorate*. This enforces the regulations. Health and safety inspectors have the right to enter premises to make inspections and at any other time if they have reason to suspect a dangerous situation. They have wide powers, and two principal weapons are:
  - Improvement notice. This is issued where the inspector believes that a statutory provision has been breached and that the occurrence is likely to be repeated. The notice will specify the breach and will lay down a period within which the situation must be remedied (minimum 21 days).
  - Prohibition notice. This is issued when the inspector is of the opinion that an activity involves a serious risk of personal injury. This notice will order the immediate cessation of the specified activity until the situation is remedied.

Appeals can be made to employment tribunals, but the employer must comply with the requirements of a prohibition notice until it is withdrawn.

WAREHOUSE HEALTH AND SAFETY RISKS

Management and operators need to be able to answer the following questions on safety.

Health and safety checklists

Layout

- Has an up to date risk assessment (see below) been done on all hazards?
- Are people/vehicles segregated?
- Are one-way systems used?
- Are aisle and gangway widths adequate to stop collision damage?
- Are emergency exits marked, open and accessible?
- Are surfaces flat and unobstructed?
- Are markings clear and visible?
- Is beam load guidance followed?
- Are rack end uprights protected?

Floors

- Is load bearing adequate?
- Are floors slip-proof?
- Are floors flat, level and free from holes/ 'sharps'?
- Do mezzanine floors have clearly marked safe load-bearing capacities?
- Are all openings and edges guarded on mezzanine floors?
- Are self closing gates fitted to mezzanine floors?

Heating

- Is a reasonable working temperature maintained for people working in the warehouse, in recommended ranges from 18 to 28 °C? (Where a high physical effort is needed, a low of 13 °C can be acceptable.)
- Where reasonable working temperatures cannot be maintained, such as in warehouses storing frozen food products, is an area available to allow employees to warm up?

Lighting and visibility

- Is lighting sufficient to give safe and workable conditions? (For example, minimum levels are receipt/despatch 30 lux, racking 60 lux, offices 100 lux.)
- Is documentation clearly written in large letters?
- Do all packages contain clear details/marking?

Noise

- Normal conversations are at 50–60 dB(A), a loud radio is 70 dB(A), and a busy road with lorry traffic is 80 dB(A). Levels over 85 dB(A) – for example, a circular saw cutting wood at a distance of 1 metre – require preventative action and levels over 140 dB(A) require immediate action. A busy warehouse with exposure to goods vehicle engine noises can lead to such preventative action being needed.

Housekeeping

- Are aisles kept clean?
- Is there a check to ensure that stock does not project from racking/shelving?
- Are spillages immediately cleaned up?
- Are packing materials used the correct ones for the job?
- Are waste packing materials contained and correctly disposed of?

Fire risk

(*Source*: www.thefpa.co.uk. Reproduced by permission of the Fire Protection Association.)

- Is a written fire risk assessment in place?
- Are fire procedures in place?
- Are there emergency escape routes?
- Is there emergency lighting?
- Are the emergency routes indicated by signs?
- What are the means of raising the alarm?
- What are the means of fire fighting?
- Is all the equipment maintained and up to date?

- Has all staff had annual fire training?
- Have the fire procedures been reviewed recently?

The Fire Precautions (Workplace) Regulations 1997 and the Fire Precautions (Workplace) (Amendment) Regulations 1999 cover the legal requirements and are published in www.hse.gov.uk (ISBN 0 11 341 1693). Meanwhile it should be noted that people cause the vast majority of fires in warehouses. Thankfully, arson is rare in warehouses, but the most common cause is human error with 40% of fires starting between 2200 and 0600 hours. The human error may be in failing to identify a risk, failing to have in place preventative measures, or failing to respond correctly and quickly to a fire that has just started. Accordingly, staff training is now a mandatory requirement of the regulations.

All open fires and hot surfaces are sources of risk, such as shrink wrapping equipment, cutting/welding equipment, smoking and heaters. Such ignition sources need to be controlled and operated correctly in the right location. Electrical equipment is another fire source emphasising the need for adequate maintenance programmes and inspections. Key exposure areas come from high-intensity discharge (HID) lamps, where violent failures can cause fragments of 1000 °C to land on vulnerable surfaces.

Organisation health and safety

- Have all health and safety aspects of the warehouse operation been assessed?
- Has an organisation (and arrangements) for securing such safety been detailed in the safety policy?
- Has a person been appointed to be responsible for warehouse safety?
- Have safe systems of work been set up?
- What monitoring is carried out to ensure that the systems are followed?
- Have all drivers/operators of mechanical equipment been adequately trained and tested?
- Is there a satisfactory formal licensing or authorisation system for equipment users/drivers?
- Have all personnel been trained, informed and instructed about safe working practices where warehousing operations are involved?

- Is there sufficient supervision?
- Has an update risk assessment been done on all hazards?
- Are people/vehicles segregated?
- Remember the Accident Pyramid:
  - For every one serious injury, there are 100 minor injuries.
  - For every 100 minor injuries, there are 1000 close calls.
  - Investigating the close calls can therefore cancel the one and the hundreds.

Warehouse external and internal roadways and aisles

- Are they of adequate dimensions?
- Are they of good construction?
- Are they well maintained?
- Are they well drained?
- Are they gritted, sanded, etc., when slippery?
- Are they kept free of debris and obstructions?
- Are they well illuminated?
- Are there sufficient and suitable warning signs?
- Are there speed limits?
- Is there a one-way system (as far as possible)?
- Is there provision for vehicles to reverse when necessary?
- Are there pedestrian walkways and crossings?
- Are there barriers by exit doors leading onto roadways?
- Is there a separate vehicle/equipment parking area?

Loading and unloading

- Do loading positions obstruct other traffic, or do pedestrian ways need to be diverted?
- Are there special hazards, e.g. flammable liquid discharge, and do pedestrians need to be kept clear?
- Is there a yard manager to supervise the traffic operation, to control vehicular movement and to act as a banks man during reversing?
- Has the yard manager received satisfactory training in the use of recognised signals, and has that person cover during absences?
- Will the layout of loading docks prevent trucks falling off or colliding with objects, or each other?

- Can any mechanical hazards be caused by dock levellers, etc?
- Are methods of loading and unloading assessed?
- Are all loads stable and secure?
- Are safe arrangements made for sheeting?
- Is there a pallet inspection scheme?

RISK ASSESSMENTS

Full risk assessments form a feature of the Health and Safety legislation. The six stages involved on conducting risk assessments are:

1. Gathering necessary information: for example, see the following manual handling task analysis.
2. Considering the elimination or reduction of hazards and assessing the level of risk.
3. Recording significant facts under 1 and 2 above.
4. Improving safety arrangements in relation to 1–3 above.
5. Recording the findings of the assessment.
6. Developing an emergency plan and carrying out necessary staff training.

Manual handling task analysis

The following questions are a guide to analysing manual handling:

Tasks

- Are loads held at a distance from the body?
- Do body movements involve stooping or twisting?
- Is excessive pushing or pulling involved?
- Is frequent and prolonged effort involved?
- Are there sufficient rest periods?

Load

- Is it heavy, bulky, difficult to grasp, unstable, hot or sharp?

Work environment

- Does the space available prevent a good posture?
- Are there uneven, slippy or unstable floors?
- Are there variations in floor levels?
- Are there poor light conditions?
- Are temperature levels satisfactory?

Individual capability

- Does the job require above average strength?
- Is the job a hazard to people with special health needs?
- Does the job require special training?

Manual handling principles

As a result of wide-ranging research, in 2003 the HSE published the following principles:

1. Think before lifting: plan the lift and decide where is it going to be placed. Use handling aids as appropriate; do you need help with the load? Remove any obstructions; think of the best way to do it. If it is a long lift, is there somewhere to rest if necessary?
2. Keep the load close to the waist.
3. Adopt a stable position: have your feet slightly apart with one leg forward.
4. Get a secure hold: keep the load as close as possible to your body (hug the load?).
5. When starting, slightly bend your back, hips and knees: this is preferable to fully flexing/stooping or squatting.
6. Do not flex your back any further when lifting or when starting to lift.
7. Avoid twisting or leaning, especially if your back is bent: keep shoulders level and in the same direction as the hips; it is better to turn by moving your feet after lifting.
8. Keep your head up when handling: after securing the load look ahead and not down.

9. Move smoothly.
10. Do not lift more than can be easily managed.
11. Put the load down, and then adjust, for example, by sliding the load into position.

Source: http://www.hse.gov.uk/research/rrhtm/rr097.htm (2003). Reproduced by permission of Her Majesty's Stationery Office.

FORK-LIFT TRUCKS: HEALTH AND SAFETY

The following principles are involved to assist in ensuring that the employer's duty of care is undertaken:

- Select only those operators who show a concern for health and safety.
- Ensure that operators and supervisors are trained.
- Ensure that driving is only undertaken by people who are authorised.
- Ensure that pre-shift equipment checks are conducted.
- Follow the manufacturer's operating handbook.
- Follow preventative maintenance practices.
- Use equipment within the rated capacities only.
- Ensure that the company complies with PUWER-98 (see above) and LOLER-98 (see below).

LOLER regulations

The Lifting Operations and Lifting Equipment Regulations 1998 state that all lifting equipment (such as fork-lift trucks, pallet trucks, tail lifts on road transport vehicles, etc.), has to be thoroughly examined:

- at least every 6 months (if lifting people, or is a lifting attachment)
- at least every 12 months for all other lifting equipment
- after installation, and before using for the first time
- each time lifting equipment has been involved in an accident.

This means that thorough inspections are required by a competent person who is sufficiently independent and impartial to make objective decisions.

It can be seen that this requirement is very similar to the MOT required for cars and large goods vehicles.

After the inspection, a report has to be completed for the customer and/or the employee, which notifies of any defects that are or could become a danger. Serious defects have to be reported to the Health and Safety Executive. Usually fork-lift truck suppliers can arrange inspections at an appropriate charge related to the speciality of the specific equipment.

Lifting operations

Preparation

When using cranes or other lifting machines, the load, the task to be performed, the lifting equipment and the site will all need investigation before undertaking the actual lift; this represents the necessary preparation to be undertaken (fuller details are available from Lifting Equipment – A User's Pocket Guide, LEEA).

The following will then need to be observed when undertaking the actual lifting:

Cooperation

- The person responsible needs to ascertain that the people who are lifting have the authority to use the equipment and to make the lift.
- The lifters should be able to clearly communicate with the crane driver and others involved by an agreed code of signals.
- The activity will not conflict with other activities in the area or in the path of the lift.

Check the equipment

- Does it have adequate capacity?
- Will the speed of the equipment make it easy to control and position the load?
- Is there adequate headroom for the height of the lift?
- Is it possible to position the hook so that it is over the centre of gravity of the load?

- If operating a special lifting installation, has it been tested and examined by a competent person?

Select the lifting gear

The person responsible for the required lifting gear should ensure the following.

- If the load cannot support itself, additional support will be provided.
- The load will stay together and pieces will not fall off.
- The safe working load (SWL) for the lifting gear will account for both weight and type of use.
- The load will not be damaged by the lifting gear or the environment.
- The load can be controlled in the air, using a tag line if required.

Check the lifting gear

- Is it fit for use?

Assemble the lifting gear

- Position the hook vertically above the centre of gravity.
- Attach the lifting gear so that all pieces can align correctly.
- Hoist up to take up the slack, keeping parts of the body clear.
- Check that the gear is correctly positioned.

Make a trial lift

- Check that the load is still not fixed down.
- Lift the load slightly off the ground.

Lift and travel with the load

- Warn exposed people to clear the area.
- Avoid obstacles and people.
- Check that the landing site is prepared.
- Lower the load, stopping just clear of the ground.

Make a trial landing

- Check the position and that packing materials/supports will support the load without trapping the slings.
- Gently lower, but do not allow the gear to go slack.
- Ensure that the load is safe and will be stable after removing the gear.
- Slack off the gear and remove it by hand.

Clear up

- Check the gear.
- Return it to safe storage.

Maintenance and care of equipment

The PUWER and LOLER regulations require that all equipment is maintained and inspected regularly so that it is kept in efficient working order. We therefore examine below what this means for fork-lift trucks and for racking.

Fork-lift truck maintenance

This will be more readily facilitated by adhering to the following:

- What is on the manufacturer's data plate?
- Are you working within this data?
- Are brakes, lights, warning devices, safety locks and overhead guards in safe and working order?
- Are all drivers properly trained and do they attend refresher courses?
- Are trucks maintained daily, weekly, six monthly, in accordance with the following checks?
- Are drivers' defect reports (see below) completed daily and acted upon?

Periodic checks

- Daily check: At the start of each shift, check by the driver/supervisor.
  - Ensure that tyre pressures are correct (for pneumatic tyres only!).
  - Note and advise on any tyre damage.

- Ensure that all brakes are operating efficiently.
- Ensure that all lights are working correctly.
- Check fluid levels, in engine trucks (fuel, water, lubricating oil, hydraulic oil).
- Ensure that batteries, where appropriate, are adequately charged.
- Ensure that lifting and tilting systems are operating correctly.

At the end of each check, a written report should be completed.

- Weekly check (or 50 hours or period recommended): Check by the supervisor/maintenance.
  - Agree with all daily checks.
  - Check the operation of steering, lifting gear and other working parts.
  - Check the condition of mast, fork, attachments and lifting mechanisms.
  - Check the hydraulic system for leaks/damage.

At the end of each check, a written report should be completed.

- Six monthly check (or 1000 hours or period recommended): Check by supervisor/maintenance.
  - Check all working parts.

At the end of the check, a certificate should be completed.

Racking maintenance and care

This will be facilitated by the following:

- Is the racking on sound and level floors?
- Was it installed in accordance with instructions?
- Are double-sided runs connected and spaced with appropriate run spaces?
- Is racking fixed securely to the floor?
- Are the aisles wide enough to allow adequate manoeuvring?
- Are the beam connector locks securely fixed at both ends?
- Are the correct maximum load notices displayed?

- Are all racks and beams aligned?
- Are the correct pallets being used?
- Is there any physical damage?
- Are end protectors fitted?
- When was the last inspection undertaken?
- Is all reasonable care taken for accident prevention and racking safety?
- Have there been any changes to product/handling equipment since the original specification?

People awareness

Most accidents are a result of people not being adequately trained and, not reporting possible hazards or 'near misses'. Remember the Accident Pyramid:

- For every one serious injury, there are 100 minor injuries.
- For every 100 minor injuries, there are 1000 close calls.

Therefore investigating the close calls can cancel the 'ones' and the 'hundreds'.

Managers, therefore, can usefully ask if all the people involved are able to:

- define the best methods of carrying out the job
- determine the right equipment to use
- know how to operate equipment
- know what dangers are associated with its use
- know what the safety precautions are
- clean equipment safely
- know how to report faulty equipment
- use the appropriate personal protective equipment.

Managers should also ensure that all people involved have undertaken formal training on safety hazards.

Recall that a manager's duty of care means that all individuals who report to them are aware of all potential hazards, that risks have been assessed and that corrective action has been taken.

Where this has not been satisfactorily done and it goes 'wrong', then Magistrate's courts can levy up to £5000 for each breach of regulations of Health & Safety at Work Regulations, plus up to £20000 for breach of the Health and Safety at Work etc. Act. Crown Courts give an unlimited fine and up to two years' imprisonment. Additionally private prosecutions from 'no win, no fee' companies are increasing, putting individual managers potentially directly 'in line'. The paperwork generated by this increasing trend causes additional work, time and effort.

8

Productivity, Cost and Service

Improvement needs to be a continuous aspect of management. Before starting to do this, however, there is a need to understand the current situation. This is necessary to give understanding on just how things actually work and also to be in measurable terms.

FRAMEWORK FOR ANALYSIS

A useful framework to adopt is to use the following basic problem-solving approach.

- **Where are we now?** This involves an analysis of the current situation in measurable terms. Measurements can be by quantity, time or cost – for example, with warehousing, the labour pick rate per hour.
- **Where do we want to be?** This involves setting clear objectives for improvement – for example, to improve the pick rate from 150 to 170 picks per hour.
- **How are we going to get there?** This involves looking at options and methods available for improvement, selection and then making a plan for implementing improvements.
- **How will we know we have arrived?** This involves comparing the new situation against the standard expected – for example, on picking, this is 150 picks per hour, against the improvement objective standard of 170 picks per hour.

So, by having a clear analytical framework managers can then work through an improvement programme and measure, objectively, the progress being made.

Let's now look at some of the key drivers in warehousing. It will be seen that these so often centre around time – that four letter word that we can never get enough of!

KEY COSTS

Costs are usually divided into two main categories, fixed and variable. Fixed costs occur every day irrespective of any activity, whereas variable costs are only incurred when there is some activity.

In warehousing the following is the usual division between these two cost categories:

Fixed costs

- Rent and/or rates.
- Heat power and light. Although this may only be a cost that occurs when there is activity, it is usually taken as a fixed cost and is usually a relatively low-cost item. However, where the cost is significant (for example, in ambient/chilled food warehouses), then it could be viewed for better control purposes, as a variable cost.
- Insurance on the premises/building.
- Depreciation on the assets, such as equipment.
- Basic wages and other people cost areas, like pensions.

Variable costs

- Overtime wage costs.
- Repairs and maintenance.
- Running costs of equipment.
- Insurance on the goods/products.

Warehouse total costs

While we will shortly examine the importance of these cost separations, the total costs to operate a warehouse will come from adding together the fixed and variable costs, for example, on a yearly basis. This will typically result in total costs as shown below, these being the typical costs for a 'normal' warehouse handling ambient goods, received and stored on pallets in adjustable pallet racking, with case picking by pallet truck and despatch on pallets.

Labour	60%
Space	25%
Equipment	15%

Labour includes basic wages, overtime, and all salary expenses; space includes rent and rates, heat, power and light; and equipment includes fixed and variable costs for plant, racking, fork-lifts, etc.

Therefore, with fork-lift trucks, the following costs could be typical for a CBT:

Fixed costs:	Wages (labour)	73%
	Finance costs	14%
Variable costs:	Running costs	8%
	Maintenance costs	5%
Total		100%

It will be seen from both of the above, that labour costs are the largest item. The question to ask is which of these costs are controllable on a daily basis and analysing labour costs by activity can be useful here. The following is a typical view:

Activity	Labour cost
Receiving	13%
Put away	12%
Picking	43%
Despatching	20%
Other	12%
	100%

As the labour cost rates (wages, overtime, and all salary expenses) are usually determined annually, then the way the daily activities are managed and organised will need to be examined. As picking is the largest item, this is the one we will examine further. For managers, this concentrates their limit analysis/improvement time onto the area that could have the biggest 'hit'.

KEY PRODUCTIVITY DRIVERS

All companies need to measure and control their cost expenditure. But cost measurement is only one side of the coin of measurement. There is also the need to measure the utilisation productivity and performance. These non-financial terms must have meaning and must be able to be identified by those who are directly involved.

It should be appreciated here, that the financial measures are always post-event, whereas productivity measures are virtually pre-event in examining the way resources are used on a daily basis. In turn, it is the input of these resources that actually determine the financial output.

It should also be appreciated that the data for measurement (by quantity, time and cost) will already exist within the operation – it only needs to be retrieved and made into useable information. Then with constant monitoring of the key productivity drivers (or indicators) an ongoing health check and early warning of problems is available.

Key productivity drivers in warehousing

In warehousing, we have seen that labour is a major cost and therefore an analysis of this cost would seem helpful. We can see the following key measures:

1. The time used/time available
2. The percentage of time used working on receiving
3. The percentage of time used working on put away
4. The percentage of time used working on picking
5. The percentage of time used working on despatching
6. The percentage of time used working on other activity

Warehouse labour productivity

With up to 60% of costs in labour, it is important to ensure effective productivity. While this is more precisely checked by the use of time study methods, a quicker method may be used to give an estimate. Assuming that the main activity is picking and delivery of single cases, then the total warehouse labour required will need to be assessed. This can be approximately assessed in the following manner:

1. Determine the time period (e.g. day or weekly or monthly).
2. Determine the cases handled in that period.
3. Determine the total warehouse hours worked, in the time period, in the following areas:

Operation	Total hours
Goods inward/receiving	
Checking/inspecting	
Put away to storage	
Picking	
Replenishment	
Checking	
Packing/load assembly	
Goods out/delivery	
Management/supervision	
Maintenance	
Others	_____
Total hours	_____

Total hours × 60 = Total minutes worked

$$\frac{\text{Total minutes worked}}{\text{Cases handled in that period}} = x \text{ minutes per case}$$

Note: 1 minute   = excellent   5 minutes = average
10 minutes = must improve   15 + minutes = poor

While warehouses are compact places, time is easily eaten away. For example, if one person can pick 150 cases per hour and takes an extra four steps for each pick, he or she travels around an extra 12000 feet in a 10-hour shift – that's around an extra 2 miles travelled each day by one person.

We have seen that picking is the major cost item, and an analysis of the average picking time could typically show that:

Travel time   60%
Pick time   20%
Looking/checking time   10%
Other time   10%

Which of these key time drivers are controllable by operations people on a daily basis? The following may help:

1. Time used/time available
2–6. Time working on activities (see page 176)

This is only controllable to a certain extent as other parties (suppliers and customers) are involved with the origination and availability of work. The time working on an activity (items 2 to 6) is the most controllable area, and it is important to establish the percentages for each activity compared with the others.

Warehouse space utilisation

As up to 25% of costs relate to the use of space, it is useful to check what percentage of the warehouse is actually taken up by the goods/products.
  The formula is simple:

$$\frac{\text{Actual cubic space used (i.e. the cubic volume of the product)}}{\text{Actual cubic space available (i.e. the cubic volume of the total warehouse)}}$$

As this answer is likely to be low (under 20%), what can you do to improve it?
  You could, for example:

• select a more appropriate mix of equipment
• use the headroom available

- select a better layout
- examine the work methods.

An alternative is to examine how the floor space is being used. The formula is simple:

$$\frac{\text{Actual floor space used}}{\text{Actual floor space available}}$$

The answer will reflect clearly the mix of equipment used. For example, with:

CBT/APR	50%
RT/APR	60%
NAT/APR	65%
DIR	75%
Hi Bay	90%

BASIC IMPROVEMENTS

We have seen in warehousing that:

- the key controllable cost driver is the labour cost
- the key controllable productivity driver is the labour picking rate.

On the improvement possibilities for warehouse picking, the first thing here is to be able to categorise throughputs. An ABC/Pareto analysis will reveal the A (fast) to C (slow) moving products. The ideal is to place the A-items where the travel distance is minimised; recall that travel time was 60% of picking time. Other options, from using an ABC analysis, may be to ensure that:

- fast items (A) are cross-docked/picked on receipt/picked by line
- medium items (B) are aisle/racked/zone picked
- slow items (C) are aisle/racked/belt picked

The principles to apply are:

- To travel less (as already illustrated)
- To travel faster, for example with powered pallet trucks using low level picking
- To pick several orders at once, for example batch picking
- To simplify/remove paperwork checking, for example, radio frequency, pick by light, and finger scanning.

A summary of the options to use is shown below.

Picking options

Aim: To minimise operatives' travel time

- Goods to operator
  - carousels, either vertical or horizontal
  - conveyors, pick to belt.

- Operator to goods
  - walking with hand or powered pallet truck at low level
  - picking trucks up to high levels
  - zigzag or switch travel patterns in the aisle
  - batch pick or zone pick.

- Performance indicators (indexed picks per hour)
  - hand truck (low level)   100
  - picking truck (high Level)   100
  - conveyor   100 to 300
  - vertical carousel   300
  - powered truck   300

Action time

It has only been possible to give a flavour of some of the improvement options. The ones used are real enough and have been used to challenge action. It has been shown that it is possible to effect improvements by closely monitoring daily operations and measuring all internal operations, and the key measurements that can be used are as follows:

Utilisation (time used/time available)

For:

- equipment
- people
- in each activity for example: receiving, put away, pick, despatch etc.
- space.

Performance (achieved/expected standard)

Examples per time period (per hour/shift/day/week/month/year, as appropriate) are:

- pallets received/unloaded
- pallets put away
- cases picked
- roll cages loaded
- inventory turns
- value of goods damaged
- customer returns
- accidents
- people absent
- stock-checking accuracy
- customer OTIF (on time, in full).

What next?

Many people know and talk about improvements, but far fewer bother doing anything. Why is this? Perhaps it is because implementing improvements means change. Perhaps it is because implementing improvements is often undertaken at the 'front end', and is therefore visible (and risky). Perhaps it is because people think they are doing it correctly anyway, after all, 'you do not know what you do not know'!

It is said that there are three kinds of people when it comes to change. Those who embrace it and go with the flow; those who disrupt it and actively try to sabotage it, and those (often the silent majority) who are subversive and have seen it all before (when it never worked as nothing ever happened).

Implementing change is very similar to the earlier basic problem-solving approach (see 'Framework for analysis' above). The following steps are needed:

- Evaluate the current reality. (Where are we now?)
- Envision with goals. (Where do we want to be?)
- Explore options. (How are we going to get there?)
- Establish what to do. (How are we going to get there?)
- Empower self and others, the essential communication and awareness programmes. (How are we going to get there?)
- Excel in the results. (How will we know we have arrived?)

Remember that, with change, success is also about combining technical competence and people's attitudes. Technical change is usually easier than cultural change – a subject we consider in Chapter 10.

We have used the following framework:

- Understand the current operation first in measurable terms.
- Set clear improvement objectives.
- Identify the key controllable cost and productivity drivers.
- Consider various options/methods to improve operations.
- Monitor and measure improvements by utilisation performance and productivity ratios.
- Effective implementation will involve combining technology with people's attitudes.

And finally

- What are your current measurements?
- Do they illustrate the key cost and the key productivity drivers?
- What is the best option for improvement?
- How will the implementation of the improvement be managed?

Improvements

The following not only represents a continued way to ensure improvements in warehouse methods, but also represents potential ways forward that can be further examined in times of change and continued dynamic developments in warehouse operations.

Labour related

- Work hours/shifts/annualised hours/overtime
- Absenteeism levels
- Incentive schemes
- Multi-functional/skilled labour
- MBWA (management by walking about)
- Training and development
- Managing managers and supervisors who supervise
- Picking methods: will batch picking of a few orders at a time improve efficiencies and accuracies? If not, what will?
- Shorter travel distances
- Unitisation of products, either by suppliers or on receipt
- Use of transport vehicle drivers, as a resource in loading/unloading.

Space related

- Cubic utilisation; very high levels are only usually found with bulk storage of slow-moving items
- Variable height racking
- Standardised pallets
- Layout re-examination.

Equipment related

- Batch picking/sortation
- Scanning
- Automation
- Radio frequency
- Specifications.

Process related

- Product lines/volumes/product obsolescence
- F/M/S, ABC analysis: understand the velocity of movements in each activity
- Order quantity
- Average/peak/low periods – daily/weekly, monthly
- On receipt, inspection is not undertaken due to having in place the appropriate supplier management/cooperation/controls
- Procedures for operational discipline
- Scheduling for each activity
- Picking is synchronised with the transport loading
- Service levels for customers: are they really needed to be at high levels for all products?
- Safety stock levels
- Customer response: are these really needed to be at high levels for all products?
- Information flows; more real-time information enables better decision-making
- KPIs that are meaningful, visible and used
- Consider the whole operation and not sub-optimisation at the expense of the whole.

Improving the warehouse by 5-S

The 5-S discipline offers a practical step by step approach to making any works improvements, be it in a factory, a warehouse or an office. The following gives an overview of 5-S, and it should be borne in mind that, in being a practical approach, it is necessary to customise and detail the approach to specific operations. This is not possible to do here, but the levels and stages give a useful indication that may well encourage taking it further.

5-S GUIDELINES

The five levels to be undertaken are as follows:

- Level 1: Sort = clearing
- Level 2: Set in order = arrange, organise
- Level 3: Shine = clean
- Level 4: Standardise = maintain levels 1–3, plus . . .
- Level 5: Sustain = continuous improvement, train.

(In the original Japanese, the 5-S mean Seiri–Seiton–Seiso–Seiketsu–Shitsuke)

The application of these levels involves moving through three stages.

Stage 1: Improving the current situation
Stage 2: Making it a habit
Stage 3: Becoming 'World Class'.

A great deal of iteration is required between these stages and levels.

Why bother with 5-S?

- It brings in 'good housekeeping' . . . plus . . .
- It reduces the wastage of time and energy spent in 'looking for things'
- It reduces frustration
- It increases 'well being' and a culture of continuous improvement.

There is a need in using 5-S to see the workplace through 'new eyes', as if you have never been there before. This can be difficult and may benefit from the use of an outside person to assist in 'opening the eyes'.

Stage 1: Improving the current situation

Level 1: What is 'sort'?

- Sort out the required and the necessary from the non-required and the unnecessary items.
- Keep near only those items that are needed today.
- Remove all unnecessary items: keep those for tomorrow away from the work area; and take those for next week to a storage area.
- Discard old, obsolete equipment, unused manuals, etc., and keep work areas and desks tidy.

Sort: Some methods to use

- Take photographs, before and after.
- 'Red tag' unnecessary items.
- Decide what to do with the red-tagged items; e.g. dispose of defectives/dead stock, put slow stock into storage, dispose of left-over materials.

Level 2: What is 'set in order'?

- Everything should be placed in order.
- Everything should be easy to find.
- It should take no time to find something. ('A place for everything and everything in its place')
- Work out the ergonomic and efficient use of work space, e.g. minimise bending, leaning, walking, lifting, etc.

Set in order: Some methods to use

The following questions are to be asked:
'Where?' (Fix the position)
'What?' (Fix the items/ID)
'How many?' (Fix the quantity)

- Follow good health and safety practice.
- Follow good work study/method study practice.

- Apply a 'lick of paint', especially to the floors and rest areas.
- Apply new lighting, signs, etc. . . .

Outcome of level 2: Re-layout and new work methods.

Level 3: What is 'shine'?

- Eliminate rubbish and dirt.
- Clean equipment, aisles, tools, floors, machines, instruments . . . everything is kept clean.
- Set up routines to keep it tidy; cleaning routines and regular inspections in the work areas (such as, check that maintenance has been done, look for leaks, loose cables, clear signs, fire exits, etc.).

Shine: Some methods to use

When: Clean every day and establish targets and schedules.
Who: Establish responsibilities.
How: Give appropriate tools and equipment.

Level 4: What is 'standardise'?

- Maintain levels 1–3 with a strong and supportive programme; e.g. team work.
- Settle down to 'what works well'.
- Establish the working practices that will continue to 'make it happen'.

Standardise: Some methods to use
Establish and use checklists/check-points for:

- Unnecessary items
- Storage
- 5-S procedural organisation
- 'Dirt'
- Cleaning.

Level 5: What is 'sustain'?

- Practice and repeat, so that it becomes 'a way of life', e.g. competitions, cross-functional inspections.
- Everyone keeps the rules . . . always.

This is when the 5-S have become 'embedded' by using the 5-S discipline and following the procedures to ensure that the hard work and results so far are not wasted. All four levels are present and it will be 'sustained' only when it has been used successfully for a period of time.

Sustain: Some methods to use

- Visual controls, so that all can see, e.g., photo displays, slogans, radar charts, etc.
- Can the improvements be seen?
- If 'no', what went wrong and why did it go wrong? Rectify the problem and start again.
- If 'yes', then the current situation has been improved and Stage 1 is complete.

Continue what has been started in Stage 1 and Levels 1–5

Next . . . after Stage 1: Improving the current situation, it is necessary to move through the following stages of:

Stage 2: Make it a habit

Stage 3: Become World Class.

Stage 2: Make it a habit

- Question stock levels strongly.
- Make it easy to return things (organise by colour, by shapes, by lines).
- Make cleaning habitual (checklists, checkpoints).
- Maintain a clean workplace (standards).
- Maintain standards (constructive criticism, correction, accept criticism).

Is it yet a habit? (A radar chart can be used to identify any weak points to be corrected.)

Stage 3: become world class

- Only move to this stage after making any corrections from Stage 2 'Make it a habit'.
- Now move from being reactive and remedial to being proactive and prevention . . . in **all** the five levels.
- 5WIH questioning.*
- Radar chart . . . are we there yet?

Who, what, where, when, why, and how.

UNDERSTANDING PRODUCTIVITY

To help to view improvements further, it is useful to understand the basic parts of productivity and the links between them. Figure 8.1 presents a model for productivity.

Inputs of resources such as labour, machinery, materials, money and time are used in a process that brings together various methods. As a result of this processing, an output results in the form of a product or service.

In our model we then consider the *utilisation* of resources, the *productivity* of the process and the *performance* of the product/service, and when we come to measure them, the following measurements are used:

- Utilisation is measured by the input used/the input that was available. So if picking activity took place for 7.5 hours in an 8-hour shift, then the utilisation is 7.5/8 = 93.75% of the time available
- Productivity of the process is measured by the output achieved/the input actually used. So, if picking is by hand pallet truck per picker over an 8-hour shift, and using the above examples, then the output achieved was 1125 cases for the input of 7.5 hours, or 150 cases per hour, divided by the output expected of 1200 cases in 8 available hours, or 200 cases per hour, which gives 150/200 = 75% picking productivity per picker using hand pallet trucks.

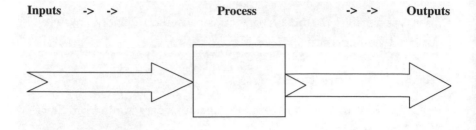

| Inputs   -> -> | Process | -> -> | Outputs |

Resources are used in......... **Producing**..........a............**Product or Service**

Utilisation	Productivity	Performance
Of resources	Of process	Of outputs

Measured by:

Used/	Output/	Actual/
Available	Input	Standard

Figure 8.1   A *model of productivity*

- Performance is measured by comparing what was achieved against the standard or KPI expected. So, if in picking, 1125 cases per shift were picked by one picker against a standard of 1600 cases per shift per picker, then the productivity of picking is 1125/1600 = 70.13% case picking performance per picker.

Planning timings

Time is that precious resource that once gone, cannot be recovered directly. So many improvements to processes and increased productivity come from the better utilisation of time. In warehouse operations, it is critical that all the times taken to undertake activities are measured. The way that different types of work are undertaken has a direct impact on the time taken. Consider, for example, the time difference when a picker is walking or is riding on a powered pallet truck.

Some simplified examples of time differences can be seen in Table 8.1. These are suitable for planning purposes with the real timings being obtained from time study methods.

Table 8.1 Simplified examples of time differences

Operation	Activity	Seconds taken	Minutes taken
Manual pick up and put down (PU/PD)	Pick up and put down a small item	10	0.16666
	Pick up and put down up to 18 kilos	20	0.33333
Manual walking	Walking, empty handed		61 metres per minute
	Walking pulling a hand pallet truck		30.5 metres a minute
Fork-lift truck	Pick up and put down a pallet	65	1.08833
	Hoist up and down (HU/HD)	20 seconds per metre of height	
	Travelling		120 metres a minute

Some immediate differences will be noted, for example, a fork-lift truck or powered pallet truck, is four times as fast as manual walking with a hand pallet truck. A worked example follows.

Operation: FLT moving 1 full pallet from goods in to storage area (75 metres); lift (2 metres) and returns empty to goods in area.

PU/PD   = 65 seconds
Travel 75 metres out/75metres back
  = 150 metres at 120 metres/minute   = 75 seconds
HU/HD 2 metres at 20 seconds   = 40 seconds
                                               = 180 seconds

(The actual sequence is PU – Travel – HU – PD – HD – Travel)

This time could also be used in determining standards; for example, it takes three standard minutes (SMs) for a FLT to move 1 full pallet from goods in to the storage area (75 metres), lift (2 metres) and return empty to goods in area.

The use of standard minutes is useful in determining pricing, as we shall see below.

DETERMINING PRICING AND CHARGING

There are many options available for warehouse owners and operators to determine rate pricing strategies. For a third party operator, taking a marketing point of view, pricing may be made low to enable a market share to be gained, pricing may be made towards 'what the market will bear', or cost plus pricing may be the favoured option. For 'own account' internal charging purposes and whatever 'third party' marketing charging method is used, a fundamental aspect for management has to be to determine all of the base line costs that are involved in operating the warehouse.

Costing a warehouse service can be very simple or can be very complex. As costing is usually done before a job is undertaken, it is therefore important to have a systematic procedure to determine the costs so that the 'before' and 'after' events can be checked and verified. Costing also helps third party companies to determine the base line from which revenue and profit can be determined. A procedure that can be used is as follows:

1. Specify clearly what the *service* is.
2. Identify what *method* is being used.
3. Estimate the *resources* that will be used in terms of the labour, equipment and miles.

This procedure can be explained further by looking at some warehouse examples for pallet storage and case handling. Please note that these financial figures are for illustration purposes and do not represent real and current figures; such figures will need to be applied as appropriate in a 'real' situation.

Example 1

Service: Pallet storage.
Method: Warehouse, 4000 square metres, fully racked 4 pallets high, with 3360 pallet spaces available.

If the estimated average pallet space utilisation is 75%, then the cost per pallet stored is: £83.33 per year (£210 000/3360/0.75); or £1.60 per week or 23 pence per day (Table 8.2).

Table 8.2   Resource/warehouse costs in £ per annum

Item	£ per annum
Rent	120 000
Rates	50 000
Heat and light	10 000
Repairs and renewals	15 000
Fire insurance	5 000
Racking depreciation	10 000
Total cost per annum	**210 000**

Clearly if a storage cost per case was needed, then this can be easily calculated by dividing the cost per pallet by the number of cases per pallet.

Storage costing is fairly straightforward but it is important to have a realistic estimate of space utilisation/pallet occupancy. Even though it is simple to cost, the cost of storage is frequently grossly underestimated.

Now we shall look at case handling in the warehouse.

Example 2

Service: Receive a case, put away, pick and delivery onto road vehicle.
(Note: There is no storage as this is a different type of calculation.)

Method: Receive on pallets by fork-lift truck (FLT)
   Check manually
   Put way into racking by FLT
   Restack to case-picking area by FLT
   Pick cases by PPT (powered pallet truck)
   Move order to loading bay by PPT
   Check manually
   Load onto vehicle by PPT

Resources: time

This method of calculating would use existing and known time calculations that are expressed in standard minutes (SMs).

Key operational assumptions used in the following example (Table 8.3) are that cases are received on pallets of 100; picking is by single cases which are then loaded onto pallets containing 60 cases. As you will see, these variables are then standardised to a cost per case.

Table 8.3   Resources and time: standardised variables

Method	Unit	No. of cases	People SMs	FLT SMs	PPT SMs
Receive	Pallet	100	2.0	2.0	
Check	Pallet	100	0.5		
Put away	Pallet	100	3.0	3.0	
Restack	Pallet	100	1.5	1.5	
Pick	Case	1	0.3		0.3
Move	Pallet	60	2.0		2.0
Check	Pallet	60	5.0		
Load	Pallet	60	3.0		3.0
Totals	**1 case**	**1**	**0.54**	**0.065**	**0.38**

Resources: costs

Key operational assumptions used here are the number of shifts available, where, for example, 225 = the working days available per annum allowing for holidays, sickness, etc.; whereas FLT/PPT equipment is available for more (300) shift days.

The time availability per shift is 8 hours for people and just under 7 hours for equipment (to allow for checking, fuelling, etc.).

The cost is therefore 7.3 pence per case (see Table 8.4)

(11.1 p × 0.54 SMs, plus 5.0 p × 0.065, plus 2.5 p × 0.38)

Table 8.4   Resources: costs

Item	People	FLT	PPT
Annual cost (£)	12 000	6000	3000
Shifts worked per year (days)	225	300	300
SMs per shift (mins)	480	400	400
Cost per SM in pence	**11.1p**	**5.0p**	**2.5p**

It will be seen that this type of methodology for costing is clear, as the key assumptions are stated. This is important, as it enables the subsequent verification of conformance and verifies the current validity.

Systematic costing 'on the back on an envelope' is fraught with problems! It will be seen that the links between costs and productivity measurements are interdependent. Both should be involved as one gives rise to the other; calculating unit costs based on guesswork is dangerous and subjective, yet it is not too difficult to calculate costs more precisely and objectively.

CUSTOMER SERVICE

Improving customer service is the key and critical aspect for all supply chain operations. Customers are both internal and external, and delivering good service can also be a key market differentiator and give competitive advantage. A service philosophy must therefore prevail from the top of the company.

There are three key measures used in distribution; unfortunately these may be interpreted differently, for example:

- Response/cycle time, e.g. the warehouse view may be: despatch within 24 hours of order receipt, but the customer's view is, time order placed to time received. Part of the 'OT' measure in OTIF (on time – in full).

- Accuracy/availability, e.g. the warehouse view may be: deliver 100% of what is available, but the customer's view is, have I got the complete 'in full' order (the IF part of OTIF).
- Quality/reliability, e.g. damage free when received.

Where the service provided is substandard, then the following can occur:

- Finance: delayed payments, penalties, extra stockholding
- Sales: enquiry, authorise return, credit notes
- Returns: transport, administration, put ways correctly
- Warehouse: unpack, repack, retransform. It can certainly be that a 1% pick error can easily bring 10% extra cost.

Improving customer service

The following methodology can be used to examine this important aspect:

1. Establish the key components of service from market research surveys, and/or see points 3 and 4 below.
     The top items in distribution that are commonly identified from surveys are (in priority order):

   - Time to deliver ('on time')
   - Reliability and 'constancy' of service
   - Availability of stock ('in full')
   - Advice and communication when non-availability
   - Quality of sales representatives/customer service department
   - Product support.

2. Identify the relative importance of each component:
   - If on time, is it 2 or 3 or 4 days?
   - If in full, is it 80 or 90 or 100%?

3. Establish 'where are we now' against the importance of each component and rate current service levels against competition by market research. As we shall look at in section 5 below, it is useful to view the competition not as the enemy, but as a source of information.

It is critical in this step, to find out, from both internal and external customers, the current level of service provided. As a bare minimum and potential starting point, this may be done by conducting a random sample of customers (10–20) and ask them to rate your operation on a 1–10 scale, as shown in the customer satisfaction survey.

CUSTOMER SATISFACTION SURVEY

What do you think of the service to you?

It would help us if you would rate this on a 1–10 scale
(1 is poor, 5 is average, 10 is excellent)

Activity	Your score	Our target
Response Time		10
Accuracy of orders		10
Complete orders		10
Product Damage		10

Thank you for your cooperation and in helping us to improve our service.

Remember that 'perception is reality', so what your customers think is important to know. This can mean learning new information and will also very likely show that different people in the customer's company will have differing views of the service being provided.

4. Analyse the competition including any 'surrogate' competition – these are those companies or products that provide a substitute to what you do; for example, e-mail for letter post. Customers will make comparisons with the competition and so should you. They may be doing new things and may have developed new markets. Use this analysis to give you knowledge, so you can improve/differentiate what you do.

5. Segment the market, for example:
   - Do all customers require the same service?
   - Which customers are sensitive to what specific service component?

6. Design the customer service package
   - Price brackets related to service levels?
   - Promotions
   - See 'using the customer's eyes', therefore manage the customer contacts, for example, with people working in reception, sales, administration, finance, warehousing, transport and, very importantly, in all written communications.

7. Establish, measure and control and ensure the distribution customer service measurements are understood by all involved:
   - Order cycle time/on time (OT)
   - Reliability/quality
   - Accuracy/availability/in full delivery (IF).

Customer's requirements are not static

E-commerce and the 'follow on' of E-fulfilment illustrate that customer service requirements change and require new and different responses. The following item illustrates such changes.

ACTION TIME 8.1: SAINSBURY'S E-FULFILMENT

WIDE EXPERIENCE OF E-TAILING METHODS

Leading supermarket group Sainsbury's has, through recent investments, become a major authority in e-tailing distribution. With e-tailing well established, but – in business terms – still in its infancy, industry standards and best practices have yet to be fully established. It is still early days for benchmarking of the market leaders. Sainsbury's has invested in a supply chain strategy that gives the company both wide local coverage and the flexibility to process orders in the most economical way. Sainsbury's employs some in-store picking by its retail store staff. This method is used where stores have the capacity to pick orders without impacting adversely on store customers; where this is not possible, the strategy is to use dedicated fulfilment centres such as the Park Royal picking facility in west London. These centres follow the in-store-picking pattern but – as they are dedicated to on-line shopping orders – there are no walk-in customers. The dedicated fulfilment centre in Park Royal employs state-of-the-art automated and semi-automated order-picking techniques designed and installed by KNAPP.

Dedicated centre lowers fulfilment costs

The new 170 000 sq. ft distribution centre (DC) has been designed around the key objective of minimising the costs of fulfilling e-commerce orders. The DC serves an area within the M25 and is ideally positioned to serve customers in central and west London. A substantial fleet of vans is deployed at the site for making deliveries directly to customers' homes. The London, Park Royal DC, which is operational 24 hours a day, can also fulfil orders for other parts of the UK, if required, by utilising trunker delivery services to regional points, from where local deliveries are completed in smaller vans. Thus, Sainsbury's has developed an integrated supply chain solution that provides the company with the flexibility to use both DC fulfilment and in-store fulfilment to balance customer demand and logistics capacity on a day-to-day basis.

Improved picking accuracy

The handling system at the Park Royal facility features computer-controlled order picking techniques which give the DC an edge in terms of picking accuracy, thereby improving customer satisfaction. The centre acts much like any other Sainsbury's retail store, in that it orders its stock from one of the group's conventional distribution warehouses, with certain fresh items being delivered daily directly from suppliers. Items arrive, in the main, as picked cases in roll containers – again, just like any of the other retail stores. The goods are then stored in carton live storage, pallet live storage and longitudinal or lateral shelving – but never outside of the physical reach of the average human frame. The 'Sainsbury's to You' home shopping range from fulfilment centres offers up to 15000 lines, compared to over 20000 in a Sainsbury's superstore.

Intelligent conveyor and pick-by-light

Customer orders are electronically segregated into three distinct sections, determined by storage and transit temperatures. Ambient, chilled and frozen goods are stored, picked and shipped separately – albeit in the same van – and only finally come together on the customer's doorstep. The three types of goods are placed into different colour plastic tote boxes, $400 \times 600 \times 350$ mm in size. Within the tote, the goods are actually placed into standard Sainsbury's plastic shopping bags so that, on delivery to the customer, the plastic totes can be retained. Picking for the ambient and chilled goods is essentially similar. Once the control system has scheduled a customer's order as ready to pick, a tote box with a unique bar code is placed onto a conveyor by an automatic tote box destacker. The intelligent conveyor system transports the totes only to the picking locations required for each particular order, speeding up the material flow. Once the tote reaches a required picking zone, it is discharged from the live conveyor onto a static conveyor line immediately in front of the picking faces. A pick-by-light system identifies the tote and the quantity of each item needed to fulfil its order. As each order line is picked, a completion button is pressed until no more pick signal lamps are lit. Once all the picking at that particular station is complete, an order confirmation button is pressed and the tote is pushed back onto the live conveyor to be transported to the next pick station required for that order.

Delivery at the right temperature and the right time

Stock awaiting picking is mostly stored in carton flow racking, and within the goods area there are approximately 80 picking stations on two levels. The chilled area has some 50 picking stations, again on two levels. The frozen goods are picked from static shelving within a special cold chamber. After order picking, totes of frozen goods are loaded into insulated roll cages, which are individually charged with dry ice to keep them at the required temperature until the point of delivery. Roll cages of ambient and chilled goods plus thermo-tainers of frozen goods are loaded into the delivery vans, with the chilled and frozen items being placed within a refrigerated section. Computer software plans the delivery routes, taking into account the customer's specified delivery window and the need to minimise the distance travelled.

Automation and flexibility – the keys to success

Automation and computer control ensures that handling costs at Sainsbury's Park Royal facility are minimised. Intelligent conveying systems, combined with pick-by-light technology, have resulted in high rates of productivity and picking accuracy. Sainsbury's strategy of utilising a combination of fulfilment methods has resulted in an enviable degree of flexibility. Computer control of order processing allows this flexibility to be exploited by directing customer orders to whichever fulfilment centre in the network will complete the order within the given time frame at the lowest cost.

TASKS

1. Describe how 'e' has changed traditional ways in supply and in the service/order fulfilment.
2. Compare your response with the next section.

Source: Warehouse News, 22 July 2002.

It should be noted, that early in 2004, the closure of the above site was announced due to lower market expectations and it changed to a picking-in-store operation – a method already favoured by Tesco and Asda.

In e-commerce, some have observed that it is the fulfilment/satisfying customer order process that separates the e-commerce winners and losers. The following is to be considered:

Growth of demand

- Ability to manage growing and unstable demand patterns?
- Appropriate core competence in warehousing and transport?
- Is a third party needed?
- What core competencies must be retained?
- Is the finance available to invest in the process and technology?
- Are customer management (CRM) processes in place?
- Can you track and trace from order acquisition to satisfactory fulfilment (which may include a significant percentage of returns)?
- Can you accept/respond to the fact that what is required today, may not be required tomorrow?

Performance quality

- Customer expectations are higher from e-commerce, such as speed and accuracy.
- Customers are able to search for competitors easily.
- Customer loyalty is as far as the last performance.
- Current internal processes need analysing:
  - What are customers needing and wanting?
  - What are the current capabilities?
  - What abilities can be added?
  - When will the required customer needs be met?
  - Is support/after sales service available?

Correct technology

- Design the services required first; then explore the technology support/enabler. For example that which:
  - Compresses through-put time
  - Operates in real time with RF
  - Decreases bottlenecks in the processing

  - Increase 'right first time' fulfilment
  - Decreases rework/returns
  - Increase customer satisfaction
  - Decreases costs.
- Technology solutions change fast, therefore view it as a process and a means and not as an end in itself.
- Do not add complexity, keep it simple and try to retain some flexibility.

Supply customised products

- Customers are individuals and may need customised products/service, for example, Levi can deliver customised, made to order, jeans in 10 days.
- Packing, assembly, labelling, etc., to present 'finished consumer products' can bring new demands to the warehousing activities.

ADDED VALUE

This has become common language in business, but is often confused in meaning. There are often two different views:

1. *Value is found when something satisfies a need, conforms to expectations and/or gives 'pride of ownership'*, i.e. it is 'valued' over something that is not.

   Here then the perception of value will differ. Customers have different perceptions of 'worth' and 'price'. For example, different customers have different perceptions of quality/lead time and the cost/service balance. Maybe, therefore, value can be seen as the balance and the pivot point between worth and price or between quality/lead time and cost/service.

2. *Value is the opposite of cost and in most processes more time is actually spent on adding cost and not on adding value*; for example:

   - In manufacturing:
     85% of time = queuing/setting up/inspecting/storing and handling = added cost
     15% of time = processing/QA = added value

- In warehousing:
  30 days in storage (added cost) yet only 1 day to pick/pack/load/transit to the customer (added value)

A business will not find it worthwhile to invest and automate wasteful non-value-added activities. Waste is the symptom rather than the root cause of the problem; so the aim must be to investigate the cause and then remove the wasteful non-value adders: those processes that take time and resources without adding any value.

Added value is, therefore, simply doing things better, by innovating and by improving the 'worth' of a product or service. Added value represents an important aspect that companies need to understand and then be able to apply. When adding value, this will go beyond a standard performance and moves more towards delivering customer success and excellence. Added value will often be seen as 'doing that something extra' which others do not do and is therefore increasingly seen as another source for competitive advantage.

The opportunities for adding value are varied and, in conceptual terms, adding value will mean looking at form, at time and at place:

- Form of the product/service offering. This means asking: What is the current form? Why is it done this way? How can we do it better?
- Time is involved in the total process/processes. How long does the process take? Why does it take that time? How can we do it better?
- Place issues. Where do we do it? When do we do it? How can we do it better?

As products have their maximum value when they are with the customer, then in the supply chain(s) there are many existing added value opportunities before the customer is 'reached'. Opportunities for added value are therefore many, and can be found within and between the processes of buying, making, moving and selling. The following form, time and place opportunities will illustrate just some of these advantages.

'Form' opportunities

These will often exist in the following areas:

- Packaging: for example, hanging garments and not flat packs; point of sale outers and not items packed within bulk outers.
- Packing postponements: for example, packing items only when ordered instead of packing in bulk outers.
- Price tagging/labelling: for example, undertaken just before the final delivery.
- Subassembly: for example, assemble to order operations and customise product only when a definite order is received.
- Sequencing: for example, scheduling to a specific and definite assembly/manufacturing 'run'.

'Time' opportunities

To examine this properly, it is necessary to establish a complete view of the lead time involved, not just for a 'narrow' operation, but across all of the broader supply chain. If sourcing products from a Hong Kong supplier to a UK wholesaler, the broader supply chain stretches back from Chinese manufacturers to their suppliers and stretches forward to UK and European retailers and consumers.

Within a supply chain all the lead times involved in the flows of goods and the flows of information should be examined. This will, in turn, involve looking at individual processes in procurement, production, warehousing, transport, stock/inventory, administrating, ordering and payment.

Clearly this examination will also raise issues for 'form' and 'place' added value opportunities. Meanwhile, specifically for the 'on time' opportunities, the following examples may be given:

- Shelf-life reductions or improvements
- Faster response rates
- Supply to order options
- Make to order options
- Inventory reductions
- Track and trace visibility
- Real-time proof of delivery provision
- Quicker performance reporting
- Faster invoicing and payments.

'Place' opportunities

These can be found in the following:

- Supplier visits: for example, to examine stock levels and response times.
- Channels used: for example, home shopping, internet buying.
- Stock positioning: for example, managed inventory at customer locations.

The wider supply chain

To go further into these opportunities again needs an examination of the 'wider' supply chain. A simple framework would be to analyse the following:

- Customer wants/needs.
- Internal processes and relationships.
- External processes and relationships.
- Trade-off analysis between and within processes on cost/service balances, on lead-time implications and on make-to-stock/make-to-order options.

This examination would fully link both the supply chain and the added value chain concepts. Doing this gives rise to the 'value chain' expression. Accordingly, in principle, everything in the supply chain will be considered as a source and an opportunity to add value (and not just to add cost). Some broad examples of adding value in supply chains are given in Table 8.5.

The relationship between cost and value

We have defined added value as simply doing things better. An examination of costs may therefore result in simply doing things cheaper, and cost reductions will certainly be a feature of any examination or analysis. In broad terms, the following cost reductions will be considered:

Table 8.5 Some broad examples of adding value in supply chains

From	To
Forecasting	Make to order
Inventory push and stockholding	Inventory pull from order placing
Storing	Sorting
Handling	Postponement
Manual ordering	Automated ordering

- Decrease the spend (by buying cheaper, the same).
- Increase the throughput for the same fixed costs (sweating the assets).
- Increase the productivity (getting more output for the same or less input).

What now becomes interesting is that by looking at those activities where cost is being added, these are usually going to be non-added-value activities. Accordingly, these added cost activities could become opportunities for added value. If we look strategically across the broad supply chain, then the following cost-adding activities can become added value opportunities:

- Forecasting involves effort and cost, whereas an added value opportunity exists in make-to-order solutions.
- Inventory involves varied costs, many of which are disguised; added value would encourage more 'pull' rather than 'push' supply chain strategies.
- Storing in bulk would be replaced by added value, sorting to order.
- Multiple handling would be reduced through added value, postponement.
- Ordering/invoicing manual processes would be replaced by added value, electronic transmission processes.

Third parties and added value

The view of a third party logistics service provider will often be one that sees added value as providing break-bulk/consolidation, pick/pack, track/trace, labelling/assembly and storage services. However, storage may not be seen as value added for a client company pursuing JIT or make-to-order supply chain options of production. But from the view of a third party provider, they will often view storage as being an added value service when they are going to provide such a service. It is a question of 'perception' (and also raises the potential confusion that can follow when using such terms as added value).

WAREHOUSE LAYOUT

We have now come to the end of looking at the technical aspects of ware-housing. All of this will be focused upon when looking at redesigning (or designing for the first time) a warehouse layout.

Current and existing warehouse layouts – unless they have been re-examined recently – will more than likely be ineffective and inefficient unless, of course, the warehouse is handling a very stable and consistent product range. This is not to say that warehouse layouts should be changed every month, but at least, if taking such a decision, it should be an objective one. This will only ever be possible by undertaking regular re-examinations and the modelling of various options. This does not need expensive computer software, and very adequate and effective results can be obtained from the use of manual drawings and applied logic – as any student who has undertaken the former Institute of Logistics and Transport Certificate and Diploma qualification programmes covering Ware-house and Resource Management will have discovered.

The model in the following section can be used when examining warehouse layouts.

Model for warehouse layout planning

1. Analyse the historic demand data:
   - SKUs volumes by numbers received per day in minimum–average–maximum volumes (i.e. what comes in).
   - SKUs volumes by numbers picked/despatched per day in minimum–average–maximum volumes (i.e. what goes out).

- SKUs by daily–weekly–monthly stock levels (i.e. what stays).
- SKU range by product-handling groups.
- Picking/issues by lines, by units, by order for daily, weekly, monthly periods.
- Receipts by SKU by frequency and volume for daily, weekly, monthly periods.
- Receipts by SKU by supplier for daily, weekly, monthly periods.
(See Chapter 2.)

2. Are there any future developments and/or changes that will alter this historic pattern? (Chapters 1 and 11 may also assist here.)

3. Calculate the internal space needed for:
   - Receiving
   - Storing
   - Picking/assembly
   - Despatching
   - Any special areas needed for quarantine, hazardous products etc.
   - Offices
   - Canteen and rest areas
   - Equipment maintenance/parking-recharging if applicable
   - Spares, packing materials, pallets (possibly kept externally)
   - Waste materials, rubbish, disposed stock (likely kept externally).

   This involves considering the organising for flow aspects covered in Chapter 4 along with the product handling groups from Chapter 2.

   It will be important with the product groups to consider any special requirements such as ABC analysis and any product specifics like temperature control, security, hazard ratings, etc., that require goods to be kept separate.

4. Choose options for MHE and Storage equipments, including the varied aisle widths/lift heights for these options, if pallet handling, then especially consider the short and long side pallet-handling decision. (See Chapter 5.)

5. If using an existing building, then with a scale floor plan drawing, check for the existing building constraints of floor loading, doors, columns, overhead lighting and all other obstructions.

6. Draw a sample layout(s) using varied options from item 4, not forgetting to allow for fire exits and regulations appertaining to emergency evacuation of personnel. (See Chapter 7.)

7. For each sample layout, calculate the people and MHE requirements, using synthetic data, and then calculate the costs. (See Chapter 8.)

8. 'Walk through' each layout for bottlenecks, flows, and 'comfort factors'. Examine especially the flow for the fast movers, ensuring there is a smooth routing and hand over to the next activity.

9. Decide using iteration for each of the above processes, if required.

10. Remember the warehouse exists in an environment, so external aspects to be considered are:
    - Access for employees, customers, suppliers
    - Parking space for cars and vehicles
    - Rest/waiting areas for visitors
    - External perimeter/security
    - Landscaping to reduce any visual intrusion.

TRAINING TOPICS

It can be useful for a company engaged in warehousing to ensure that all concerned personnel have a common understanding of what is involved. The following is an example of the contents from one such training programme:

- *The role of the warehouse*
  - The alternative uses, for example, storing or sorting?
  - Definitions and uses of warehouses
  - Checklist to undertake an initial analysis of operations.

- *Product classification*
  - Supply and demand variables
  - ABC analysis to show where to concentrate limited resources
  - Product handling groups and classifying for effective operations
  - Checklists to help on the analysis.

- *Layout options*
  - The trade-off between using floor and height space
  - Organising for flow from receipts, picking/assembly to despatching
  - Picking/selecting options and improvements
  - Checklists to help on deciding the best option.

- *Methods and equipment*
  - Handling equipment
  - Warehouse structure checklist
  - Storage options and key features of racking types
  - Pick/pack equipment
  - Checklists on equipment selection
  - Checklist on how to complete time planning
  - Video on equipment types.

- *Health and safety*
  - Roles and responsibility
  - Maintenance
  - Accident awareness
  - Risk checklist
  - Video on safe fork-lift truck driving.

- *Security and loss*
  - Internal theft
  - External theft
  - Preventative measures.

- *Productivity, cost and service*
  - Identifying the typical costs involved
  - Getting costs under control by targeting and measurement
  - Checklists on labour and space productivity
  - Service level analysis
  - Checklist on customer service sampling.

- *The 7-step model for better warehouse management*
  - A structured approach to ensure all elements are considered
  - Checklist on warehouse improvements
  - The top 20 warehousing ideals.

9

Outsourcing

USERS' VIEWS OF THIRD PARTIES AND THE MARKETPLACE

While names are important in defining what third party (3P) companies do, different names are often given to the same things and user confusion results. The following therefore attempts to give a view on what the various name definitions are for third party logistics service provider companies (3PLSP).

First, a few words of explanation. Fixed terms arrangements in the following definitions, means a dedicated provision of services for a specified timed/term contract and *ad hoc* arrangements mean common user/shared provision as required/on demand.

- *Contract distribution/logistics*
  This is a fixed term agreement for provision of dedicated vehicles and/or warehouse resources. It is usually offered by large companies with access to capital to support such operations who also will offer a high range of services.

- *Haulage companies/warehouse companies*
  These companies offer fixed or *ad hoc* arrangements for dedicated but usually, common user/consolidated services. They are usually medium to smaller sized companies operating nationally or regionally with, sometimes, access to a network of other regional companies. They offer specific services.

- *Integrators*
These companies offer fixed or *ad hoc* on demand arrangements, using multi-modal transport. These are often multinational companies operating world wide.

- *Express companies*
These companies offer fixed or *ad hoc* on demand arrangements for local/national express next day deliveries. They are either large companies with owned networks or smaller companies with access to a network of other companies, often on a franchised basis.

- *Forwarding agents, forwarders and 4PL*
These agents mainly offer *ad hoc* on demand arrangements; they may be traditional shipping and forwarding agents with some transport and warehousing resource. Forwarders are usually smaller and local companies although there a few large companies who operate with owned facilities on a more global basis. In the UK, there are around 3000 forwarders, with less than a hundred companies employing over 100 people. Forwarders are involved in numerous activities, such as:

  - selection of the carrier/operator/service provider
  - organising/supervising the movement
  - providing documentation and insurance
  - ensuring compliance with regulations (customs, banking, consular, etc.)
  - advising on packing, warehousing, supply chain management, etc.

Traditionally, freight forwarders act as agents on behalf of shippers. They will do anything, anytime, for anyone, to any place in the world, by any means of transport, for a profit. They are perhaps a partial original 4PL (fourth party logistics provider), a term coined in the late 1990s by Anderson Consulting who defined this as: 'a 4PL is a supply chain manager which can combine its own resources, capacities and technologies with those of other service providers to offer companies complete solutions.'

However, some forwarders also act as principles and are the actual service operators. In this role, for example, the forwarder 'buys in bulk' from the freight services carrier/operator, per full container load (FCL) for sea freight, or per unit load device (ULD) for air freight. They then sell on a LCL/consolidated/groupage service, which will operate on a terminal-to-terminal basis with additional services such as collection/delivery, documentation being provided.

- *Shipping lines and airlines*
  These are basic terminal-to-terminal providers who may have expanded into offering door-to-door land-based services. Fixed or *ad hoc* arrangements are offered.

- *Postal companies*
  Formerly these were state-owned nationally based companies with access to other postal authorities' networks. Since privatisation, many have bought into privately owned contract distribution/integrators/forwarding companies. They are mainly considered to be available for *ad hoc* on demand arrangements, but fixed term contracts are also an important part of their business.

- *Parcel companies*
  These companies mainly offer *ad hoc* on demand arrangements for non-time-sensitive consignments. These companies are of a comparable size to Express companies.

- *Couriers*
  Couriers offer fixed or *ad hoc* on demand arrangements for hand carried/small packages requiring urgent time delivery.

Using third parties

The following questions can be used to enhance your concepts of outsourcing:

- Are your objectives for warehousing achievable with outsourcing?
- Are the suppliers available to perform at least your current expectations?
- Have you any agreements that limit your capability to outsource?
- What exactly do you want to outsource? For example, the physical handling in your retained premises with your equipment (basically a managed labour service supply), through to the whole operation including transport delivery (involving also the provision of all warehouse and transport assets)?

Outsourcing is not only applicable to warehousing but is often a strategic direction that most companies face. The following 'secrets' have been identified by *Supply Management* (29 June 2000):

- Concentrate on what you do well and allow specialists in other areas to handle the non-core services.
- Adapt to new ideas and developments, as what was acceptable in the past may not be so in the future.
- Choose a provider who understands all your needs.
- It is crucial to fully know your current costs/service level.
- Ensure that outsourcing delivers planned benefits such as cost/service/time targets.
- Acknowledge that information equals power in areas such as service level requirements.
- Develop a strategic partnership with the provider, based on mutual trust.
- Start with a phase controlled service with monitored cost/service levels at all stages.
- Develop the right company culture which supports outsourcing.
- Monitor the outsource function with performance measurement regularly.

The following also provides a view on whether to use third parties for distribution:

- *Is distribution a non-core activity?* Whatever the answer, management control must remain a core activity, as should customer contact.
- *Can we release some capital?* The 3 Party industries have reported low ROCE ratios, typically 10%, probably well below that expected by many other companies/sectors.
- *Will we retain some operations in house?* It may be useful to do this for cost comparisons and service benchmarking.
- *Will we retain management expertise?* This is important to do; companies should never fully subcontract control.
- *What increased monitoring will be needed?* This should be the same as is currently done, but there is often a need to especially watch closely the customer service standards.

- *What are the risks of committing to one contractor?* Flexibility in the contract may be possible; alternatively, multi-sourcing could be the answer.
- *Will flexibility be increased?* It should be flexible as in theory, the third party operator can perhaps divert non-specialised resources elsewhere, as, after all, transport/distribution is their core business.
- *Will costs be reduced, while service is increased?* This is the ideal.
- *How will we account for future changes?* Presumably in the same way as without the contractor; but contract terms and 'get outs' are the issues to be considered here.
- *Are there any Transport of Undertaking Protection of Employees (TUPE) legislation implications?* There probably will not be if there are less than five people, or if some direct control is retained of, say, routeing, or, if relocated. There probably will be if the assets or the whole business is being transferred.

The levels of transport and warehousing outsourcing have remained relatively steady throughout the 1990s, with domestic transport outsourcing at around 75/80% of all freight transport activities and warehousing around 30/35% of companies that were surveyed. Profitable and successful third party companies are those that have:

- created an open dialogue and understood customers' needs
- priced according to the resources used and/or the value delivered
- been open on productivity measurements
- used the appropriate technology
- demonstrated flexibility
- desired to implement change and best practice.

Information needed

If considering using third party suppliers of warehousing and distribution, then the following questions will need detailed answers and indicate the information that will be required by the third party.

Giving third parties inadequate information can mean inadequate responses and if, for example, comparisons are being looked for in order to benchmark against incumbent operators, then a distorted picture will certainly be found when giving out poor information. Meanwhile the incumbent operator will have knowledge of all the key parameters/details, and is in a favourable position.

Key information must also be made known to the alternative suppliers that are being sought. It is surprising that, so often, this is not correctly undertaken, perhaps reflecting that the company is no longer fully aware of what is involved or that they 'only go through the motions' of re-tendering and have no real intention to change.

Product format

- What are the product size/shape?
- What is the weight?
- What is the value?
- What is the packaging?
- How is product identified?
- Is there any fragility?
- Is there any perishables?
- Any hazards involved?
- Any special handling needed?

Throughputs

- What is the frequency (e.g. daily, weekly)?
- What is the seasonality (e.g. over the year, in the month, during the week, during the day)?
- What are the usual patterns/requirements?
- How often does the 'usual' change?

Collection/delivery points

- Where are the geographical locations?
- What are the 'features':
  - Limited access?
  - Limited 'windows'?
  - Loading docks?
  - Side loading?
  - Height?
  - Day/night working?

Company policy

- What service level is required?
- What is the 'returns' policy?
- What is the order size policy?

Infrastructure/environment

- What are the road congestion places?
- How can these be avoided?
- Any there are legal restrictions that may affect us?
- Are there any specific climatic conditions?

Financial issues

- Is capital released?
- Is off-balance sheet finance needed?
- What is the asset utilisation?
- Are there any economies of scale?
- What are the planned and the known costs?
- Has a cost comparison, involving 'total acquisition cost' been used?

Operational issues

- What is the flexibility in 'spreading' peaks/troughs; in delivery times; in future changes?
- Will we get response to special requests?
- What are the management role changes on existing management?
- How will we keep control? (Management control MUST remain a core activity.)

Strategic issues

- After the decision, what is the ability to change?
- Have we got 'all eggs in the one basket'?
- What is our ability to bring some of the operations back in house?
- Are we able to use another third party?
- What are the full internal implications?
- Have we spread the risk?

- What will be our customers' reactions? (Customer contact MUST remain a core activity.)
- Have we completed a fair and complete comparison?
- Will the change assist in any internal change/new strategies/ expansion.

Some of the reported advantages and disadvantages from using third party contractors are summarised in Tables 9.1 and 9.2. It should be noted that while these have come from specific examples of outsourcing, they do show the wide range of opinion and that various views can be found. For example, innovation is seen as both an advantage and a disadvantage; as has been said, 'one man's meat is another man's poison'.

Clearly the listings in Tables 9.1 and 9.2 also have much to say not only about how outsourcing is approached, but also about how the work was previously conducted by the companies involved. There is no 'one size fits all', and again various views are reflected. *Caveat emptor*, or 'Let the buyer beware!'.

Table 9.1 Advantages of using third party contractors

Cost factors	Service factors
• Less capital on the balance sheet	• Flexibility against future legislation changes
• Costs now fully on the profit and loss statement	• Flexibility for sickness, holidays
• Less depreciation risk	• Less risk of IR disruptions
• More economies of scale	• Less employment risk
• Less administration and access to fully trained staff and up to date technology	• Improved service levels
• Increase business ratios e.g. ROCE	• More professionalism and expertise
• Cash return for sold off assets	• More innovation and new thinking
• Tax advantages if leasing	
• Planned and more fixed cost levels	

Table 9.2   Disadvantages of using third party contractors

Cost factors	Service factors
• Less cost control as costs 'fixed'	• Less direct control on service
• More hidden costs for unforeseen 'extras'	• Less feedback from drivers on customers
• Long-term contracts	• Less response to request
• Paying a contractor a profit	• No innovation

SELECTING THIRD PARTIES

Users will generally look for the following three characteristics from third party companies:

- Cost/price/rates
- Speed in transit
- Reliability.

The order and priority of these issues will usually vary dependent on a company's requirements and its specific offerings in a marketplace.

Users may wish to ensure that they obtain satisfactory answers to the following questions that can be asked of 3P companies:

- What are your experiences in our industry?
- What are your experiences with our customers?
- What problems have you had setting up third party operations for other companies and why?
- What successes have you had and why?
- How long will the implementation take?
- How will I know that things are working correctly?
- What are the performance measures?
- How can we better interface?
- What do you require from us?
- Why do you want our business?
- Why should you be selected?

Many different surveys have been undertaken in the UK on distribution services, and a brief summary of these surveys follows:

Important factors in the decision of which 3P to use:
- Service   98% response
- Quality of people   94%
- Cost   90%

Important factors that 3P see they have:
- Quality of service   100%
- Reputation   100%
- Experience   60%

Why was a particular 3P operator selected?
- Cost   58%
- Service   34%
- Reputation   20%

The benefits obtained were:
- Lower cost
- Focus on core activity
- More flexibility
- Higher efficiency
- Improved service

Implementation fears were:
- Fall in service   30%
- Lack of control   26%
- Higher costs   14%
- Staff will not approve   12%

Implementation 'reality' was:
- No Problems   40%
- Had Problems   60%

Implementation problems reported were:
- 35% – IT issues

- 22% – people issues ('hide', 'fear', changed)
- 11% – service levels were not what expected
- 10% – more resource/costs involved
- 8% – initial data found to be suspect
- 14% – other reasons, e.g. culture clash, no clear agreements before commencement, no planning or thought to implications.

Implementation will not always be easy and automatically trouble free. Implementation will nearly always involve managing change – a topic that is fully discussed in Chapter 10.

ACTION TIME 9.1: NEW LOOK AND P&O (RETAIL FASHION AND 3PL DISTRIBUTION)

Maintaining an efficient supply chain is a major priority for women's fashion retailer New Look in its ambitious plans for growth. The company is upgrading its stores and is widening its appeal beyond its traditional 16–24-year-old customers to older age groups, and needs the slickest possible logistics operation to support its strategy.

Logistics director Alan Osborne has control of both inbound and outbound movements to maximise the smooth-running of the operation and to allow the company to respond quickly to the volatile fashion market. 'That approach is absolutely critical in fashion. Speed to market – from sheep to shop is fundamental,' he says.

The business strategy has already reaped benefits. Profit for the year to 30 March had more than doubled to £62.3 million and by July sales revenues were up 12.3%. But the company has plans for further growth which the logistics department must support. Project Heartland aims to double overall retail floor space within five years to 200000 square metres and will involve relocating stores to larger premises in key towns and cities – so far 41 stores have undergone the process with another 119 to go. The company is also refurbishing 300 smaller stores over two years in Project 300, intended to boost sales through existing space. Originally New

Look had a strong southern bias and most of its stores were in south coast resort towns. This has changed as it has expanded and its distribution network has altered accordingly.

The company's main distribution centre, run in-house, is based at its Weymouth headquarters, where it has around 50000 square metres of warehouse space arranged over three floors. New Look is the town's largest employer and, at peak, 700 staff are employed in the distribution centre. 'We have no plans to change that. We have a very loyal and reliable set of staff,' Osborne says. 'The distribution centre is next to the buying office which is a great advantage. I am able to have regular contact with the buying and merchandising director and I am constantly talking to distribution centre staff as well.'

However, the geographic shift in the business has made it necessary to use an additional facility in Doncaster to serve the North and Midlands. The warehouse opened last September and is owned and operated by P&O TransEuropean. Goods are trunked from Weymouth overnight and merged with those at Doncaster and sent out to the stores on New Look's fleet. Around 48% of the company's deliveries to stores are now made through the facility. P&O TransEuropean also uses the site for a contract with Flymo manufacturer Electrolux Outdoor Products.

As well as benefiting from shared overheads, the two companies have different trading peaks and the resources they use can be flexed accordingly. 'There is a good mix of demand. They have a summer peak whereas we are more winter based,' Osborne says. This part of the operation was outsourced because New Look did not want to invest large amounts of capital in a distribution centre. 'It was also a case of P&O having the resource available to allow us to make the move quickly,' says Osborne.

As well as distribution to stores, New Look is paying a great deal of attention to inbound logistics. In future it intends to store more stock overseas, where storage costs are cheaper; and use cross-docking when goods arrive in the UK. The company is setting up overseas consolidation centres for this purpose and one of these has opened in Greece, with another planned in Turkey.

Rather than packing single items, New Look is moving to ratio packs, where possible, to reduce handling. These contain several of the same garments in the most popular sizes – for example, packs might include a size 8, a 10, two 12s and a 14.

IT systems will play a major part in making the inbound operation work more efficiently and Osborne says that the company will use fourth party logistics. It is currently talking to the major providers about the work. 'We'll be using a company with global representation. We want them to give us one systems solution so that we can have visibility of stock movements all around the world,' Osborne explains.

Traditionally New Look has owned all its vehicles, mainly Scanias, and has 44 trucks, either 25 feet or 30 feet long. However, it is currently switching to leasing and has signed up to take 28 demountable Scanias. This followed its decision to lease six Renaults last year. 'By the time we are finished we will have ten company-owned vehicles left, all under three years old,' says transport manager Paul Bennett. Although there is a full servicing and maintenance contract, all the work will be carried out on site, using New Look's garage but adhering to Scania's servicing schedules.

The drivers at the Weymouth depot are employed directly by New Look and those at Doncaster are contracted from BRS, although no trucks are taken from BRS. Despite the national driver shortage there have been few recruitment problems at Weymouth, where a 48-hour contract was introduced in April to fit in with the Working Time Directive. 'Last year we took volunteers from the distribution centre's picking staff and gave them the chance to do Class HGV driver training,' Bennett says.

Store deliveries are made at night, a policy brought in some years ago which other fashion chains are beginning to follow. Security risks are reduced because each vehicle is double-manned; where there are local authority restrictions, deliveries are made before a certain time in the evening or after a certain time in the morning.

'We have to work around those situations but in a large percentage of cases there is no problem at all. Most of our journeys take place on empty roads,' Bennett says.

TASKS

1. Describe the supply chain strategy aspects that are covered here.
2. Identify the strengths and weaknesses in the warehousing, outsourcing and supplier aspects.

Source: Motor Transport, 29 August 2002. Reproduced by permission of Reed Business Information.

TRAINING TOPICS

It can be useful for a company considering outsourcing to ensure that all concerned personnel have a common understanding of what is involved. The following is an example of the contents from one such training programme:

- *Understanding the UK distribution market*
  - The UK distribution market size and trends
  - Strategy aspects of, own operation or third party supplier(s)
  - Suppliers in common user and contract services, and market size
  - Cost/service balance and being clear on what we want
  - Keys to successful supplier selection

- *Cost and productivity variables*
  - Fixed and variable costs
  - Key cost drivers
  - Productivity measures
  - Key productivity drivers
  - Service provider variables and options

- *Looking for added value*
  - Supply chain and logistics viewpoints
  - Time
  - Postponement
  - Changing form

- *Selecting the 3PLSP*
  - What is available?
  - Specifications/tenders
  - Negotiation/selection
  - Agreement/contracts

- *Ongoing monitoring*
  - Performance reports
  - Partnerships
  - Inspections

- *The 5-step approach*
  - The Model (understand the distribution market, understand the key cost/productivity variables, looking for added value in the supply chain, select the supplier, and monitor/review performance).

10

People Management

Warehousing can use all the best and efficient equipment, but without effective management the operations will fail. Even if the technical systems are the best, unmotivated people can still cause failures. Management is therefore ultimately all about people. Getting the best from people is the major and critical task for a business.

A reflection of having unmotivated people comes from company staff turnover rates and absenteeism rates (running nationally at between 3 and 4% per annum). These measures, as with absence for example, can be a reflection that people are taking time off because they are 'fed up'. It is also a proven fact from an analysis of distribution centres in large company networks, that those centres with high levels of absenteeism and staff turnover also have relatively low rates of productivity with higher operating costs. Here it seems that one aspect is 'feeding' the other, in a perpetual spiral.

But getting the best for people is not always going to be an easy or an automatic process. People operate on at least three levels: as individuals 'in their own right', in 'collective' groups and teams, who will then 'combine' into a company/culture. We will look at these levels, starting first, with company culture.

COMPANY CULTURE

People working for a specific company find that it has its own way of doing things, and those people who leave one company to join another to do a similar job will appreciate the urgent and early need to 'fit in'. A company therefore has its own culture, which can be defined as the 'way we do things around here' and is shown both formally and informally.

'Formal' culture

Company culture can therefore be shown by the overt and published vision, mission and goals and in the company's rules, norms and procedures. This formal expression of company culture may be seen in statements of vision, mission, and goals/objectives, for example:

- Vision incorporates the timeless values and beliefs.
- Mission incorporates the purpose, policies, and power structures to achieve the task.
- Goals are the strategic, tactical and operational objectives, right down to people's individual roles and responsibilities.

All of these are important for the efficient running of the company and also to give overall direction, guidance and 'checkpoints'.

Rules are needed which set standards of conduct and show the way people should behave by clarifying what is expected. Rules need to be:

- kept simple, clear and easy to understand
- in writing
- displayed publicly
- kept up to date.

Procedures are also needed to help people to keep to the rules and establish the methods used to deal with the rules. Procedures maintain/apply the standards, demonstrate a fair/consistent approach and also bring clarity. Such rules and procedures, therefore, represent a form and overt demonstration of the company's culture.

'Informal' culture

However, culture is also often covert and informal, with values and beliefs that can remain unnamed. For example, contrast the difference between a charity and a private sector company, between the army and a football team, between the civil service and a retailer, between the Royal Mail and TNT. As well as things like dress, office styles and types of buildings, differences will be found in the human 'software' represented by the attitudes, values and beliefs that operate behind the scenes and determine how decisions are made.

'Total' culture

In all forms of management, therefore, there are hard, objective and clearly defined ways of managing and the more subjective beliefs, values and soft skills are also involved. Culture, therefore, will embody the following:

1. *Purpose, policies and roles:*
   - What are the structures/processes?
   - Where are the key decision-makers?
   This is the 'why?' and the 'what?' of the company.

2. *Power:*
   - Who has access to which resources?
   - Where is the central authority?
   This is the 'where' and the 'when' of the company.

3. *People partnerships:*
   - What is the degree of support and trust?
   - What is 'valued' and what are the associated reward structures?
   This is the 'who?' and the 'how?' of the company.

It may be that purpose and power are in fact easier to change than the beliefs, attitudes and behaviour of the individuals that make up one part of the company culture. The following 'test' can therefore be undertaken by talking to or observing the people in a company. This will give indications of the real 'people' aspects of the company.

Is the 'culture' climate friendly or unfriendly?

This quick test (Table 10.1) will show some management tasks that may be needed to improve work:

Table 10.1   'Culture' climate: friendly or unfriendly

Friendly ☺	Unfriendly ☹
People take the initiative	People feel boxed in
Team work flourishes	Friction and a lack of appreciation between team members
People understand their contribution	People have little understanding of their role
Clear direction is found	Conflicting goals are found
Good communication exists	Mixed messages and little understanding
An even workload allowing for individual skills/abilities	Work is spread unevenly
Teams know other team members' skills/abilities	Little understanding exists of what makes the team tick
Work environment is conducive to good performance	Physical environment prevents good performance

- Communicating regularly: for example, what do people think about their work and what do they want to do?
- Creating a shared vision: for example, to ensure that everyone knows where they are going.
- Improving the physical environment: for example; lighting.
- Using ideas from the team to make improvements to the work.
- Using people playing to their strengths: for example, consider people's skills and aspirations and allocate work accordingly.

All of these aspects shall be examined later, but first we shall look further at the management task and process.

MANAGEMENT

Management is variously defined and some of the definitions are as follows:

- *Getting people to do things.*
- *To achieve a task and build a team and develop individuals.*

Managing work involves dealing with the four fundamental management activities: planning, organising, directing and controlling. These activities are summarised below.

Planning

- Identifies the current situation.
- Determines the outcome required/desired.
- Sets aims and objectives.
- Prepares budgets and develops standards.
- Determines what has to be done.
- Sets deadlines and timescales.
- Establishes policies.
- Develops programmes and procedures.
- Sets plans of action.

Organising plans into action

- Determining what resources to use (money, machinery, and materials, methods, time).
- Determining how to make the best use of resources.
- Defining and designing jobs, responsibilities and authority levels.
- Structuring work relationships.
- Designing systems of work.
- Allocating work.

Directing actions to achieve results

- Developing communication channels.
- Coordinating actions with teams/groups.
- Assessing leadership styles of individuals.

Table 10.2 Warehouse job roles

Job titles	Tasks	Accountability	Outcomes
Level one: Operative or labourer	• Basic skills in using tools, plant, equipment • Applies knowledge of procedures • Performs physical job requirements • Has some related training in the job • May require a licence to drive/operate equipment	• Under immediate supervision • Works from verbal and written instructions • Follows operational procedures • Follows health and safety procedures • Is able to resolve basic questions and problems	Safe, successful and timely completion of all the assigned tasks
Level two: Storekeeper or senior operative	• Knowledge of all regulations that apply in the specific operation • Undertakes varied duties such as unloading, picking, loading • Has skills in operating equipment and may need a licence to do this	• Works under direct supervision • Selects from a variety of procedures to accomplish assigned tasks • Resolves routine questions and problems but refers complex issues to the next level • May be responsible for leading other people	Accurate work completion in accordance with procedures

Level three: Senior store keeper, or supervisor or first line manager	• Applies knowledge of specific warehouse operations • May plan, but will coordinate single or several activities • Resolves competing demands from customers and users • Applies supervisory management practices and principles	• Has strong technical and supervisory skills • Organises, directs and controls staff • Measures employees' outcomes and takes any appropriate action • Is able to independently resolve daily operational problems	Efficient and safe/secure handling of goods/ materials giving good customer service
Level four: Manager	• Plans, organises, directs, prioritises and assigns work to staff • Controls and evaluates the effectiveness of operations • Plans and implements operational and procedural improvements • Manages using extensive warehouse and management experience	• Has strong technical and managerial skills • Independently resolves any management issues that involve people, customers, resources, procedures and practices	All warehouse operations to be efficient, safe/secure and within company budget and company goals/targets

- Training and developing individuals.
- Identifying opportunities for learning.
- Recognising what needs to be learned.
- Determining the effectiveness of operation and people.
- Knowing what's going on.

Controlling the outcomes/results of actions

- Using standards to monitor performance.
- Creating controls and measures.
- Evaluating results.
- Recognising problems.
- Continually monitoring.
- Conducting appraisals of performance.
- Taking corrective action.
- Making improvements.

Some of these activities may be carried out more than others, for example, with a specific job function such as a work planner/scheduler; and some may be undertaken more than others. However, over time, all the activities will usually be undertaken many times per day by management staff.

These four functions cover all supervisory and management tasks and the relationship to all the people's roles and functions in stores and warehouse operations can be seen in the job roles given in Table 10.2.

Management styles

The way people actually undertake the above four fundamental management activities can differ, as individual people have a 'style'. Styles are such things as being aggressive, being passive and being assertive, and these will be more fully considered later when we discuss behaviour.

Management styles themselves are subject to change and, for example, 'old' and the 'new' ways of management can be seen in the following view:

- Managing with a command and control style
  - keeps control
  - people are 'held onto'

- – judgemental
- – 'tells'
- – see though a 'pinhole'
- – directive
- – 'push' approach.

- Managing with a coaching or empowering style
  - – lets people try
  - – people are given a 'self release'
  - – non-judgemental
  - – 'sells'
  - – sees the wider view
  - – supportive
  - – 'pull' approach.

People differ

People will differ; for example, some people are more oriented to planning, or organising, or directing or controlling; some are more autocratic and directive; some are more democratic and want a consensus view; some are more charismatic and supportive; and some are 'utility players' and flexible. Teams, for example, require the right blend of unique individual strengths and we shall look at teams later. As people are different, managers should recognise that it is usually better to build and develop an individual's strengths, while continuing the need to manage that person's weaknesses. Unfortunately some managers continually concentrate on their people's weaknesses, leaving them to wonder what their strengths are. Such managers are simply getting the praise/criticise balance wrong, but they often create serious consequences and ramifications.

WORK OBJECTIVES AND PERFORMANCE

These should be traceable back to company objectives, so, for example, if a competitive advantage is found in the speed of delivery, it is important for the company to know how quickly things are done.

All measurements are of different processes (as we have seen in an earlier chapter on productivity), and all processes have common components of inputs, activity/process and outputs. So, important management tasks are ensuring the efficient usage/utilisation of inputs, the efficiency of the activity and the effectiveness of the output. The output is sometimes the most difficult one to measure and when this is so, it can help to see it from the perspective of the user/customer of the output; for example, what is 'success' for them?

Remember that the purpose of setting measurable objectives is to give guidance and allow people to improve. They should be not be 'a stick to be used to beat up' on people. The following guidelines will assist in determining measurable objectives to give guidance and allow for improvement.

Smart objectives

- SMART means specific/simple, measurable, achievable/attainable, realistic, time based.
- SMART objectives give a clear view of the performance standard expected.

Determining SMART objectives, standards and targets.

- Objectives are about the job purpose. They identify 5 to 7 key job outcomes in a maximum of 30 words. Example: To reduce, to increase, to improve, to implement, etc.
- Standards and targets are the measurable outcomes. They use measures of quantity, quality, and time/speed/frequency and cost/money.
- Standards are achievable by all; they are the norm, and are common and long term. Example: To reduce the cost by 10% within 12 months.
- Targets are, however, individually agreed with those who are able to exceed the common standard and they will tend to be short term. Example: To reduce the cost by 12% within 2 months.

In writing work objectives it is useful to think about the company and the work place (problems, processes, practices). Think about what the person is to do and draft a verb/action component. Think about why that action is wanted (results, outcomes, effects, why it is important, what is the value) and change the verb/action component if necessary.

Think about ways of measuring the work and then draft the measurable standards (quality, quantity, time/speed/frequency, cost/money).

If necessary, modify the action component.

Next, think about the time frames in which the work is to be accomplished and specify the dead lines, due dates, etc. Rethink it and ask the person who is to be accountable what he or she thinks it means. Finally, rewrite it if necessary.

Key performance indicators

Key performance indicators (KPIs) are standards, targets or outcomes that enable people to determine when they have done a job in accordance with expectations. They also provide a benchmark for a comparison with what actually happened (the actual outcome) against what should have happened (the outcome expected). These form some of the measures of productivity that we have already referred to above.

KPIs can be grouped into the following five categories: quality, costs, delivery, safety and morale/motivation. We shall look at each in turn.

Quality

- Are products or services delivered to an agreed specification?
- Do you analyse rejects?
- What is the quality of communication and paperwork?
- What is the quality of relationships with suppliers/customers?

Examples of measures

- Functionality
- Service
- Defects
- Returns

- Rework
- Complaints

Costs

- Are costs kept within agreed limits?
- Are cost reduction programmes in place?
- How much is cost attributable to purchasing decisions (TAC)?

Examples of measures

- Stock value
- Activities
- Productivity
- Over time
- Expenses

Delivery/speed

- Are goods or services delivered at the right time/place/quantity/condition?
- Are products packaged correctly?
- Are throughput speeds acceptable?

Examples of measures:

- On time, in full (OTIF)
- Reliability

Safety

- What is the accident record?
- How are the legal requirements effectively carried out?

Examples of measures:

- Accidents
- Suggestions

Morale/motivation

- Are people there, because they want to be or have to be?
- What is the 'temperature' of the people interactions?

Examples of measures:

- Absences
- Lateness
- Staff turnover rate
- Suggestions
- Job satisfaction
- Promotions
- Training days
- Appraisal ratings
- Contacts managers/staff

Troubleshooting performance problems

Despite having all the appropriate planning and control measures, performance could still suffer. When this happens, the following questions can be asked before, perhaps, pursuing the formal discipline procedures:

- Can the person assigned fully describe the process and the results expected?
- Does the person assigned to the task acknowledge that he or she is accountable for its completion?
- Does the person assigned the task have the knowledge and skill to carry it out?
- Has the assigned person done that task before?
- Are there any consequences that discourage the task from being performed?
- Are there any competing tasks to be performed at the same time?
- Does the person performing it see the task as worth while?
- Can the assigned person explain why it needs to be done?
- Is the working environment conducive to performing?
- Are the appropriate tools and equipment available?
- If cooperation is required from others, is it forthcoming?
- Are the right standards in place and are they understood?
- Are the standards referring to performance that the individual can control?
- Is feedback given on performance?

- Is the task adequately designed?
- Are diagnostic tools available for repetitive tasks?
- Are the expectations realistic?

Discipline and grievance

Despite having good management practices, there will be times when employees do not perform as expected. Therefore disciplining may be needed. The key aim of discipline is to encourage unsatisfactory employees to improve, and by definition this means to teach and mould.

Discipline must have as its 'root' a concern about unacceptable performance. This simply is work performance that is not up to the standard expected. It is important to use this definition, as then any type of misconduct is clearly going to be all about standards that were expected, but have not been met. Being very clear on the standards expected is therefore important, and it will be of assistance to have SMART objectives and standards. Having these will give a clear view when performance is below the standard expected.

When performance is not met, there is a need to establish whether the person cannot do it or will not do it. The former is usually clear and noticeable, however, the latter may be camouflaged and not easily seen. The under-pinning reasons for the non-performance will have to be looked into. There are many possible reasons when someone cannot do a job as required, for example, insufficient training. Common factors, however, will be a lack of competence and not having the knowledge/skills to do the job required.

When someone will not do it as required, there can be many possible reasons – for example, dissatisfaction over something. But the common factors will be a lack of personal commitment in not having the confidence or the motivation/desire to do the job as required.

Disciplining should be used only relatively infrequently. If it is being used continuously, then there is something else wrong. Discipline and grievance handling are therefore a management practice to be used only 'in the final analysis', when everything else has failed. However, how managers see things is important (perception is reality) and this is shown in Table 10.3, where list A is all about blame, and list B is more about gain.

Table 10.3   Different perceptions

List A	List B
'I am right, I know best'	'I would like to know your opinion'
'Listen to me'	'Let me listen to your view'
Sees obstacles and problems	Sees solutions and opportunities
Finds fault	Gives support
Feels frustrated when with people	Feels calm when with people
Makes others feel guilty	Makes people learn
Looks for who is wrong	Looks for what is wrong
Mistakes are to be punished	Mistakes are opportunities to learn

As perception is reality, then seeing discipline as punishment will involve managers taking more of a 'blame' view. This will not help and will reflect and be shown in the handling of discipline and grievance issues as well as in the manager's style and also possibly in the culture of the company.

Company Codes of Practice

Company Codes of Practice for discipline will normally cover the following discipline and grievance issues.

Discipline misconduct offences

These offences can always be categorised as performance issues or relationship/behavioural issues.

- Work performance issues are about:
  - poor attendance and absence
  - poor/careless work output
  - failure to follow rules, such as Health and Safety.
- Work relationship issues are about:
  - refusal to obey reasonable instructions
  - disruptive behaviour

Note: Misconduct offences normally lead to disciplinary action, with the following gross misconduct offences normally lead to dismissal.

Discipline gross misconduct offences

These offences can be categorised as performance or relationship issues.

- Work performance issues are about:
  - gross negligence causing loss, damage
  - serious disregard of health and safety legislation
  - deliberate damage to company property.
- Work relationship issues are about:
  - theft, fraud
  - assault, fighting
  - conduct prejudicial to the company's reputation
  - serious incapability due to alcohol, illegal drugs
  - gross insubordination.

Typical grievance issues

These cover a multitude of problems:

- Work relationship issues could be:
  - 'I am treated badly by *x*'
  - 'I cannot get on with *y*'
  - 'I am made to feel small'
  - 'I am not appreciated by the company'
- Company aspects could be:
  - on policy: 'We were told to work on a Saturday and we never do that'
  - on administration: 'it takes three months to get back expenses'
  - on work conditions: 'this place is too cold and too dirty'
  - on wages: '*x* is paid more than me and we do the same job'
  - on the canteen: 'the food is poor and expensive'.

Handling disciplines and grievances is an important procedure for management and one that needs 'doing by the book'. This section does not attempt to do this and readers wanting more information on this topic are referred to *The Discipline Pocketbook* (2001) by the author.

Behaviour

Understanding how people behave is fundamental to understanding people and being able to manage them more effectively. However, let us first consider a few definitions on behaviour and related matters:

- Behaviour is 'what we say or do'.
- Attitudes are the 'way we see and think about things'.
- Beliefs/values are 'what we know to be true'.
- Habits represent repeated and learned behaviour.

The relationship of these may be seen in Figure 10.1.

Identifying those specific incentives that motivate and create action/ behaviour (towards that which satisfies needs) can be one way to change

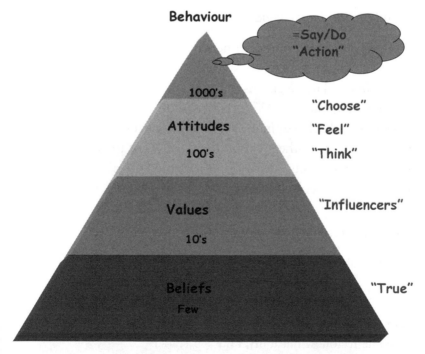

Figure 10.1 Understanding how people behave

a person's behaviour. However, people will view in different ways the incentives and their needs. People will see these differently as 'perception is 90% behind the eyes', 'whether you see it wrong or see it right, you are right', and 'as a person thinks, so they are'.

People, therefore, can individually behave differently when they face common circumstances; and three general types of behaviour patterns can be identified: passive, aggressive and assertive.

Aggressive and autocratic behaviour

This type of person is also a hard positional negotiator, who:

- drives and pushes people but is not a leader
- has a 'single', 'my' viewpoint
- is a one-way communicator
- demanding, 'do it my way, now'
- takes 'fixed my way positions' and engages in a contest of will
- makes threats and applies pressure.

Passive and procrastinator behaviour

This person is also a soft positional negotiator, who:

- abdicates from taking decisions
- uses group viewpoints
- is indecisive and believes in always being democratic
- leaves everything to others: 'what do you all want to do, whenever'
- changes positions easily and avoids any contest
- makes offers and yields to pressure.

Assertive and charismatic behaviour

This person is also a partnership negotiator, who:

- pulls more than pushes
- is a two-way communicator
- gets people to follow naturally, and is a leader
- makes concessions, 'I think this, what do we think'

- problem solves and explores interests
- has partnership views and gives reasons
- looks for objective criteria and yields to principles, not pressure.

Key points here are that individuals differ in their own style and will also respond differently to other styles. Therefore, a manager who 'does things one way with everyone, is like the clock that has stopped; it is correct only twice a day'. Selective adapting and responding is needed.

MOTIVATING PEOPLE

Motivation is a topic seen by many managers as central to their being able to get the best from people; it is indeed essential to improving performance, yet motivation is a commonly misunderstood topic. Motivation requires that the following is found:

- Competence, which is having the knowledge and skills, for example from training.
- Commitment, which is having the confidence and motivation to do the job in the work place.

Competence may therefore be provided, but without commitment; then performance may well suffer. Simply 'telling' and 'showing' will not always work, as commitment is always finally 'an inside job'. Motivation is therefore all about:

- 'Getting people to do things, willingly and well.'
- 'The motives to act.'
- 'Positive valued rewards.'
- 'Goal-directed behaviour.'
- 'Getting people to do what they want to do' (using the carrot approach), which is the opposite to manipulation, which is 'getting people to do what we want' (the stick approach).

The results of poor motivation, at work, can be a depressing reality for many companies, as shown in Table 10.4.

Table 10.4   Results of poor motivation

Reduced	Increased
Quality of work	Absenteeism
Work performance	Wasted time on breaks and private tasks
Willingness of people	Gossip and grievances
Attention and interest	Disciplining
Positive company culture	'Playing the system'
Creativity	Negative compliance
Job satisfaction	Bureaucratic controls
Direction	Rule breaking
Team spirit	'Them and us'
Feedback	Unacceptable behaviour

Theories of motivation

Motivations have been studied for a long time and it is certainly recognised by these studies that those who look for the 'one magic key to unlock people' will be disappointed. We will therefore look briefly at some of these studies.

Herzburg has identified the following hygiene and motivating factors:

- *Dissatisfiers: the hygiene factors.* These are factors that need 'to be cleaned up', for example:
  - company policy/administration
  - supervision
  - working conditions
  - personal relationships
  - salary/pay/benefits
  - job security.

The hygiene factors can be seen as those things that pull people away from being motivated. These are largely external/extrinsic to the person. Although, the removal of these factors does not automatically mean that people are then motivated.

- Satisfiers: the motivating factors. These are factors that need 'to be promoted', for example:

- achievement
- recognition
- participation
- growth
- feedback.

The motivators help to 'push' people towards being motivated; these are largely 'intrinsic'/internal to the person.

Further research has been done on what people 'need'. The idea here is that if we can be clear what people want or 'need', then if managers are able to provide them, it can mean that their people are more satisfied. Such views on 'needs' are shown is Table 10.5, where level 5 is a high level need; level 1 is a more basic level need.

Table 10.5   Views on the needs of employees

Maslow's hierarchy of needs	Covey levels of needs
5. Self-transcending	Spiritual: 'To leave a legacy'
4. Self-fulfilment	
3. Self-esteem	Psychological: 'Learning and loving'
2. Socially belong	
1. Security/safety	Physical survival: 'Living'

The key points revealed in the table are that we attempt to move from the lower to the medium/higher levels in order to satisfy our needs. If we are threatened at our current level, we then drop down a level. For example, if people at level 3 in employed work are faced with redundancy, they will then immediately drop down to level 1 and think about how they will survive. Similarly, a starving person at level 1 is not going to be looking beyond satisfying this level and will not be spending time and effort on the higher level needs until level 1 has been satisfied.

Motivation at work

Therefore, to provide motivation at work, the following incentives are required according to theories on motivation.

- Incentives 'to be promoted' and to increase the sources for motivation are:
  - Achievements: for example, targets, SMART objectives, interesting work.
  - Recognition: for example, create heroes, appreciation.
  - Participation/responsibility: for example, involvement, consensus management.
  - Growth/prospects: for example, personal development, life-long learning.
  - Feedback/communication: for example, praise and criticise fairly.

Key aspects with incentives are that, once provided, motivators do not last; when our needs are satisfied the incentive reduces its impact. So, for example, money by itself is not a motivator, and it is therefore important to always have the 'motivation encore' ready to go beyond the temporary effect of a single motivator.

- Disincentives are 'to be cleaned up' so that the sources of discontent are removed, for example:
  - Policy/administration: for example, paperwork, rules and procedures.
  - Supervision: for example, management styles, communication.
  - Working conditions: for example, heat, light, tidiness, safety equipment.
  - Personal relationships: for example, harassment, social facilities, shift patterns.
  - Salary/pay/benefits: for example, compare with others, times of reviewing.
  - Job security: for example, communication, job descriptions.

Key points with disincentives are that removing discontent does not bring motivation as it just removes the discontent and stops that particular source of 'groan and moans'. If the discontent is not removed, it can create resentment and grow into a problem = grievance = dissatisfaction = depression = frustration = poor work = discipline procedures.

Implementing motivation

As mentioned above, motivation does not last as there is the need to look for the 'encore', and you could run out of 'encores'. For example, where motivation is by fear ('do or else') or by reward ('do this and you get a prize'), the motivation has gone when the fear or reward has gone.

The only motivation that will ever last is one that satisfies an individual's core value/belief; for example, a belief that he or she will 'live life to the full'. This gives an internal drive, which has an irresistible momentum. This links to what people believe and is also shown by the following statements:

- 'You are what you think.'
- 'You get what you expect.'
- 'The impossible is what no one can do, until someone does.'
- 'Seeing yourself as a "winner".'
- 'Dreaming big dreams.'
- 'Choosing to be what you love.'

It is helpful, therefore, when dealing with other people to really know them and what needs are important to them. It will help to appreciate that people can be different but interesting, and that some people need more direction and guidance than others. Seeing things from other people's perspective will also help. All of this therefore involves a manager or supervisor being able to:

- link motivation to specific staff
- plan and organise what to do
- develop positive personal habits
- plan motivating action points, by calendar events (e.g. Christmas), by company events (e.g. new recruits), by communication events (e.g. newsletters) and by personal events (e.g. five years service awards)
- keep a record on motivation actions for specific staff
- review and check the results, and modify them as appropriate.

Effective motivation does really make a difference and it has been said:

> 'There are more chrysalises than butterflies – a manager's job
> is to encourage the chrysalis to hatch and to encourage
> the butterfly to fly.'
>
> 'It is like getting a plant to bloom.'

Motivation is not therefore, just about what you do to someone; it is more about what you allow them to do for themselves. This is also what empowerment is about, as we shall see shortly. However, there is always much that can be encouraged and supported by managers in the workplace and the following motivation model will help to ensure that this is done.

The motivation model

Step 1: Expect the best from your people

- Believe that people want to do a good job
- Tell people what is expected
- Have clear rules and procedures (but do not be bureaucratic)
- Set SMART objectives/targets
- Involve people in determining these objectives/targets
- Communicate
- Be flexible, recognising that people are different.

Step 2: Eliminate barriers to 'being the best'

- Check out all the disincentives and remove/improve as appropriate
- Check out all the incentives and apply as appropriate
- Make work interesting, meaningful and valuable
- Ensure that people have the appropriate resources to do the job as required.

Step 3: Encourage people to 'be the best'

- Recognise good work
- Give feedback
- Be accessible, ask and listen for feedback
- Reward with good pay, promotions and personal loyalty.

EMPOWERING

This is a concept that is related to motivation, the word meaning literally 'to give power'. It involves looking at the management areas of responsibility, training, trust and support and it is more towards the 'coaching' style of management that was referred to earlier.

In 'normal' management, the 'manager' is *accountable* and *responsible*, but individual subordinates are only *responsible*. In 'collective' teams, however, both accountability and responsibility are shared and agreed. Accountability is represented by the view of 'the referee' who has the ultimate control, which cannot be delegated or passed on by the team; for example, 'the buck stops here'. Responsibility comes from all the players, who carry out simply what has to be done – for example, the 'duty of care' in Law and in Health and Safety.

Empowerment gives people a sense of ownership to enable them to see the bigger picture of how what they do fits elsewhere. Empowered people should therefore be able to:

- evaluate the work of others
- plan and schedule work
- recruit and select
- give presentations
- determine the pace of work
- set targets.

Trust is also needed but this is difficult to define, despite the fact that we are aware when it is there and when it is not. Trust usually needs to be earned, and works together with integrity and honesty. The key ingredients of trust are:

- creditability
- dependability
- honesty
- admitting mistakes
- openness
- willingness to listen

- sharing information
- giving accurate feedback.

Managers still need to give people support, but many managers often ignore this requirement. Indeed, giving support is so often the key differentiator between a good manager and an average manager. Support not only involves giving feedback and assistance, but it also involves:

- being appreciative
- listening
- questioning
- challenging thinking
- coaching
- developing.

TEAMS

Teams involve a small number of people who have a common shared and accepted goal. The goal is the 'performance purpose' and the team players, the participants, have a complementary contribution with mutual accountability. The team is a unit in which the aims of team are put before those of individuals. The following sayings are true of teams:

- 'Individual success is dependent on others.'
- 'Work out problems together, individual blame is banished.'
- 'Where the whole is more than the sum of the parts.'
- 'Teams require individuals to connect to something bigger than them.'
- 'Where you need to be awake, aware and in tune with others.'
- 'United we stand but divided we fall.'
- 'There is none of us as strong as all of us.'

Teams are not a universal 'cure all' panacea for everything. For example, they are not suitable when creativity is needed with individual specialised talent, or where there is committee/group working with no unified common goal.

Teams case study

Sports teams offer some good analogies for work teams, and the following aspects identified from the British Lions Rugby team of 1997 can be checked and compared with teams in business and in companies:

- Inspired leadership
- Clear goal
- Meticulous planning
- Picking the right players
- Clear communication
- Excellent team spirit
- Committed team member
- A learning culture
- Desire and passion
- Focus on results
- Shared values
- Self and team belief
- Confidence in ability
- Pride
- Celebrate success.

A key principle that is also demonstrated here is that teams require the right blending of unique individual strengths. When managing people, it is important to be able to build and develop strengths, and to recognise and manage weaknesses. Recognising diversity can therefore be seen as a strength as some people are better at planning, some are better at organising processes and methods, some are better able to meet deadlines, to be directive, or creative and thoughtful, or are better being supportive or more 'utility players' and flexible. After all, if all people were exactly the same, then we would all go rapidly in one direction and cause casualties en route!

Effective teams

Effective teams are those that have selected the right mix of people and have determined the team vision and objectives. They will communicate and understand each other while also motivating and supporting each other. The behaviours needed involve a blended mix of 'togetherness' and 'self' Involvement and commitment require openness and, sometimes, confrontation with honesty and truthfulness in a supporting and trusting way.

COMMUNICATION

Communicating involves sharing information between people, 'up/down and side/side' with the objective of communication being to prevent misunderstanding. Unfortunately much of what passes for communication is actually one way and also makes no attempt to check on whether it has been understood, as demonstrated, for example, in one FTSE 100 company who renamed all their notice boards as 'communication' boards. (The former description was the correct one.)

The following questions focus on how communication should actually work in a company:

- Is there evidence of an interchange of ideas?
- Do employees know the reasons for the job they are being asked to do?
- Can changes be introduced without major upsets?
- Are ideas used that are put forward and, if not, is it explained why?
- Are those nearest to the job consulted on matters affecting them?
- Are new employees carefully inducted?
- Do all people know what their jobs are?
- Do people show a sustained interest in their jobs?
- Is there a smooth flow of work?
- Are people seldom bypassed in the flow of information?
- Is the 'grapevine' a very small one?

Giving feedback

Communications at work involves giving and receiving feedback on work-related issues. Managers will get more out of people if they are sensitive to their situation and treat them like adults by concentrating on their behaviour and not on personal traits/characteristics. It is necessary to balance both positive and negative messages and not just to concentrate on weaknesses but to always balance weaknesses by emphasising strengths and by directing towards the behaviour that the person can do something about.

It will be necessary to choose the appropriate tone and language and to check, at the end, for understanding, for example, by asking them to repeat back the feedback given. Then, and always, end on a positive note.

Communication and consistency in management

Finally, some steps of consistency for managers; it will be seen that communication is only one of the many issues that have been discussed in this chapter:

- Develop an awareness of your impact on others.
- Always try to involve people in decision-making.
- Believe that teamwork is the best approach.
- Have a consistent management style.
- Spend time coaching and developing.
- Build a positive climate in the team.
- Empower and support team members rather than control them.
- Develop appropriate performance review systems and methods.
- Set challenging but achievable and measurable objectives.
- Communicate one on one.
- Reward success.
- Agree improvements and personal development plans.
- Give regular feedback.
- Tackle poor performance.

MANAGING CHANGE

Change is the one constant of modern life. As the world changes, then so does work. The only certain aspect of the future is that it will be different – a future of stable turbulence. It is in the dealing with this uncertainty in the future that managing change becomes a key management function. In today's intensively changing world, a central management challenge is involved in managing change, and at the same time, ensuring that people continue to contribute to company goals by being willing participants with trust and commitment.

Sources of change

There are many sources of change, and some of these general categories are as follows:

- Political, e.g. trade agreements.
- Economic, e.g. currency fluctuations, inflation levels.
- Social, e.g. lifestyles, increased leisure.
- Technological, e.g. IT.
- Legal, e.g. legislation.
- Organisational, e.g. take-overs, closures, new start ups.

Generally, most people will have noticed the following trends and resultant changes in recent times:

Table 10.6   Recent trends and resultant changes

From old ways	Towards new ways
Technology/product/supply	Customer/market/demand
'Push' product flows	'Pull' product flows
Product sells	Customer buys
Manage people	Manage messages
Specialist skills	Broad skills
Bureaucratic control	Empowerment
Instruction/telling	Consulting/selling
Job for life	Portfolio jobs
Earning a living	Learning a living
Adversarial	Partnership
Fire-fighting	Fire-lighting

Reactions to change

Change can be dramatic and can, if handled wrongly, be traumatic and cause a company to become extinct. A choice often has to be made when facing change, as to whether the response needed is to be either revolutionary or evolutionary.

Change will always have some impact on people. The impact will vary, but all those people involved will experience the same stages – usually however at different times. Table 10.7 shows the stages involved and some typical responses; stage one commences when a person first hears about the change.

Table 10.7   Impact of change on people

Stage	Comments	'Here' to 'there'
1. Shock, immobilised	'They cannot do it'	Past orientation
2. Denial	'We will never do it'	Past
3. Frustration and defensive	'It is just too difficult'	Past
4. Acceptance and discarding	'I might try'	Past/future
5. Testing	'Let's try'	Future
6. Search for meaning	'It seems to work'	Future
7. Integration	'I can do it'	Future

Attitudes to change will therefore vary in any group of individuals, and these attitudes can be very emotional and as wide ranging as those mentioned below.

- From stimulating to resisting
- From exciting to denying
- From dynamic to fear
- From anticipation to anger
- From enthusiasm to stress
- From exciting to concern
- From challenging to worry
- From opportunity to certainty
- From visionary, looking forward, to staying with the current situation.

It is critical to appreciate that all people will go through such emotional responses, but they do it differently and at different times. Managers need to be alert to such variations and to manage them effectively. After all, people have to change one at a time.

Dynamics of change

These are found in any change situation, and two forces are dynamically involved: the driving forces and the restraining forces.

- Examples of driving forces:
  - Job enrichment
  - Upgrading
  - Broadening
  - More responsibility
  - More reward
  - More status
  - Better conditions
  - Easier work.
- Examples of restraining forces:
  - De-skilling
  - No discretion
  - Changed jobs
  - More difficult work
  - Degrading
  - No promotions
  - Redundancy.

One force represents the 'foot on the gas', while the other represents the 'foot on the brake'. A key action, therefore, is to identify the driving/'backing' and the restraining/'blocking' forces in a change situation/context. Next, recognise that if we move forward by increasing the driving forces, then resistance may well increase to maintain the balance. Consequently, the best way to move forward is by analysing the restraining forces and trying to minimise their impact.

Resistance to change can also be minimised when the change:

- is agreed by all
- is owned by individuals
- is supported by management
- follows culture and values
- decreases current problems
- increases new experiences and interests.

Resistance can also be minimised when:

- management understand the consequent emotions
- management allows reactions to be discussed
- management ensures that personal security is not threatened.

The manager's role in implementing change

Managing change is a skilful process, and an essential skill in dealing with change is communication. As we noted earlier, the objective of communication is to prevent misunderstanding, and doing this effectively involves the following:

- Not 'telling' propaganda, but 'selling' proper communication
- Informing at all stages
- Asking questions to uncover feeling
- Listening carefully to answers
- Using written communications only where appropriate
- Concentrating on face-to-face methods
- Consulting wherever possible
- Admitting any mistakes and learning from them
- Celebrating individuals and group success
- Being as open as possible.

It is critical therefore to involve people, communicate, listen, give people a chance to air objections and time to adapt.

Managing change will be a routine activity in a changing future, which involves learning to learn and being continuous learners with active continuous personal development plans. Managing change also involves the full and complete management repertoire; unfortunately it is estimated that the majority of change fails – a statement that is also about the quality of the management involved.

Some case study examples on change follow to show that it is not impossible for some companies to manage change 'properly'.

CASE STUDY 10.1: MANUFACTURER (1)

The 'problem'

- Long-established stable company in an industry that was changing.
- Had traditional structure with top-down communication.

The 'future' was identified as needing:

- Team work across the functions
- New plant and machinery
- New annualised hours, therefore abolishing the overtime wage structure
- New graduate managers to be the core management.

The 'approach'

- Coaching one to one
- Business application workshops
- Group meetings of coaches to build common purpose/plans/projects

The 'results'

- All changes made on time.
- Moved from a 'problem performer' to a 'star performer'.

CASE STUDY 10.2: MANUFACTURER (2)

Important points identified:

- Tailored approach was needed
- Top management commitment was vital
- Long-term view needed
- Communicating was very important
- Involvement
- Listening (more than anticipated)
- Partnership with trade union
- Third party facilitation and assistance
- Visit/learn from others
- Training needed.

CASE STUDY 10.3: RETAILER

The 'problem'

- Not customer focused
- Low-quality product
- Family focus ownership of a plc.

The 'plan'

The plan used was to:

- establish a mission statement: for example, on value for money, customer service, friendly environment in stores
- establish a set of values: for example, trust, respect, communication
- plan the change programme: for example, current and future cultures identified
- work on the top managers' behavioural styles: for example, less 'tell'

- work on the mid-managers' behavioural styles: for example, teams, interactions
- work on branch managers'/'department managers' behavioural styles: for example, customer service.

Other initiatives were:

- Focus groups, internal cross-functional, external on customer service
- Annual conference
- Monthly area meetings
- Weekly trading meetings.

WAREHOUSE PICKING OPERATIVES

This essential people resource needs some special mention and attention. There is a growing reluctance of people to undertake such work; additionally, attention is also needed to the poor way that some managements actually 'manage' and motivate their people.

At best such people management problems are dealt with incrementally and in isolation from one another by the large companies and, at worst, are only dealt with by the poaching of staff, with inevitable consequences for rising costs.

Warehouse operatives, however, are often unanimous in what they like and dislike about their work; for example, they like:

- being site based
- being part of a team with communication 'crack' and social activity
- being able to have some control over the daily work load;

and they dislike:

- not having career prospects
- the low status of the job
- the remuneration.

Until warehouse management is effectively able to tackle such aspects (and some individual companies are trying), then it is possible that labour requirements will be reduced more quickly through automation, and as the costs of technology fall the take-up of, say, automated picking will increase.

With warehousing operations, the core personnel involved are at the same place of work all the time and are therefore a 'collective' workforce, and face-to-face management contact is possible at any time during working hours. However, with transport drivers, for example, this is not always possible, which effectively means that face-to-face contact with transport vehicle drivers will need to be handled much more efficiently during the limited time that is available.

Referring to the earlier section on motivation, and applying this to warehouse operatives, the following would seem to be essential steps.

- *Incentives* should be 'promoted' to increase the sources for motivation.
  - *Achievements*: for example, stressing the importance of the work done, and how this fits into customer/consumer requirements; increase the job status/importance; after all, it is an important and vital job.
  - *Recognition*: for example, appreciation of overcoming daily difficulties with changing demand patterns; tackling known internal delays.
  - *Participation/responsibility*: for example, involvement in decisions that affect the job; involving operatives in what has been done over internal delays.
  - *Growth/prospects*: for example, personal development plans; moves into management; opportunities for advancement.
  - *Feedback/communication*: for example, praise and criticise fairly; what do the customers say; how the business promotes and markets itself and what the pickers can do to help on this; creating a supportive culture.

- *Disincentives* should be 'cleaned up' to remove the sources of discontent.
  - *Policy/administration*: for example, removing unnecessary paperwork, rules and procedures; clarity in rules and procedures.
  - *Supervision*: for example, improving management styles and communication.

- *Working conditions*: for example, user friendly equipment, fair work allowances and shared workloads.
- *Personal relationships*: for example, tackling unsocial hour shift patterns, recognising personal needs and making adjustments; tackling negative 'grapevines' by creating opposite positive cultures.
- *Salary/pay/benefits*: for example, salaried pay with holiday and sickness benefits; demonstrated fair pay, terms and conditions.
- *Job security*: for example, communication on developments.

These examples are not meant to be extensive but are meant to illustrate what can be done by effective people management. As stated in the earlier section on motivation: there is always something that can be done. None of these examples is 'rocket science' but then managers do not know what they do not know, therefore they do not do it. Ignorance, however, is really no longer a valid excuse; ignoring such aspects is not a good management option and will ultimately lead to a poorly motivated workforce and effectively damage the company.

People management matters and effective policies can make real differences: 'on one site we have cut £400000 worth of agency costs just by retaining good people for longer through better human resource policies' (Bibby Distribution in *International Freighting Weekly*, 28 April 2003). Why cannot all companies take such a proactive approach to people management?

TRAINING TOPICS

It can be useful for a company engaged in managing people to ensure that all concerned personnel have a common understanding of what is involved. The following is an example of the contents from one such training programme:

- *Understanding management and leadership*
  - Definitions
  - The linking and connected activities
  - Appreciating different styles and approaches
  - Getting the balance right.

- *Supervising people*
  - Differences with people in groups and as individuals
  - Building on strengths and managing weaknesses
  - Team development, forming and building
  - Team working, roles, responsibility and relationships
  - Characteristics of performing teams.

- *Managing change*
  - Why change?
  - Attitudes to change
  - Types and levels of change
  - Moving from 'here' to 'there'
  - Steps of change
  - Model for handling change.

- *The role of planning in a company*
  - Corporate planning
  - Operational planning
  - Control mechanisms.

- *Defining performance management*
  - What it is and what it is not
  - Why it is needed
  - Being consistent.

- *Understanding productivity*
  - Setting standards
  - Utilisation and performance
  - Financial and non-financial measures
  - Benefits of taking a 'systems' view.

- *Objectives and goals*
  - Work performance
  - Objectives/goals and standards/targets
  - Authority and responsibility.

- *Appraisals*
  - Conducting appraisals (and not pay reviews)
  - Benefits of appraisals
  - What managers want from appraisals

- What individuals want from appraisals
- Handling and conducting appraisal interviews.

- *Motivating*
  - Behaviour styles of people
  - The links between attitudes and behaviour
  - Assertive and aggressive behaviour
  - Exploring what motivates people
  - Understanding why people come to work
  - Theories of motivation
  - Practical applications of motivation.

- *Communicating*
  - Communication methods
  - Problems with communication
  - Best practice
  - Verbal and non-verbal communication
  - Body language, words, voice tone impacts
  - The difference between understanding and agreeing
  - Handling diverse viewpoints.

- *Employing and dismissing people*
  - Recruiting and hiring
  - Job analysis
  - Job descriptions
  - Job advertising
  - Interview preparations
  - Selection
  - Defining unacceptable performance, competence or commitment
  - Defining unacceptable attendance and relationships/behaviour
  - Deciding whether to counsel, coach or discipline
  - The model approach to handle typical problems
  - Interview preparations
  - Spending time on prevention
  - Recognising the improvement/punishment balance
  - Following the appropriate legislation throughout.

- *Financial control*
  - Accounting
  - Profit and loss accounts
  - Balance sheets
  - Capital.

- *Commercial activities*
  - Credit control
  - Payments
  - Financial advice
  - Funding.

- *Budget control*
  - Budgeting
  - Cash flow.

- *Company law*
  - Statues
  - Liabilities
  - Contracts
  - Agency
  - Sole traders
  - Partnerships
  - Limited companies
  - Starting and ceasing a business.

11

Developments and Trends

SUPPLY CHAIN IMPACTS ON STORES AND WAREHOUSING

The supply chain involves far more than managing warehouses. The supply chain involves processes such as:

- Purchase/supply/buying/trading
- Manufacturing/production/assembly
- Distribution/warehouse/transport/shipping
- Marketing/selling/customer service
- Finance/accounts/treasury
- Stock/inventory.

In fact, the whole business process of an organisation must become integrated and coordinated, when a supply chain viewpoint is undertaken.

The Distribution Charter for Cask Marque (covering the delivery of beers into pubs), provides a practical example of how the warehouse activities link to other supply chain activities:

- The objective of the charter is to highlight best practice in the supply chain to ensure that there are the highest standards of service, thus ensuring that beer is delivered in prime condition.
- The warehouse should have refrigerated areas for storage with temperatures maintained between 12 and 14°C. (Warehousing)

- Operate a first-in, first-out stock policy. (Inventory)
- Goods received from production should be a maximum of 7 days from rack. (Production)
- Delivery to outlets must be at least 14 days prior to the 'best before' date. (Transport and customer service)
- Load on the day of delivery to ensure that there is no heat build up. (Warehouse and Transport)
- Auditable QC procedures. (Customer service)
- All deliveries are made in Health and Safety standards with draymen trained in the handling of cask ale. (Transport)

Accordingly, with a whole, complete and holistic supply chain view, all the relevant processes must be looked at. What might seem to be the best from one single individual basis may not, in fact, be the best when viewed from a total supply chain perspective. This will then involve 'trading off' processes and functions to find the right balance in the overall supply chain.

The concept of total acquisition cost (TAC) from purchasing is one way to examine trade-offs in the supply chain. Cost is seen not just as the price paid for something but as the whole cost of a purchase. The essential components of TAC are as follows:

- The price paid for the goods, say on an ex-works basis.
- The costs of quality: for example, defects, errors causing inspection/reworking costs.
- The delivery costs: for example, the transport charges.
- The performance costs: for example, reliability, KPI measures.
- The lead-time costs: for example, money investment, delivery frequency issues.
- The packaging costs: for example repacks.
- The warehousing costs: for example, break bulk handling storage.
- The stock/inventory costs: for example, for raw material, work in progress, finished goods.
- The costs for a new supplier: for example, start-up costs, negotiations.
- The administration costs: for example, ordering, payments.

The price paid may well be the largest item but all other costs will have many variations. If these costs were equal or of little significance, then the price paid would be the determining factor. Rarely, however, are all the other costs equal. So with TAC, the principle is that all relevant costs have to be allowed for.

GLOBAL LOGISTICS

A growing trend in many industries is the extent and reach of supply chains with global trading strategies and operations. Economies of scale with global media contribute to more global business and to the death of size and distance.

As consumers, we are all involved in this global reach of supply chains. Consider the traditional English Sunday roast. The beef may be from Australia, the green beans from Thailand, the carrots from East Africa, the broccoli from Guatemala, and the potatoes from Italy. As the fruit may from Chile, this example represents an overall global travel well in excess of 40 000 miles.

A current business driver for UK organisations is the perceived customer expectations for more product complexity/variation, coupled with 'I want it now' urgency. This will often result in revising the company objectives for the product value/service offering and the following wider and potential global issues will likely be involved:

- Do we need to work more closely with suppliers?
- Do we move manufacturing to offshore or outsource the whole or part of the operation?
- What are the effects of product complexity? For example, shorter product life cycles and increasing product customising of products, may mean assemble to order manufacturing instead of make to stock methods of manufacturing.
- What are the effects of transport complexity? For example, increasing distances travelled between manufacturing sites and markets; parts may be made in Mexico and Brazil for assembly in Taiwan with the finished products supplied to a world market.

Likely consequences of these wider issues could be:

- Distances change in the supply chain; meaning examination of the total process and associated lead times.

- Improving the visibility; meaning coordinating functions by a proactive real-time monitoring of goods and information flows.
- Managing the whole supply chain; meaning integrating the processes while effecting trade-off analysis and TAC examinations.
- As is normal for international trade, this involves both imports and exports in the overall trade between countries; meaning attendant threats and opportunities for companies, such as cheap imports of substituting products that are manufactured locally and/or more export opportunities.

REVERSE LOGISTICS AND CUSTOMER RETURNS

In many operations a high volume of return traffic has to be managed; for example, clothing catalogue goods have between 18 and 35% of their delivered goods returned, whereas electrical catalogue companies report 'only' 4 or 5% returns.

This return traffic is often referred to as 'reverse logistics' and can comprise any of the following traffics:

- Pallets, roll-cages and other unit-load devices making the empty homeward journey.
- Unwanted, damaged or defective goods being returned, for credit, replacement, or repair. In catalogue clothing, for example, it is well expected that customers do order goods to 'try out' and that they have no intention of buying everything they order (there is at least some degree of planning certainty for these unwanted goods).
- Products recalled due to quality or safety defects. This, however, will be more random and therefore more unpredictable than catalogue clothing.
- Used packaging being returned for re-use, recycling or for disposal as waste.

It is important to know why goods are being returned. Therefore the customer contact information and supporting technology should be adequate. While some returns may be expected in overall volume terms, returns could arise due to some unexpected event; for example, the contamination of food products. These particular situations may be further complicated by police insistence on secrecy if blackmail is involved. Even if this is not the case, very often the perishable nature of the goods will have ensured that they were distributed very quickly across a large geographical area. If goods are defective in some way that is not life-threatening, but where the consumers' reactions to the products may tarnish the company's reputation in the marketplace, then a rapid resolution of the matter may even enhance the standing of the company in the consumers' eyes.

Organising the physical return process will include transport and the 'rechecking in' operations at the warehouse, ensuring that the quality and condition are verified and that action is taken as appropriate. Isolating and quarantining returned goods can be necessary to avoid inadvertently despatching them again until they have been checked fully. This will be important where the reason for collection is not always immediately obvious.

Finally, there is a requirement to determine the disposition options, for example: repair, re-use, refurbish, and resale, recycle, or scrap/dispose of. There will need to be a definite policy covering these options.

CASE STUDY 11.1: REVERSE LOGISTICS (WEEE) AND SALVESEN

Reverse logistics (RL) is an expression that we are going to hear more about, particularly with the growth in home delivery services and the coming of legislation such as the WEEE directive.

The meaning of WEEE

The Waste Electrical and Electronic Equipment (WEEE) Directive (2002) affects anyone involved in manufacturing, selling, distributing, recycling or treating electrical and electronic equipment. It aims to reduce the waste arising from electrical and electronic equipment, and improve the environmental performance of those involved. The Directive is due to be brought into force in the UK by 13 August 2005.

By 13 August 2005, private householders will be able to return their WEEE to collection facilities free of charge, and producers (manufacturers, sellers, distributors) will be responsible for financing the collection, treatment, recovery and disposal of it.

Producers will also be responsible for financing the management of WEEE from products placed on the market before 13 August 2005.

By 31 December 2006, producers will be required to achieve a series of recycling and recovery targets for different categories of appliance, and the UK must have reached an average WEEE collection rate of four kilograms for each private householder annually.

It covers not just the return of faulty goods, but handling goods ordered by mistake, overstock items, display goods and also product recalls. It is an area with many pitfalls but also significant opportunities.

Reverse logistics deals with not just the product itself, but also waste products and information about the product and customer. Many companies claim to have expertise in RL, but few can point to much substantial experience.

Relationship

One that can is Christian Salvesen, which has had a long relationship with Marks & Spencer in non-food distribution. Consumer development director David Hughes has some strong views on what makes it work – and what doesn't.

'Unless you manage big ticket returns well you can severely dent the margin on sales,' he says. For example, for full credit on a returned TV some manufacturers will demand not only the TV itself, but also the original box, the instructions, all the leads and the remote control. And there are more complex items still, such as PCs.

Time is of the essence in returning these, says Hughes. 'PCs are becoming obsolete in about four months now, although some components can be re-used.'

The key to the relationship between supplier and retailer is the returns agreement (RA) – or often the no-returns agreement (NRA). An NRA is typical for imported goods – particularly those with a relatively short shelf-life like PCs – but a retailer should expect a higher level of discount. Alternatively, the RA may incorporate a returns quota – say, no more than 2% of items may be returned.

'While you had specialist electrical retailers selling electrical goods, they learned long ago how to deal with returns. But the supermarkets haven't got that luxury – and this also applies to the DIY market and furniture retailing.'

Damaged

Furniture has its own problems. 'It's so easily damaged, just like white goods. It has high handling costs, high cube, it is difficult to store and it is difficult to realise a value from it. Developing a secondary market in furniture is difficult – but I think we could get involved there. That's what we're trying to develop – a business where we can release the value for our customers.'

Another area of returns is what Hughes calls Trading Standards returns – product recalls, for example. 'Typically if retailers can return it they will – they take the path of least resistance,' Hughes says.

One of the thorniest issues of reverse logistics is cost, and how one charges for it. Hughes suggests three options for charging:

- Open book
- Fixed price (but only if the level of returns can be very well predicted)
- Unitary pricing, with a sliding scale of charges. 'As you scale up the efficiencies do improve,' he says, 'and returns handling lends itself to both dedicated and shared-user applications.'

Waste, particularly packaging waste, is a considerable element of this, and Christian Salvesen runs the recycling and waste operations for all Tesco and Asda RDCs. The M&S account generates millions of plastic coat hangers, which are sold to a recycling company; conversely, the polypropylene intermediate bulk containers (IBCs) used by industrial liquids suppliers are often returned to the factory.

When handling returns, many of the same issues apply as in conventional retail logistics – shrinkage, for one. 'You have to put in place the same sort of security measures you would in a distribution setup,' he says.

But it is not just employees you have to watch for; customer fraud is rife too, particularly with electronic goods. With digital cameras, for example, customers will remove memory cards or rechargeable batteries, replacing them with defective or less desirable ones. Inkjet printers can have a full cartridge replaced with an empty one.

'People will buy a lawn-mower, go home, cut the grass and bring it back saying it won't work!' says Hughes. Dinner jackets are another item favoured by the 'use once, and then return' consumer.

'Manufacturers may dispute return credits if a product works – and they will tell you that a high proportion of products returned have no fault.' So an RL contractor has to be a broker and a policeman as well as a returns processor.

'This is more like manufacturing; it's a processing centre rather than a warehouse – it's a flow-through process. As a logistics company we are good at this.' Hughes himself has a background in manufacturing – primarily brewing – so he is used to process management and product flow.

Batches

And one of the things Salvesen is manufacturing is information – lots of it. Handling batches of hundreds or thousands of items at a time is not enough. 'You need to deal with everything at item level – identify product number, identify the store that sent it, and even attach customer information.'

Building customer relationships is a given now, even a cliché, but it isn't easy – especially when a large superstore may have

60 000 regular customers. 'There is some specialisation in the IT needed for this – you cannot use a warehouse management system alone. There are only a few IT systems in the world we've found that can do this job.' US-sourced systems are not necessarily suited to UK operations – US and UK retailing is still quite different – and they can be expensive. 'Some US companies quote up to £1 million for an installation,' says Hughes. Nevertheless, the US is ahead of us in some aspects of RL – not least the setting up of national returns centres.

Retailer
But the WEEE Directive is not an entirely known quantity yet. 'Every country is now interpreting it . . . the details are not fixed at all. Retailers are hoping they won't have too many responsibilities – it might make some retailers think about whether they want to import directly.'

The economics of recycling are likely to change, too. 'Some retailers are putting goods into a skip in store – when WEEE comes in they will be in breach.' However, Hughes emphasises that he doesn't want to get involved in every aspect of goods processing. 'We'll be an enabler, not a repairer or reseller.'

So how has Christian Salvesen approached the issue of reverse logistics? Hughes sees it in terms of the physical processing of goods, credit recovery and the duty of care for disposal. The purely physical side of returns processing costs a lot, but benefits enormously from economies of scale, according to Hughes.

'To process an outbound item through an RDC typically costs 10 pence. Some retailers manage returns in stores: we've costed it at more than £20 an item; in a central processing centre, that cost can be reduced to somewhere between 80p and £2. But it's a much higher cost than an RDC because everything has to be dealt with as a single item.'

While the physical processing is far from trivial, 'the real added value is in these last two. The skill set to do the second group is definitely here,' he says.

'We're building intellectual capital,' Hughes adds. 'For instance, we've built relationships with secondary markets.' Examples of these are auctioneers, charities and jobbing firms, which can dispose of items in other countries.

Hughes believes that this experience is particularly valuable in competition with other firms which claim RL expertise. 'We'll have an eye for the deal that they don't have,' he says, pointing out that 'jobbers can be swamped – then you can end up with unsellable stock. The important thing is to keep shifting the stock. You can't sit on the stuff – its value is dropping all the time,' he says.

Reputation

It is vital, however, to think about brand value at all times. 'As a retailer you've got to worry about your reputation, about where your product is being sold off.'

There are specialist areas within RL; for instance, home entertainment products such as DVDs. Handling a huge number of items when they are launched means that a significant number of them will be unsold, and will have to be discounted – or destroyed.

David Hughes is convinced that reverse logistics will be a massive issue, brought to prominence by legislation. 'I think this market is just about to break; everybody's been talking it up, but the WEEE directive is moving things along. That what's concentrating minds.'

More information on WEEE is available from: www.environment-aqency.gov.uk/netreqs/ legislation.

Source: Motor Transport, 17 July 2003. Reproduced by permission of Reed Business Information.

RISK

As supply chains become more responsive and integrated with lean and agile responses, then with any disruptions to this leanness, the supply chain could become fragile with no flow and with slow or, at worst, stopped supply chains. Also as supply chains become more lean and agile and deliver smaller quantities with lower stock holding and an increased volume product range being supplied, then the demand they are satisfying is more susceptible to breaks in the links. A chain is as strong as its weakest link and small changes in one part of the supply chain can cause massive changes elsewhere. Uncertainty therefore exists and plans need to be made for this. This means identifying where the weak and choke parts are in a supply chain and developing contingency plans – for example, alternative methods and back-up operations. Focusing only on internal contingency planning is not enough as there are also risks from lack of supply and from other external factors, such as terrorism. The key is to have a full knowledge of the way the supply chain works, how it is managed internally and externally by all players and participants, and to have both internal and external contingency plans available.

ROADS

In the UK, road congestion is a major growing concern and the impacts of traffic congestion on journey times for freight traffic are expected to be dramatic, unless there is a fall in economic and social activity. Journeys that take longer mean that more vehicles are needed to carry the same freight volumes, a simple basic point that can easily be illustrated by any transport scheduler. Road congestion can mean late arrivals, delayed deliveries, missed book in times, rejected deliveries, stock-outs, lost sales and loss of customers; leading to higher costs, falls in productivity, unreliability and to that major supply chain disrupter: uncertainty.

In recent times, road building has not kept up with the growth in road traffic and in the last 50 years the number of cars has increased some 15-fold, whereas goods vehicles have increased by five-fold (although goods vehicles became much larger over this period). Road congestion that lengthens journey times can mean the need for more regional stocking warehouses to meet required customer availability. In turn, this can affect the distribution logistics network and mean that warehouse locations need to be re-examined.

LEGISLATION

The effect of the Work Time Directive on the distribution industry will impact on transport operations and affect companies' distribution, logistics and supply chain strategies. This should at the very least force companies to look more closely at how they can better use a key resource: the transport driver. This could make changes to operations, such as two drivers working a vehicle separately over 7 days, the use of three shifts in 24 hours, vehicle/trailer interchanges and possibly more use of drawbar/swap body techniques. This, in turn, will probably mean that changes to depot networks will also be required.

The Waste Electrical and Electronic Equipment (WEEE) Directive (2002), commented on above under 'reverse logistics', also shows how recent legislation can significantly 'change the ways we (may have to) do things' in the future.

TECHNOLOGY

Tagging and identifying individual packages is technically available, and if the time sensitive/reliability aspects of supply chain management continue, then increased usage of such technology will occur.

PEOPLE DEVELOPMENT

Competence is not a constant, therefore keeping up with 'what's new' is a critical function for individuals in companies and for companies to acknowledge and therefore encourage and support people's learning. One way to advance learning is by following a process of continuing professional development (CPD).

One definition of CPD is the systematic learning and improvement of knowledge, skills and competence throughout a professional's working life.

Personal learning lies at the heart of CPD which is the method and process that uses personal power, knowledge and experience to:

- make sense of things (by thinking)
- make things happen (by doing)
- bring about change (by moving from one position to another).

Learning is not a passive activity or an automatic process; it requires an active and thoughtful approach and it can be hard work.

No one is likely to force individuals to learn and develop. CPD is therefore all about individuals being committed to their own growth, success and survival. Many people may think that personal learning does not need to take place. However, in the current climate of change, continual challenge and new developments, this view is both outdated and dangerous. In a changing and developing world, development needs to be dynamic in order to keep up with factors such as rapid changes in technology, new and shifting markets and requirements for better standards, more rapid processes and at lower cost. Those people who abdicate responsibility for managing their own development will surely be less valuable to companies in the future.

All these changes place emphasis on the continuing need to be professionally competent. Those who remain in the past can quickly have outdated knowledge and skills. A company only develops and learns through its people. Individuals are the constant in companies' learning and development and individuals do the learning in companies; it is therefore clearly the responsibility of individuals to promote their own learning.

POLITICAL INFLUENCES

The EU has a view on distribution policy, and the following represents a summary of the key issues they see. Most of these have already been commented on, but this will serve as a summary of the future possible influencing events.

Growing conflict is foreseen for road transport due to the increasing demand giving worsening congestion, poor quality services, environment damages and safety. The issues involved here are:

- Imbalance in transport modes with road being dominant.
- Rising congestion, unless something is done.
- Growth in demand.
- Integrating transport into sustainable development.

Possible strategies to solve this are seen as:

- A reduction in mobility.
- Redistribution among modes.
- Road freight charging 'taxes'.
- Revitalisation of other modes.
- Targeted investment in networks.

These effectively look to shift the current balance of transport which, in turn, can mean changes to distribution networks and will also need to be considered in the context of other EU policies, such as those on economics, land use, social and education working patterns, budget and fiscal, competition and research.

Some of the policy guidelines that have been made are as follows:

- Framework directive on principles of road charging.
- Harmonise fuel taxes.
- Road: working time directives, introducing a 'drivers' certificate and compulsory training with the tightening of controls and penalties.
- Rail: to be integrated by allowing cabotage, setting high standards, creating a dedicated freight network.
- Air: to have common regulation on air space, rethinking of airport capacity, encouraging intermodality with rail.
- Water: to simplify port rules and, for inland waterways, to establish better links.
- Intermodal: to create favourable technical conditions and standardise swap bodies sizes.

How far the political will is able to further these proposals remains to be seen. The 'knock-on' effects to distribution networks and the warehouses/depots within such networks could be immense.

Clearly this is an involved and dynamic situation and readers who wish to keep up to date can monitor the EU website at http://europa.eu.int/comm/transport.

THE SUPPLY CHAIN

Clearly, warehouses exist to serve the various multiple supply chains of a business. In evaluating warehouse activities, therefore, it is necessary to examine the supply chain(s) and ensure that they are effective, adaptive and profitable. The main areas to be examined for company profitability from the supply chain are as follows:

- Product and service portfolio management
  - Detect product life cycle shifts and modify underlying models.
  - Customer segmentation can allow for targeted service offerings that will increase margins.
  - New products can capture the market potential more directly.
- Working capital efficiency
  - Reduction of inventory and payment cycles.
  - Ensuring rapid flows of goods and information.
- Cost to serve
  - Cost management is reported by both product and by channel to market.
  - Checking of the 'planned to actual' profitability of each customer order.
  - Using of total acquisition cost models by the buyers.
- Asset efficiency
  - Recognising that the utilisation of assets goes straight to the bottom line.
  - Outsourcing can reduce the working capital.

The impacts of these profitability aspects on warehousing can be seen in Table 11.1.

Clearly these examples will vary in specific contexts. Suffice to note, however, that many impacts will be found and while some will merely reinforce current known trends and developments, some also serve to

Table 11.1 The impact of profitability on warehousing

Profitability aspects	Warehouse effects examples
Product life cycle shifts	Returns of unsold items
Targeted customer offerings	Smaller order despatches to 'unusual' places
New products	Smaller order despatches to new customers
Reduced inventory	More frequent deliveries of smaller quantity
Rapid goods flows	Speed and reliability of operations
Cost management	More control on costs/productivity
TAC models by buyers	Emphasis on the previous 'hidden' warehouse costs
Asset utilisation	More productivity analysis
Outsourcing	More third party usage and more leasing/subcontracting by existing 3PL companies

confirm once again the importance of, for example, effectively managing cost and productivity and change (as explained more fully in earlier chapters).

Designing supply chains

In designing the supply chain and the associated distribution network, the following can be noted:

- Customer demand
  - Design the supply chain on market needs – as it is demand that 'kick starts' the whole process.
  - Understand the supply chain requirement for customer segments (and tailor as appropriate).
- Product
  - This will vary: for example standard, segmented standard, customised standard, tailored customised and pure customised.

- Design products for interchangeability, ease of assembly and standardised parts.
- Assemble to order, customised products.
- Postpone final product differentiation until the product is required.
- Strategic
  - Need a top recognition and commitment to the supply chain purpose/vision that recognises it is fundamental to integrate processes for interdependency.
  - Concentrate on areas that have maximum business impact.
  - Leverage e-business to link assets and process across partners.
  - Minimise fixed costs, keeping assets and resources flexible.
  - As supply chains are collections of business that add value, focus on the core value drivers, then perform more added value work.
  - Outsource non-strategic and non-competitive activity (DIY or Buy In).
  - Adopt and enforce common performance and quality standards throughout the supply chain.
  - Use flow logistics by designing all processes for the continuous flow of goods and information, therefore minimising lead times and stockholding.
  - Design and manage adaptable supply chain networks.
  - Manage through a cross-functional organisation and structure.
  - Appreciate flexible relationships across the supply chain.
  - Continuously develop the people, so that they will continuously improve.

The future supply chains will be dynamic, hopefully more collaborative, and with end to end visibility being fully recognised in both the supply side (capacity, availability, compliance, fulfilment and settlement) and the demand side (orders, inquiries, promotions and inventory).

In operating environments of greater customer expectations on speed, flexibility and quality of products, combined with cost, speed and reliability of delivery, warehouse and supply chain excellence will need to involve:

- Accessible, accurate, and timely customer, product and supply information throughout the supply chain.

- Enhanced customer relationships leading to repeat business through fast, accurate, product delivery and professional customer response services.
- Integration of internal and external information and material flows.
- Flexible infrastructures and partnering.
- Analytical assessment, on demand, of freight movement, price and placement actions.
- Coordinated, rapid decision-making environment that synchronises any global supply chain events.

This can be summarised in Table 11.2 where the connections and links to warehouse activities can be specifically noticed.

As will have been seen, warehousing in the supply chain covers many topics and aspects and it is hoped that this book has provided areas for further investigation and improvement.

Table 11.2 Summary of expectations linked with warehouse activity

Aspect	Traditional supply chain	New supply chain
Orders	Predictable	Variable/small lots
Order cycle time	Weekly	Short/daily-hourly
Customer	Strategic customers only	Broader based
Customer service	Reactive and rigid	Responsive and flexible
Replenishment	Scheduled	Real time
Distribution model	Supply driven/push	Demand driven/pull
Demand	Stable and consistent	Cyclical
Shipment size	Bulk	Smaller lots
Destinations	Concentrated	Dispersed
Warehouse re-configuration	Monthly/yearly	Continual
International trade compliance	Manual	Automated

Finally, the following aims and ideals provide a view of 'perfection' when managing warehouse and stores in the supply chain and also summarises all the aspects and topics that are involved.

WAREHOUSING AIMS/IDEALS

The following represents a view of 'perfection'.

1. *Professionalism*: Warehousing will be viewed as a critical step in the material flow cycle and not as a necessary evil.
2. *Customer awareness*: Successful warehouse operations will have a high regard for the customer, will know the customer requirements and will consistently meet these requirements.
3. *Measurement*: Warehouse standards will be established, performance will be measured against these standards and timely action will be taken to overcome any deviations.
4. *Operations planning*: Systems and procedures will be put into effect that allow the warehouse manager to proactively plan the operations as opposed to reactively responding to external circumstances.
5. *Centralisation*: The trend will be towards larger, centralised warehouses instead of smaller, decentralised warehouses.
6. *Third party warehouses*: More intelligent use of third party public warehouses to handle peaks will be commonplace.
7. *Pace*: The reduction of lead times, shorter product lives, and increased inventory turnover will result in an increase in the pace of the warehouse.
8. *Variety*: Different SKUs and additional special customer requirements will result in an increase in the variety of tasks performed in the warehouse.
9. *Flexibility*: Due to the increase in warehouse pace and variety, all warehouse systems, equipment and people will be more flexible.
10. *Uncertainty*: All uncertainty will be minimised; discipline will be increased.
11. *Integration*: Activities within the warehouse (receiving, storing, picking and delivery) will be more integrated and the warehouse will be more integrated within the overall material flow cycle.

12. *Inventory accuracy*: Cycle counting will be used to manage inventory accuracy, and accuracy above 95% will be the norm.

13. *Space utilisation*: Space will be more efficiently and effectively utilised.

14. *Housekeeping*: Quality housekeeping will be a priority and a source of employee pride.

15. *Order picking*: The criticality of order picking will be understood and procedures and layouts will be designed to maximise picking efficiency and effectiveness.

16. *Human resources*: Every manager will be dedicated to creating an environment in which every employee is motivated and happy.

17. *Team players*: Suppliers, customers and a wide variety of functions within the warehouse will be integrated into a single service-providing facility.

18. *Automation*: Advanced technologies will be more easily embraced and economically justified.

19. *Automatic identification*: Automatic identification systems will become the norm for data acquisition and transfer.

20. *Control systems*: Real-time, paperless control systems will be used throughout modern warehouses.

Useful Information and Websites (UK Sources)

These may be obtained from web searches under specific topics or from the following:

INSTITUTES/ASSOCIATIONS/ COMPANIES

Chartered Institute of Logistics and Transport: www.ciltuk.org.uk.
Chartered Institute of Purchasing and Supply: www.cips.org
Fork Lift Truck Association: www.fork-truck.org.uk
Health and Safety Executive: www.hse.gov.uk
Lifting Equipment Engineers Association: www.leea.co.uk
Storage Equipment Manufacturers Association: www.sema.org.uk
The Fire Protection Association: www.thefpa.co.uk
UK Warehousing Association: www.ukwa.co.uk
(Hundreds of links are also available from the above sites)

JOURNALS/MAGAZINES

Better Safer Storage: The Redirack Guide to Safe Storage (undated). Redirack
    Limited: www.redirack.co.uk
Distribution Business, now *Supply Chain Business*: www.uktpl.com
Focus (magazine of Chartered Institute of Logistics and Transport):
    www.ciltuk.org.uk.

Guide to Picking, Dexion Limited (1993): www.dexion.co.uk

Guide to Safe Storage, Dexion Limited (1994): www.dexion.co.uk

Handling and Storage Solutions: www.western-bp.co.uk

Heath and Safety: www.western-bp.co.uk

Industrial Handling and Storage: www.dmgworldmedia.com

International Journal of Logistics Research and Applications: www.tandf.co.uk/journals

Logistics Business: www.logisticsbusiness.com

Logistics Europe: www.logisticse.com

Logistics Manager: www.sevenkingspublications.co.uk

Materials Handling News: www.nexusmedia.com

Motor Transport: www.reedbusiness.co.uk

Storage Handling and Distribution: www.turret-rai.co.uk

Supply Management (magazine of Chartered Institute of Purchasing and Supply): www.cips.org

Supply Chain Business: www.supplychainbusiness.com

Warehouse News: www.warehousenews.co.uk

Bibliography

Distribution, June 2001. (Reed Boardall)

Distribution Business, December 2002. (Entertainment UK)

How to Mentor and Support Learning, Stuart Emmett. Spiro Press, January 2003. ISBN 1-90429-865-6: www.capita-ld.co.uk

Health & Safety Executive: www.hse.gov.uk

'Improving Freight Transport and Warehouse Operations', Stuart Emmett, in *Focus* (Institute of Logistics and Transport), March 2000, and includes references to Logistics Training International Limited and to 'The Effect of Traffic Congestion on the Efficiency of Logistical Operations' by Alan McKinnon, in *International Journal of Logistics Research and Applications*, Vol. 2, July 1999.

Improving Learning for Individuals and Companies, Stuart Emmett. Chandos Publishing (Oxford) Ltd/Spiro Press, June 2002. ISBN 1-90429-831-1; www.capita-ld.co.uk

Industrial Handling and Storage, October/November 2001. (BMW)

International Logistics, Cheltenham TC (for Chartered Institute of Purchasing and Supply qualification), 2002.

Lifting Equipment – A User's Pocket Guide, Second Edition, Lifting Equipment Engineers Association, 2004.

Logistics Europe, November 2002. (Sorter types/speeds)

Managing with Systems Thinking, Michael Balle. McGraw-Hill Book Company, 1994. ISBN 0-07-707951-5.

Motor Transport, 29 August 2002. (New Look/P&O)

Motor Transport, 17 July 2003. (WEEE/Salvesen)

Open Learning Material for the Introductory Certificate in Logistics, Institute of Logistics and Transport, 2003.

Stock Control, IPS (now CIPS), 1991.

Storage Handling and Distribution, March 2003. (Wilkinson)

Storage Handling and Distribution, June 2004. (Unwins)

Stores and Distribution in the Supply Chain, Cheltenham TC (for Chartered Institute of Purchasing and Supply Professional Stage qualification), 2002.

The Discipline Pocketbook, Stuart Emmett. Management Pocketbooks, 2001. ISBN 1-870471-90-3: www.pocketbook.co.uk

The Fire Protection Association: www.thefpa.co.uk

The Supply Chain in 90 Minutes, Stuart Emmett. Management Books 2000 Ltd, 2005. ISBN 1-85252-467-6

Warehouse News, 22 July 2002. (Sainsbury's/E-fulfilment)

Index

Index compiled by Annette Musker